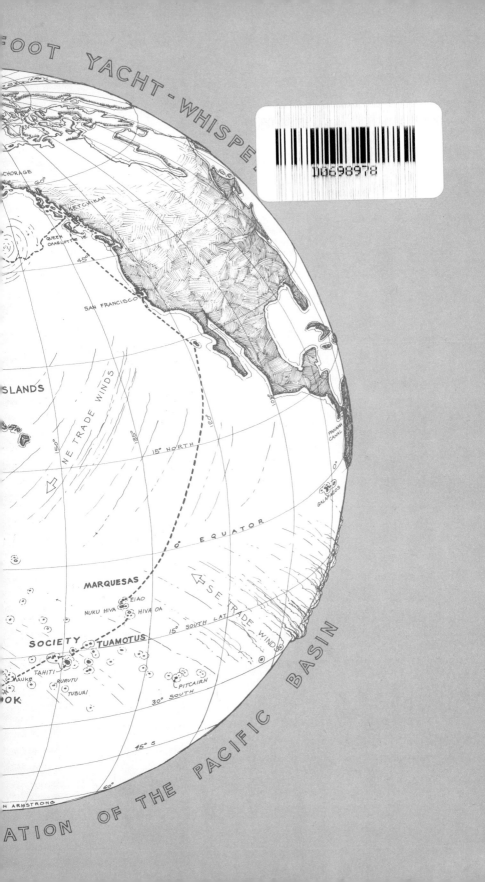

Two on a Big Ocean

Books by Hal Roth:

Pathway in the Sky
Two on a Big Ocean
After 50,000 Miles

HAL ROTH

Two on a Big Ocean

The story of the first circumnavigation of

the Pacific basin in a small sailing ship

Maps by John Armstrong

W · W · NORTON & COMPANY

New York · London

Library of Congress Cataloging in Publication Data
Roth, Hal.
  Two on a big ocean.
  Includes bibliographical references.
  1. Pacific area—Description and travel.
  2. Whisper (Yacht).   3.   Roth, Hal. I.   Title.
[DU23.R66   1978]   910'.09164   78–3731
  ISBN 0–393–03216–7

2 3 4 5 6 7 8 9 0

ACKNOWLEDGMENTS

I would like to thank Joe Brown the editor of
Oceans, Hans Strepp of *Die Yacht*, Bill Robinson
of *Yachting*, Gerry Kidd of *Pacific Yachting*, and
Bernard Hayman of *Yachting World* for their
kind permission to use some of the material which
appeared originally in these magazines. The Gilbert
Island song is from *We Chose The Islands* by
Arthur Grimble, New York, William Morrow,
1952, and is used by permission.

This book is dedicated to
Bobby Uriburu, the veteran
sailor from Argentina, whose
constant encouragement, assistance,
common sense, and good humor
might well be copied by men
everywhere.

CONTENTS

Even in a little thing
(A leaf, a child's hand, a star's flicker)
I shall find a song worth singing
If my eyes are wide, and sleep not.

Even in a laughable thing
(Oh hark! The children are laughing!)
There is that which fills the heart to overflowing,
And makes dreams wistful.

Small is the life of a man
(Not too sad, not too happy):
I shall find my songs in a man's small life.
                    Behold them soaring!

Very low on earth are the frigate-birds hatched,
Yet they soar as high as the sun.

—Song from the Gilbert Islands

Two on a Big Ocean

1 / ~~~~~~~~~~

An Idea

AS WITH MOST GRAND SCHEMES OUR PLAN WAS SIMPLE. We wanted to sail a small yacht from our home in San Francisco to Japan via the islands of the South Pacific, and then to return to the United States on the great circle northern route by way of the Aleutian Islands, Alaska, and finally the Queen Charlotte Islands on the west coast of Canada. The proposal called for 19,000 miles of sailing on a roughly oval-shaped course that followed the sweep of the major surface currents of the Pacific. During the nineteen-month trip we would call at some seventy-five ports and sail in both warm and cold waters. In the South Pacific our biggest hazard would be coral reefs. In the North Pacific our difficulty would be fog.

We were two. Margaret and I decided after examining the records of many small-yacht trips that crew problems were often more severe than the trips themselves. We would man the ship ourselves, although we realized that meant watch and watch in turn, not so easy sometimes, especially when the going was difficult. However, we weren't worried about the troublesome moments. What we thought of were lovely anchorages in turquoise lagoons, weeks of splendid sailing with the warm trade winds behind us, getting to know such places as Samoa, Moorea, Rarotonga, Kusaie . . . and the fun of meeting Polynesians and Micronesians. I was anxious to hear Tahitian music at first hand. Margaret was keen to see a coral atoll. Japan and the northern islands were unknown mysteries.

We planned to stay entirely in the Pacific and to begin with French Polynesia, the Cook Islands, and Samoa. Then we would shape our course to the northwest and sail to the Ellice, Gilbert, and Eastern Caroline islands, before stopping at Guam and crossing the Philippine Sea on the way to Japan.

It all seemed a long way and a big undertaking. Could we do it?

I learned long ago that travel is more worthwhile if you spend a little time reading about where you are going. There was certainly no lack of writing about most of our goals in the Pacific. The shelves in the libraries bulged with reports of exploration, memoirs of English and French navigators, dusty histories, reminiscences of early travelers, surveys of modern governments, and various long-haired studies. The books about Japan and the Far East often filled a whole room— even in small libraries.

However, when we tried to find out something about the Ellice and Gilbert islands the librarians shook their heads.

"Not much on those places," they said. "Hardly anyone goes there. No steamship or air service. In fact the Ellice and Gilbert islands are not even on most maps."

"Just the islands for me," said Margaret eagerly. "I want to discover some new places. I want to sing and dance with strange people. I want to sit in the kitchens of the women and see how they cook. I want to find out how their clothes are made and I would like to look at their houses. But I guess the only way we can visit such forgotten islands is in our own ship."

Our own ship! Our own ship! The phrase sounded nice, but it was only talk. At that time we didn't own a ship or even know what to buy, though we had been getting plenty of ideas from the splendid shelf of sailing books we had found in the library. More suggestions came from yachting magazines. But most of the advice was from our acquaintances on the docks of Sausalito, a small community just north of the Golden Gate Bridge inside San Francisco Bay.

"What kind of a ship shall I get?" I asked my expert sailing friends.

"A ketch with a powerful engine," said one.

"By all means buy a schooner," said another. "It's the traditional ship of America and the best for going anywhere."

"A cutter is the only yacht to have," said a third. "The two headsail rig is easy to handle and . . ."

Ralph Holloway, my neighbor in Sausalito, owned a trim blue-and-white gaff yawl. "It's just the sail plan you need," he said enthusiastically, unrolling the blueprints on his living-room floor. "Everybody knows that a gaff rig is the best for offshore work. A yawl sail plan is perfect."

Four answers to the same question. I should have known better, but like a fool I held out my burned hand toward the flame.

"What is the best material for a ship?" I asked.

"Wood is the only thing for small ships," said Bill Hauselt, who owned a ten-ton schooner and who spoke with authority. "You can always fix wood yourself and the repairs are simple and quick."

Nipper Riddell, a veteran of a long Pacific cruise, had other ideas. "Bah! Wood is the worst choice you can make for a cruising yacht," he said menacingly. "Forget wood. It's only a homestead for worms. Get yourself a good steel ship. You want strength in case you hit anything. *Steel* is best."

I mentioned Nipper's suggestion to Bob Van Blaricom, an expert sailor who was a civil engineer.

"Steel! Wood! Are you mad?" said Bob. "Do you want to spend the rest of your life replacing rotten planks and soft frames? Or scraping rust and painting steel? Forget woodies and tin boats. Get with the times. Buy a fiberglass ship. Plastic is the best choice these days."

My head was spinning from all these opinions, each of which seemed to go off on a different point of the compass. Only one thing was certain. Small sailing-ship owners were an outspoken, fiercely independent lot who delighted in expressing forceful, earnestly argued views.

The yacht brokers had more ideas. In fact once they started talking they never stopped. They sounded like violin players entranced by the sound of their own fiddling. The brokers never asked us what *we* wanted; they only tried to sell us what *they* wanted. They kept telling us what we should have. The brokers asked nosy questions about our finances and suggested schemes for buying harbor-type, cocktail-hour yachts that would have had us in debt forever. Margaret and I fled in horror.

We began to read newspaper advertisements and to tramp the San Francisco Bay docks seeking FOR SALE signs. We shopped diligently for months and inspected several dozen yachts. A ship we could afford was generally too small, too old, in bad condition, or perhaps all three. The cost of big, handsome yachts was beyond us. One ship had a splendid hull but we didn't like the interior. A Hong Kong-built cutter seemed a good choice until an expert told us the frames and deck beams were too light for offshore cruising. We were shown a forty-two-foot cutter named *Helaine* that had been constructed by a famous Alameda shipyard. We looked, we liked it, we hesitated . . . and a friend bought it.

We drove to the Pacific Northwest to see what yachts were for sale. One Sunday morning in October at the Shilshole Bay Marina in Seattle we saw a sleek black-hulled sloop about to go out for a race. The yacht seemed much larger than her thirty-five feet. We liked the ship right away but sighed at the probable cost of a fiberglass hull.

The craft turned out to be a Spencer 35, a design with a good racing record that was built in Canada, just across the border. We traveled to Vancouver and looked up the tiny boat works on Mitchell Island, where we met the builder and later the naval architect, John Brandlmayr. The price was more than we had planned, but we were thrilled at the prospect of a sleek new yacht beautifully finished in teak below decks. I outlined the Pacific trip proposal to Brandlmayr and he thought the ship could do it. We had barely enough money, so I agreed to do a little of the interior finishing and to shop for the Diesel engine, rigging fittings, ground tackle, and the sails myself.

We decided on the name *Whisper* for our new ship. The builder started construction in November 1965, and she was launched the following February. We spent March fitting her out and installing a Hasler wind vane automatic steering gear which we hoped would reduce tedious watches. In April we sailed *Whisper* south to San Francisco, covering the 1,000 miles in eleven days.

We soon learned that a new ship needs many modifications, refinements, and a continuing supply of equipment. We threw out an expensive Diesel cooking and heating stove because the depth of the ship made a proper draft impossible. The ship lacked conventional bilge drainage, so we ran a hose from the chain locker to the engine bilge. The floor of the head compartment had no drainage and had to be rebuilt. We put the hand bilge pump in three places before it found a permanent home. We installed larger outlet pipes and valves in the self-draining cockpit. We had trouble with deck leaks around the chain plates and in the after section of the forepeak. A friend, Doug Duane, a magician with metal, made us a dozen special stainless-steel fittings, including a fifteen-gallon kerosene tank that we needed to hold the fuel for lamps, a new cooking stove, and a cabin heater from England.

Margaret and I both kept our regular jobs, but we spent every spare hour of 1966 working on *Whisper*. Our problems fell into two classes:

(1) Instead of stockpiling money for the trip we found we were spending large sums outfitting the ship ($55 to Paris for charts of French Polynesia, $14 for two mushroom ventilators, $9 for fire-extinguisher refills, $150 for a spare sextant, etc.).

(2) For every job we scratched off our project list we found two more to do. For example, on April 30 I had a list with thirty-eight projects (drill locker ventilation holes, improve cockpit locker drainage, install windlass spring, make dinghy chocks, and so forth). That day I completed four jobs but found six new ones, so the list increased to forty!

The following March we began to lay in stores. One evening at dusk a driver from a wholesale grocer unloaded most of his truck on the dock. We almost fainted when we saw the mountain of canned goods ("Opening a grocery?" inquired a man walking his dog). However, little by little we tucked away the thirty cases of canned meats, vegetables, and fruits, a sack of rice, long skinny boxes of spaghetti, and giant cans of onion flakes, instant potatoes, and dried eggs. Fang, the ship's cat, was mystified by all the containers, and while we were putting the stores away she liked to hide behind the boxes and to jump among the cans.

By now we had both given up our jobs and were living and working full time on *Whisper*. There was so much to do that even day and night weren't long enough. We constructed shelves underneath the cockpit and strapped in such items as eight gallons of bottom paint, varnish, fiberglassing chemicals, and various solvents and sealants. We tucked away a dozen lamp chimneys, extra winch handles, spares for the Primus stoves, and a large box of engine parts. We slipped 130 charts beneath the forepeak bunks, which began to rise alarmingly. Doctors whom we knew loaded us down with enough drugs to start a pharmacy.

"I don't approve of your trip particularly," said Dr. Hank Turkell, the Coroner of San Francisco, who owned a nearby motor-sailer, "but if you're really going you had better take these antibiotics along," he said, generously handing me a small box.

A dentist, Jerry Williams, who had the ship next to us obligingly fitted out a kit for emergency tooth fillings.

We hired an expert to adjust the compass.

We had both shorts and swimming suits for the tropics, and heavy sweaters, thermal underwear, sea boots, and oilskins for the North Pacific. We had light bulbs, nose drops, Stillson wrenches, birthday candles, metric taps, ukulele strings . . .

We had thousands of items on board, so many that Margaret was obliged to keep lists in order to find things. For foodstuffs she kept one notebook with locations and a second that listed the quantity. We got visas in our passports for the countries we planned to visit. We went to the doctor for various traveler's injections and booster shots. It seemed that we were working twice as hard and twice as long as we did when we had regular jobs.

But sometimes we stopped work to go sailing, which after all was what the ship was for. San Francisco is a lovely place to sail, for the winds are good and the seas slight. At dawn the sky above the bay was often a delicate garden of daffodil yellow and wild rose. In the afternoon, tongues of cottony white fog would slip in from the Pacific and gently drift past the massive towers of the Golden Gate Bridge. At dusk the lights of San Francisco spun a web of silver that floated above the strong, silent water. In our little ship we would glide along and marvel at it all.

The word had gotten around that we were soon to leave on a long trip. The number of curious visitors on weekends became a problem. Although we had many jobs we were glad to see people and to explain the working of the automatic wind vane steering gear which was a novelty. However, on some Sundays twenty-five or thirty people would appear, some expecting to be fed, given drinks, and generally entertained. Hardly anyone took off his shoes, and by Sunday night the decks and cabin sole would be black with tracked-on dirt.

Sometimes we solved the weekend problem by slipping out for a sail and anchoring in a cove somewhere, often with our friends, Bob and Jane Van Blaricom, who helped us immensely. They had a new baby, Anne, who Bob carried on board in a basket. Bob and Jane had purchased a forty-foot cutter in England and had sailed it across the Atlantic, through the Panama Canal, and up to San Francisco, where they had sold it at a big profit.

"And hated ourselves ever since," said Bob wistfully, wishing that he still owned *Armorel*. "Cruising in small boats is the real life. We certainly wish we were going with you. What fools we were to sell *Armorel*."

"Some of our friends think us quite adventurous and brave," I said. "Others think us quite mad. One thing is certain. We'll be entirely on our own when we're out there. We'll have to be self-sufficient and to look out for ourselves. Of course the first question most people ask when they hear about the trip is: 'How powerful is your radio transmitter?' I tell them that we have no transmitter and that even if we did there would be no one to call far out in the Pacific, certainly no U.S. Coast Guard. Many people profess to like boating but they have a genuine fear of the sea—or maybe it's a fear of the unknown. I don't wish to sound cocky, but I am supremely confident."

"You won't have any problems at all," replied Bob. "The biggest problem for adventurers is to get away from home. The world is full of talkers and dreamers. Not many people do anything."

Neither Margaret nor I had ever visited the South Pacific or the Far East. Although we had sailed a little in the West Indies, in Greece, in Scotland, and up and down the west coast of the United States, we had never undertaken a major ocean crossing by ourselves. There was much talk about the Pacific being too large for a small yacht. We would have to find out. . . .

We were ready to go. We had a good ship, hopefully were well prepared, and had an exciting itinerary.

The table was set. The meal was in front of us.

2 / ⌇⌇⌇⌇⌇⌇ ⌇⌇⌇⌇⌇⌇⌇ ⌇⌇⌇⌇⌇

The Long Crossing

ON OUR TWELFTH DAY AT SEA, MAY 15, WE WERE HALF-way between California and the Marquesas, the northernmost islands of French Polynesia. We had forgotten about land. Civilization seemed remote and unbelievable. Our position that day was 15° 15′ north of the equator and 125° west of Greenwich. San Francisco was 1,560 miles to the north. Hilo, Hawaii, lay 1,740 miles in a direction a little north of west, and my chart showed that El Salvador, in Central America, was 2,340 miles to the east.

When I stood in the companionway and looked around I saw only the ocean, the sky, and the trade wind clouds—small rabbit tails of cotton that lay stacked overhead like puffs from a giant pipe. We had seen no ships since leaving California, and we were emphatically alone—alone in a world of blue. A feathery turquoise glowed in the sky; around me as I turned I could see a hard rim of ink-bottle blue where the sky stopped and the sea began. The etched line of the horizon was firm and definitive and it almost seemed to enclose a private world. It was a delight to be by ourselves, and how free we were! Our lives lay in our hands alone—no one knew where we were—and the independence was a good feeling. I felt exuberant and reassured somehow. I knew that I was in charge of the ship and what we did, but I also had the notion that I was in control of the sea that I could see around me—a foolish idea, I suppose, for it is manifest that the sea knows no master. Yet as long as we paid proper respect to the might of the ocean I felt sure that our tiny ship would be safe.

On that sun-drenched day *Whisper* flew along with the strong northeast trade wind blowing hard on her port quarter. We had eased the mainsail to starboard so the wind blew directly against the big sail, which we balanced with a jib held out to port on a long pole set at right angles to the following wind. In general we had found the northeast trades stronger than we had reckoned. The arrows on the Pilot charts indicated winds of Force 4, eleven to sixteen knots, but we often experienced Force 6, twenty-two to twenty-seven knots, and sometimes more. However, the winds were fair and behind us.

The trade wind sailing was glorious. *Whisper* seemed totally alive and as responsive as a lady in love. How we rushed along! With the sails full and straining we would ride up on a big swell and whoosh forward as a white-topped crest raced past. The air was fresh and you took in great lungfuls of the clean stuff. The sun felt hot on my bare shoulders, and Margaret and I often sat on the side decks and let our feet hang over the edge into the 75° water. When I looked aloft the sun glinted on the warm brown of the spruce mast and sparkled on bits of the rigging. *Whisper* rolled steadily from side to side, and I looked up through half-closed eyes to see the white sails dancing beneath the blue of the sky. Was the ship moving and the sky steady or was it the other way? The white embraced the blue and waltzed around and around. The white pirouetted. The blue bowed. It was a dream; it was heaven!

We steered *Whisper* largely with an automatic mechanism, a Hasler wind vane steering gear. The device was a valuable crewman who was always alert and working, never grumbled, never got hungry, and was particularly good on long night watches. As time went on we found the steering gear more and more useful. It gave Margaret and me time to navigate, do odd jobs, read, and get plenty of sleep. Steering hour after hour at sea is a bore; we had plenty of other things to do.

The wind vane gear was similar to the devices used to steer model yachts—the trim little ships I remember so well in San Francisco's Golden Gate Park on Sunday afternoons. You put the model ship on the course you wanted and trimmed the sails for the wind. Then if the ship changed direction for any reason when sailing across the pond a small wind blade near the stern turned and its corrective movements were linked to the rudder, which put the ship back on its proper course. On a model yacht the wind blade was coupled directly to the rudder, but on a larger ship the force of the wind blade was not strong enough to move the tiller. On *Whisper* we had a clever mechanism invented by Blondie Hasler, the English sailing expert, which mechanically amplified the movements of a wind blade and exerted a powerful steering force on the tiller.

Our automatic steering gear meant we were relieved of the slavery of steering most of the time. We had to know what the wind was doing, of course, and adjust the setting of the steering vane from time to time, but sometimes we didn't touch it for hours or days. Without a hand on the tiller we could keep a better lookout because you could stand up and move around. In the neighborhood of ships it was easier to keep track of steamers, and along a coastline the person on watch could navigate instead of going cross-eyed watching the compass. Around land or near shipping lanes where there was a risk of collision, Margaret and I kept watches twenty-four hours a day, generally four hours on and four hours off. But when we were a thousand miles from shore and far from shipping lanes I eased the rigid watch schedule. At night one of us would sleep deeply while the other read or dozed below, going on deck every twenty or thirty minutes for a look around. You got used to the creaking of the ship and the water gurgling along the hull, and like a mother with a new baby you were instantly alerted by any unusual sound.

There was a different dimension to nighttime sailing. The log for May 9, read:

2045. Tearing along with the sails unchanged for over 24 hours. Margaret and the cat sound asleep. The night is so black that only after I look around for a few minutes do my eyes become aware of faint stars through a thin layer of cloud. The wind has picked up to 20 knots or so. Although we're only traveling at something like six miles an hour, the illusion of speed is tremendous; we hurtle along through the black night like an express train in a tunnel. Rivers of phosphorescence stream from the stern and our wake is a luminous, glowing ribbon of milky froth that is pure magic. The wind has veered a trifle and I have lowered our course to put us back on 175°M. The barometer has been reading low and unchanged for over two weeks and I am sure it is broken. Better forget about it. No one can predict weather anyway.

When the winds blew stronger our little ship churned through the seas. On one day our sleek hull knifed through 151 miles in twenty-four hours, a record run for us and good time for a ship only twenty-five feet on the waterline. But we paid for the speed by rolling heavily. With winds from astern we had trimmed the sails for running, and with little fore and aft canvas effectively set, *Whisper* rolled a good deal. The faster we sailed the more we rolled. We had to hold on grimly when below, and on deck we crawled around. The endurance of the crew became the limiting factor. We got exhausted. The ordinary acts of living became perilous adventures. It was time to slow down.

We reduced the area of the mainsail by rolling up half a dozen turns around the main boom. We replaced the jib with one only 75 percent as big. With the drive of less horsepower we slowed from six knots to five knots or a little less. The small reduction in speed caused a big reduction in the violent motion; no longer were we dolls controlled by a palsied puppeteer, but human beings on a peaceful trip.

A few days later the wind increased to Force 7, twenty-eight to thirty-three knots, a moderate gale, and though it was behind us we found the sea conditions too rough for us to continue. We hove to— that is, we headed into the wind and arranged the sails and tiller so the ship almost stopped. I went on deck a little after midnight, hauled down the working jib, and hanked on the storm jib. However, *Whisper* lay so smoothly under the triple reefed mainsail alone that I left her without any headsail. As I turned to go below I looked around. The clouds were gone and overhead the world was all sky and stars. Deep in the darkness of the southern sky I saw a small cluster of stars. It was a new constellation, the Southern Cross, one I had never seen before. I was enthralled. I thumbed through a star chart and added Acrux, Gacrux, Hadar, and Rigil Kent to my friends up there.

The next morning we dropped the mainsail, hoisted the storm jib, and bent on and raised the trysail, a small boomless storm sail used in place of the mainsail in bad weather. We squared away before the northeast wind again, and with only the two small scraps of sails flying we logged runs of 107 and 108 miles during the next forty-eight hours. The wind then moderated to fifteen knots and we hoisted our regular canvas.

Mariners, especially sailing people, plan their routes and try to minimize adverse currents and headwinds by studying Pilot charts. These special weather maps cover the world in various sheets and are prepared for each month or every other month. The information is based on thousands and thousands of observations and dates back to the pioneering work of Matthew Fontaine Maury, a lieutenant in the U.S. Navy, who provided nineteenth century sailing-ship masters with special logbooks in which to record the weather they found. On Pilot charts every ten-degree square of latitude and longitude is broken into four smaller squares, each with a blue wind quadrant that tells the percentage of time and force the wind has been observed to blow from a certain direction. You can read about the weather generally and inspect diagrams that detail barometric pressure and the chances of gales. The Pilot charts show the air temperature in dotted red, magnetic variation in gray, ocean currents in small blue arrows, storm tracks in solid red, fog in dotted blue, and the type and limits of ice in patterned red lines.

On our passage to French Polynesia we were concerned with the trade winds and doldrums. A straight-line course between San Francisco and the Marquesas measured about 3,000 miles. We picked up the northeast trades roughly 250 miles south of the United States–Mexican border when we were an equal distance west of the mainland. According to the Pilot chart for May, we could expect to stay in the fair northeast trades to about 8° N. and 132° W., or some 1,140 miles. But after passing through the doldrums and into the southeast trades we would have wind forward of the beam. We could improve this prospect by keeping farther east in the northeast trades so that when we finally struck the southeast trades we would have a fair wind. We also wished to cross from one trade wind belt to the other through an area where the doldrums, the place of fickle winds and prolonged calms, were narrow. Further complications were the equatorial surface currents. After studying the Pilot charts and reading accounts of other voyages, we headed for 125° W. and 10° N., a reasonable compromise that made our route some 200 miles longer but augured better winds.

"Time!" shouted Margaret from on deck. I was below with a second-setting watch in my hand. I wrote down 09:28:57.

"I read 42° 41′," called Margaret. I noted the angle in the workbook and repeated it aloud. Margaret handed down the sextant and I stowed it away in its box.

We navigated in turn. I would find our position one day. Margaret would do it the next. This way both of us kept in practice, and if one of us were sick or busy, the other could carry on. It was exciting to cross one position line with a second and to find where we were to within a mile or two. Sometimes I would be so anxious for the final cross that my hands would shake with excitement.

I think the difficulties of celestial navigation are highly overrated. We learned it ourselves, mainly from Eric Hiscock's *Voyaging Under*

Sail. You have an almanac—issued yearly—which gives the position of each navigational body for every second of time for each day. You measure the angle between the horizon and a heavenly body—generally the sun—with an angle-measuring device called a sextant. You make three slight corrections to the sextant angle, extract two figures from the almanac, and enter a second book—H.O. 249—from which in effect you take out half of your position. Observations of two heavenly bodies at the same time or of one heavenly body at different hours of the day give you two position lines and a precise fix.

Margaret and I generally made a sun sight between 0900 and 1000 and a second around noon. Or if the moon was up and we could find it we used it. (My favorite sights were simultaneous observations of the sun and moon.) Sometimes we shot stars, three of which gave a precise position. We found the main difficulty with celestial navigation was not the calculations but the observations. It was important to see the horizon sharply at the instant of measurement when no intervening waves were in the way. You waited until the ship lifted on a wave, the horizon was clear, and then turned the micrometer screw on the sextant until the reflected sun just met the horizon. At this instant you noted the exact time. Of course when the weather was rough and the ship was rolling heavily it was hard to get a good sight, but, like everything else on earth, practice was the answer.

In the old days a sailing-ship master had trouble knowing his exact position because he lacked the precise time needed to find his longitude. Chronometers helped greatly, but the invention of radio solved the problem. On *Whisper* we tuned our Zenith transistor radio to WWV and WWVH, powerful U.S. stations that broadcast special time signals. In the Western Pacific we got a time signal sent out before news broadcasts from Radio Australia. Later we got time checks from Guam and Tokyo before returning to the range of U.S. stations. On no day during our nineteen-month trip did we fail to receive time signals on one of our two receivers. In addition we carried two rated timepieces.

Shortly after we had left California we had had trouble with deck leaks, supposedly an impossibility in a fiberglass yacht. We didn't mind a few drops of water, but a steady drip from the shelves along both sides of the forepeak soon turned the books, bedding, and a hundred other things into a soggy mess. South of San Francisco we had hit contrary winds which had resulted in a lot of water over the foredeck. So much water had gotten below that I began to fear for the safety of the ship. We had two bilge pumps that drew from beneath the engine compartment, but the rest of the bottom of the hull was partitioned off into tanks and sections without conventional fore and aft drainage beneath them. Water from forward couldn't drain aft to be pumped out until it collected to the point where it flooded over the cabin floor. We mopped up the water with sponges and buckets. I was alarmed ("Would the leaks get worse?") and put back into Southern California from several hundred miles offshore. Once in port Margaret hosed off the wet things and hung them out to dry. I called on experts to help me with the leak.

We pulled off the port toerail and found that the hull-deck joint underneath, though strong, had been fabricated in such a way that water could work down inside the joint and get below through the toerail bolt holes. We sealed the top of the hull-deck joint as best we could, put plenty of bedding compound underneath the toerail, and bolted it back in place. We also caulked a leak in the front hatch coaming.

"If you'll take my advice you'll seal that front hatch with heavy tape all around the outside," counseled an old sailor. "Then she'll never leak."

We followed his suggestion, filled our water tanks, and headed out to sea determined to carry on. *Whisper* sailed beautifully with her magnificent hull, but at that moment I had a poisonous opinion of naval architects and yacht builders after a week of expensive, difficult, inconclusive, frustrating, and time-wasting leak-hunting. I formulated a thought I was to recall many times in the months ahead: "If only the naval architect and the builder had to sail their creation across an ocean!"

Now many days later and far to the south the leaks were largely forgotten. The warm northeast trade wind blew behind us. The sun was hot, all the ports were open, and the decks were dry. The cat slept stretched out under the shade of the dinghy, and I stood on the foredeck dumping buckets of sea water over my head to cool off. All the blankets and heavy clothes and shoes had been tucked away. We slept under one sheet. Our uniforms were sun hats, shorts, and bare feet.

Margaret cooked on a two-burner Primus stove that used kerosene

under pressure from a three-gallon tank. We had taken twelve dozen freshly laid eggs (which kept perfectly when coated with Vaseline) and generally had eggs and tea and toast for breakfast. Sometimes we ate cold cereal with milk made from powdered whole milk, which became a creamy, rich liquid when stirred with a little water. We often lunched on soup or bouillon and sandwiches made with tinned meat. We started off with eight loaves of bread, which kept reasonably well for several weeks. Margaret then trimmed off the moldy bits and made toast. When the bread got beyond salvage we heaved the remains over the side and changed to ship's biscuit.

We always had a hot meal for dinner: spaghetti with tinned meat, salmon or tuna in a white sauce, roast beef and rice, corned beef and cabbage. . . . We had a large box of fruits and vegetables in the forepeak, and just before we left, a friend, Mabel Rolley, gave us an enormous bag of big, tree-ripened oranges. How we enjoyed those oranges on the long crossing! How many times I blessed Mabel. When the sun beat down and the ship had rolled away your appetite the sweet juicy segments were cool and refreshing and almost seemed to pour energy into your bones.

Margaret's cooking was first-rate. She would open a can or two, ask me for a few potatoes or carrots from the vegetable bin, rattle around in the galley, and shortly afterward hand me a warm and savory plate of buttered diced beets, fluffy steaming rice, and spicy chicken curry. Or maybe creamed carrots, roast beef braised with wine, and sautéed potatoes. You always find corned beef at sea because it is cheap, keeps well, and is wholesome and solid. But you get tired of it. Margaret was a wizard at disguising corned beef. Sometimes she would dip slices of the meat into beaten egg, roll them in coarse brown flour, and fry them crispy and golden. She made a special chile con carne with corned beef. Sometimes we ate it on crackers together with white-hot mustard and pickles. Her steamed dumplings gave corned beef and cabbage a new dimension.

I saw clever work in the galley. With no refrigeration we couldn't keep leftovers long, but we hated to waste food. Margaret often stuffed the remains of the evening meal into an omelet the next morning. A little peppery spaghetti and meat did wonders to the eggs. My favorite meal was beef stroganoff made with canned button mushrooms, thick canned cream, and tinned roast beef from Colorado.

The last few paragraphs may give the idea that we dined on starched linen with gold knives and forks after consulting menus chiseled in marble. Hardly! We ate well. Margaret was a wonder with modest ingredients, but there were plenty of days when the weather was bad and we had stew, or macaroni and cheese served in bowls. Then we ate wedged in somewhere, generally with our backs pushed firmly against the corner formed by a bulkhead and a settee and our feet jammed against the opposite settee.

Whisper continued to leak a little forward, which was disappointing after our repair efforts in California. There wasn't much we could do except to move things out of the way, try to dry them out a little, and to mop up.

One night when we were hurrying along with a strong following wind, a small jib, and a deep reef in the main, there was a terrible crash and *bang! bang!* I rushed outside to find that the roller reefing gear had slipped somehow and the reefed mainsail had unrolled from the boom. Without the support of the sail, the end of the boom had dropped, and with every roll of the ship the eighteen-foot boom crashed into the dinghy, which was stowed upside down on the coachroof. Already there was a dent in the aluminum skiff, and I felt splinters from the spruce boom under my bare feet as I stood on deck. I raised the boom end with the topping lift and inspected the expensive roller reefing gear with a flashlight. Unintentional unwinding was supposed to have been impossible; clearly the roller reefing gear was faulty, which meant that every time I reefed the mainsail I had to leave the handle in place and lash it to prevent the boom from unrolling. I cursed the makers and the builder who installed such unrepairable junk. Every time I used the roller reefing gear on the trip thereafter—several hundred times—I had to tie the handle in place.

On May 15 the log read:

> *1500. Very hot as we sail on and on toward the equator. Temperature of 86° in the cabin and we are dressed only in shorts. Three squalls today—the first at 0500— and a lovely refreshing shower with each. The rain pelts down and feels like needles at first but the soothing effect is marvelous. Noon position of 9° 44' N. and 126° 20' W. We have traveled 1,698 miles from San Francisco. Eiao in the Marquesas is 1,372 miles away. Good star sights of Sirius and Dubhe and the moon at dusk yesterday. Complicated to plot because the star fixes need to be moved for precession before the position line of the moon is drawn. I have never heard this problem discussed. 138 miles noon to noon.*

The next day the strong northeast winds fell away as we worked south into the doldrums, the area of calms and variables that I had reckoned would last for 175 miles before we got into the southeast trades. I wondered what was going to happen? Would we be be-calmed for weeks and finally run out of food? *Whisper*'s light weight and easily driven hull were advantages now, and with the full main and a big genoa headsail we glided along on a calm blue sea. Tall banks of cumulus clouds towered into the hot reddish sky around us, and I counted eight rain squalls spaced around the horizon. The clouds were all tints of green, blue, and gray whose shades changed as fast as you turned your head. To describe such a scene was hopeless. While I was wondering how to do it a squall providentially erased my problem in a flood of rain and darkness.

I learned that squalls were short-lived heavy gusts of wind and rain (or snow) that could occur anywhere but appeared more often in the tropics and especially in the doldrums, where the air was partic-ularly hot and moist. During the day you would see a bank of clouds, well worried with slashes of gray, advancing toward you. Sometimes you would realize that a squall was coming when you saw the sea under a low cloud suddenly kicked up into short whitecaps that danced beneath the wind. At night you learned to recognize an unreal quiet before a squall struck. When a squall hit the ship Margaret or I would race up on the foredeck and let the jib halyard fly to lower the headsail to ease the wind pressure on *Whisper*. Heavy rain would pour down for perhaps ten minutes (a good time for a freshwater shower) and the squall would pass. Then up with the sail again and back on course. Sometimes the squalls were bigger, as I found out on May 16:

> *Last night at 0300 I heard the wind coming. The ship heeled, the rain started, and I eased off to the west with the wind behind me. But the rain! It began lightly and soon increased. It poured. Then the volume doubled and doubled again! The rain fell so heavily that it blotted out the sails, the ship, the cabin—everything. I began to wonder where I was and what I was doing out in the middle of the Pacific in such a deluge. Then the rain increased again! Were we caught under a waterspout? I couldn't even see the kerosene cabin light only a few feet away.*
>
> *The water beat down on my head and back and sloshed on the floor of the cockpit which filled faster than the drains could empty it. Suddenly there was a big crash next to me as the cat's box filled to the top and tipped off the cockpit seat. I was aware that the rain had eased a little when lightning jerked across the sky, igniting the low clouds with blue fire. I began to count one-one-thousandth, two-one-thousandth, etc., to work out how far the lightning was*

from the ship by the number of seconds later the accompanying
thunder roared, but I had forgotten how to do it and gave up such
useless calculations of doom. There was so much thunder that
I would have mixed up the various peals anyway.

I was dressed only in shorts and a cotton T-shirt and I got very
cold. I finally called to Margaret to pass me an oilskin jacket.
I had no idea whether the squall had lasted ten minutes or half an
hour. I clicked on a flashlight and wiped the water from my watch.
The storm had lasted two hours.

We had good luck getting through the doldrums and began to pick
up southeast winds only thirty-six hours after leaving the northeast
trades. On the two days in the doldrums we made daily runs of 120
and 97 miles, remarkable times in such an area, but *Whisper* was at
her best in light going.

Sometimes we saw flying fish, silvery bluish creatures eight or ten
or twelve inches long that would suddenly appear a few feet out of
the water and soar parallel to the waves for perhaps a quarter or
half a mile. Once in a while Fang would find one of the fish on deck.
She then became a wild animal. Growling hoarsely, she would seize
the fish in her mouth and rush off to a secluded corner to work on her
victim, first playing with the poor creature until it was a bloody mess
before she ate it. For some reason Fang liked to drag the fish into the
toilet compartment. She soon had blood and fish scales all over the
floor. I couldn't stand this and banished the cat and her blasted fish
to the cockpit. For a while she tried to sneak the fish below, but she
gave herself away because she always growled when she had a fish.
She finally got the idea: *no fish below.*

One morning when we were 570 miles from Eiao and below eating breakfast we heard a ship's whistle alongside. We jumped up to
see the U.S.N.S. *Richfield*, a large gray military vessel with yellow
rings painted on her stack. She was the first ship we had seen since
California more than three weeks before. The whole crew appeared
to be on deck and everyone was waving and smiling. We couldn't
imagine where the ship was going or why she was in such an isolated
part of the Pacific. From her heading she seemed outbound from
Panama. Her speed was easily two or three times that of our five
knots, and as we waved she was already pulling ahead. In a little
while she was out of sight and we were alone again. What excitement to see a ship!

On May 24 I got an excellent five-star fix from Arcturus, Spica,

Acrux, Canopus, and Sirius. We were now south of the equator and 310 miles from the Marquesas. At the time I knew it was ridiculous, but after I had plotted our position I went on deck and looked for land.

The sea voyage was long, perhaps too long. After three weeks I was impatient for land. The 64,000,000 square miles of the Pacific were too much. I took a pair of scissors and a map of the world and cut out the North Atlantic and laid its pattern over the Pacific. It took four North Atlantics to fill the Pacific. The distance from Ecuador to the Philippines along the equator measured 9,300 miles!

"Just as I thought," I said to Margaret when I showed her my paper dolls. "The blasted Pacific is endless."

Yet it was beautiful out there, and after a time you learned a rhythm from the sea. The day would break, the sun would rise in the eastern sky, the sun would beat down from overhead, and then the light would fall away to the west and the day was gone. Your life was measured in pulse beats of the sun, ticks on a colossal clock whose pendulum had its pivot among the stars and its weight on the wave tops.

The sea was calm. The sea was stormy. The sea was always there, regular and sure, swelling up and down, massive and huge. You were in its embrace and its arms were strong. Sometimes my breath came in

gasps when I felt its throbbing presence so closely. But what am I talking about? The relationship between the sea and a man is the same sort of stuff as between a man and a woman. The best parts of it are unspoken matters of the senses and the guts. You can't talk about it because no one is skilled enough. The words don't exist. It is personal and private and if you know it you feel it. If you don't you don't. There is no nonsense with mere words. That's how it was between the might of the sea and me.

Strange birds sometimes circled around and around the ship. We would get out our bird books and the binoculars and spend hours trying to identify them. One morning a beautiful red-billed tropicbird flew around *Whisper*, perhaps attracted by the white sails. When he got near the cockpit he fluttered his wings and slowed down, almost treading air, so he could have a close look at the peculiar creatures beneath him. He saw two sunburned human beings dressed in bits of cotton cloth and straw hats.

We looked up at the tropicbird and saw a slender white bird about two and a half feet in length, with two extremely long central tail feathers that extended behind him in a graceful arc perhaps eighteen inches long. He had a thick, heavy, orange-reddish bill and a long black patch on each cheek. His wing tips on top were black and his white back had fine crosswise dark lines. He was a powerful flier, and the curious bird stopped in mid-air again and again only a few feet from us. He seemed to say: "Just who are you anyway? What are you doing here?" It was a thrill to see him so near, a completely wild and uninhibited creature.

Long ago, sailors gave the tropicbird the nickname bosun bird because of the marlinspike—the long feathers—he carried in his tail.

At 0700 on May 25 I figured that we were 167 miles from land. I began to spend more time with the sextant and navigation books, and we made a big effort to steer a good course. I had no cause to doubt our position, but I was nervous nevertheless, since the distance from California to the Marquesas was more than 3,000 miles. What if I had made a constant error in navigation? To ease my mind I calculated *Whisper*'s position with H.O. 211, an alternate scheme of celestial navigation. I checked the time with the radio anew and took separate observations with the sextant. Our position appeared to be accurate.

That afternoon I replaced a chafed line from the steering vane to the tiller, but while I was tucking an eye splice in the 3/8″ line I kept peering ahead. We had seen a few land birds and the excitement at being close began to grow.

"O.K., mighty navigator," Margaret shouted a few hours later. "Wake up. It's star time."

I rubbed my eyes, got up from the starboard berth, grabbed the sextant, and climbed sleepily on deck. The sun was down in the west, and the sky was just dark enough to see the first stars. The warm southeast wind blew about fifteen knots and we galloped along at between five and six knots under the full main and the working jib.

"I've got Canopus, Sirius, and Arcturus in sight," said Margaret. "And Venus and Mars. You'd better hurry before the clouds cover them."

I braced myself on deck and shot sights of the stars and planets while Margaret used a small flashlight to read the watch and to write down the time and sextant angles. The 1900 star fix put us sixty-two miles east-northeast of Hatutu; the position lines from Mars and Venus crossed at a point fifty-five miles from land, or seven miles closer. Eiao, our destination, was a few miles farther. The wind had eased a little, and I thought we wouldn't see the islands until the next day.

One thing in our favor was that the land we were headed toward was high and mountainous and had no coral reefs. With deep water all around except for a shoal to the north, I wasn't afraid to stand in closely at night. A partial moon would give us enough light to see the islands. Surely we would see and hear breakers if we got too close.

As I sat in the cockpit and looked at the inky night I wondered how many other navigators had pondered their calculations and worried about landfalls. I thought how fortunate I was to have a good sextant, precise time, and advice on their use from generations of seamen. A small bird fluttered around the ship, the fourth I had seen since noon. I kept *Whisper* on a heading of 235° and peered ahead until midnight, when Margaret took over.

At 0300 Margaret called me. "There's something ahead," she said. I scrambled topsides and we both stared into the darkness. The light from the waning moon filtered through the trade wind clouds and cast a weak glow on the sea in front of us.

"Look a little to starboard," said Margaret excitedly. "I see two long mountainous islands."

3 / ~~~~~~~~~~
~~~~~~~~~~~~
~~~~~~~

So Lofty and Green

HISTORIANS OF THE WESTERN WORLD TELL US THAT THE
Marquesas Islands were discovered by Alvaro de Mendaña y Castro
in 1595. A captain during the golden age of Spain, Mendaña was in
charge of four ships carrying settlers from Peru to the Solomon Islands
far to the west. Halfway to his goal and 3,700 miles from Peru,
Mendaña blundered onto four volcanic islands whose mountains were
tall and dark and whose valleys grew lush and green. The navigation in those days was so shaky that at first the Spaniards thought
they had reached the Solomons, but instead of being greeted by natives who were short and black, the people who came out to the ships
were tall, fair, clear-skinned, and had long, loose hair. The natives
brought gifts of coconuts, plantains, and water in bamboo joints.

Quiros, the chief pilot, wrote of the excellent water, the luxuriant
trees, and the splendid climate. He noted the thirty or forty paddlers
in the great canoes carved from a single trunk, the houses of wood
and cane that were roofed with leaves, and the regal women, graceful
and nearly white, who seemed more lovely than even the beautiful
women of Lima.

Mendaña solemnly bestowed the name Las Islas Marquesas de
Don Garcia Hurtado de Mendoza de Cañete on the tropical islands,
naming them for the viceroy of Peru. The friars on the ships zealously
thought of new souls to save from purgatory, but as usual the Spanish
needed little provocation to demonstrate their skill in musketry—
especially on pagans—and the soldiers freely killed the friendly

Marquesans. As soon as it became certain that the all-important gold and jewels were not to be found, the islands were declared useless. After two weeks Mendaña sailed, leaving at least 200 dead Marquesans and three crosses erected to the glory of God.[1]

The islands lay undisturbed for 179 years. Then in 1774 Captain James Cook arrived in the *Resolution*. "The Inhabitents of these Isles are without exceptions as fine a race of people as any in this Sea or perhaps in any whatever," wrote the famous explorer.[2]

One of Cook's artists made engravings of Marquesan chiefs that showed elaborate facial tattooing and ornate headdresses. Under the steep cliffs of Vaitahu Bay on Tahuata the artist sketched slender outrigger canoes with delicately upcurved prows and decorated sterns that were driven by lofty spritsails of pandanus thatch. The muscular Marquesan paddlers sported extensive body tattoos of blue, and high, plumed headwear. The scientists of the expedition collected plants, studied the language, and worked on many useful projects, but in the end Cook and the natives came to blows. Again the Marquesans were killed.

Both Mendaña and Cook had looked at a Polynesian society near the peak of its development.

In the Marquesas the deep, isolated, high-walled valleys encouraged self-sufficient, independent tribes, some of whom were fierce, warring cannibals. Hereditary chiefs, often distinguished by feather headdresses, complete body tattooing, and whale tooth necklaces, ruled the tribes. The chiefs held all the tribal lands and parceled them out in return for a share of the chickens, yams, taro, etc., that was raised on them. With this income the chiefs supported extensive temples and ceremonial plazas. The Marquesan homes were built on elevated stone platforms, and the chiefs, who surrounded themselves with tough warriors, lived in large houses and had beautiful wives renowned for their sexuality. Below the chief but often on a par with him in authority stood the inspirational priest who controlled all religious affairs.

The houses, cooking sheds, and storage huts were clustered in hamlets along streams on the valley floors. Quantities of fermenting bread paste from the breadfruit, a Marquesan staple, were stored in deep holes. Other pits served as earth ovens, cooking arrangements that used hot rocks covered with leaves to steam food. The people ate pigs, chickens, dogs, taro, sweet potatoes, yams, coconuts, bananas, and breadfruit. From the sea came shellfish, tuna, octopus, manta rays, sharks, and lobsters.

The Marquesan society had many specialists and craftsmen. Fishing masters managed complicated net systems, tattoo artists decorated the skins of the people, and canoe builders produced graceful, high-prowed sailing outriggers. Wood carvers engraved superb primitive sculpture on bowls, war clubs, and statues. Officer warriors spent their time planning raids on neighboring tribes and perfecting fortifications for the home valley.

The Marquesans worshiped dozens of Polynesian and local deities, and the people erected splendid temples to various gods and placed offerings before elaborate images. The ceremonial area of each chief was a stone terrace several hundred feet long, with the corpses and the heads of recent victims displayed at one end. Dances were impressive affairs. Dozens of plumed and painted partakers danced, sang, chanted, drank, and ate. Troops of naked girls whirled through involved routines, and the feasting and dancing were uninhibited and sensuous.

The complex life of the Marquesans was taught from infancy. Not only did children learn to take care of their younger brothers and

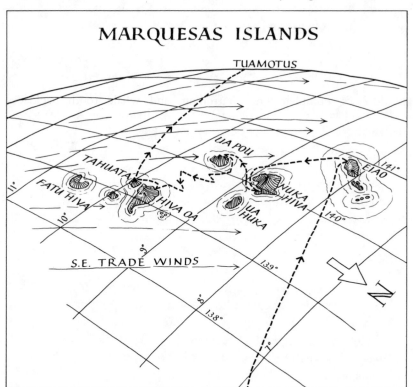

MARQUESAS ISLANDS

sisters but the boys were taught fishing, canoeing, navigation, and farming. The girls learned mat weaving, basketmaking, cooking, medicinal arts, and clothmaking.

This was the society the early explorers had found, but now the influence of the Western world speeded up. After 1790 Yankee traders and whalers began to round Cape Horn and to stop at the islands. Since sperm whales were caught near the equator it was natural that ships would call at the excellent Marquesan harbors for supplies and rest.

During the War of 1812, Captain David Porter of the U.S. Navy used Taiohae Bay in Nuka Hiva as headquarters for his two ships. Porter's job was to sink British shipping, but he soon got involved in intertribal Marquesan conflicts. However, when his men weren't fighting they were busy making eyes at the shapely Marquesan women. "With the common sailors and their girls, all was helter-skelter," wrote Porter.[3]

The American sailors, their British prisoners, the earlier explorers, the whalers—all had consorted with the native women. Venereal diseases became widespread. By now the Marquesan men had rifles, and the whalers not only passed on dreadful diseases but taught the natives how to distill alcohol.

The Marquesan society was wounded but still quite alive when Herman Melville visited Taipivai Valley on Nuka Hiva in 1842. A new menace, however, was the missionaries. The first Protestants failed and left, but the French Catholics who followed were tough, energetic, and practical as nails. Beginning in 1838 in Tahuata, they soon learned the language, mastered the customs, and gained the respect and friendship of the natives. By 1842, when Admiral Dupetit-Thouars claimed the islands for France, the work of the missionaries had created a favorable native attitude toward the new rulers. However, the understanding and tactful early missionaries were withdrawn and replaced with hard-core Catholics who under the shadow of French musketry severely repressed the Marquesan culture.

The power of the native leaders was diluted by intrigue, and the men in black robes fought against all native arts. Singing and dancing were forbidden. New churches were erected everywhere, but a dull Christian theology could scarcely replace the vibrant culture of the islanders. The natives were confused and frightened by the contradictions of the alien religion.

"Tattooing, a matter of great pride to both male and female, next fell under the ban," wrote Robert C. Suggs in *The Hidden Worlds of Polynesia*. "Tattooed adults would not be allowed to take the communion!"[4]

Even blackbirding, the worst of all offenses, was practiced. Unsuspecting Marquesan men would be lured on board ships, seized, and spirited away to South America to become slaves in Chilean mines. In 1863 a shipload of islanders contracted smallpox from the crew. The demonic captain dumped the infected natives on the beach at Taiohae. In a short time whole families and villages were infected. Large valleys became silent, inhabited only by the ghosts of hundreds and hundreds of rotting bodies. The culture had been tottering; disease pushed out the bottom block; the birth rate plummeted.[5]

In 1774 Captain Cook had estimated the Marquesan population to be between 50,000 and 100,000 for the five southern islands, half of the group. In the 1830s the French gave the population as 20,000 to 25,000 for all ten islands. A missionary wrote in 1838 of the infrequent birth of a child because of the excess of debauchery. Fifty years later the Marquesans were still declining. Their fine villages were deserted, their splendid canoes rotten and forgotten, and their temples tumbled and overgrown. Now charged with European alcohol and doped with opium supplied by Chinese traders, the shattered remnants of the people lost all respect for themselves and often spent their days in marathon orgies. Tuberculosis flamed among the weakened islanders, and by 1936, the low point, only 1,300 natives were left, pathetic remnants of the fierce and proud thousands that Mendaña had seen some 300 years earlier.[6]

With this melancholy history behind us we approached the lovely islands—so lofty and green—with misgivings. We brought no dogma, suffered no contagion, and wanted no jewels. We came only to look and to sample the islands for a little while.

In the yellowish light of early morning on May 26, we rounded the squarish volcanic cliffs on the southern side of Eiao. Dozens of birds spiraled above our mast, their high-pitched calls knifing through the warm air. We saw a large bird new to us, a black, swift-flying giant with a seven-foot wing span that we identified as a frigate bird from its angular profile, enormous beak, and scissorslike tail. After so long at sea and thinking about the islands so much we could scarcely believe what we saw. Eiao burst out of the ocean in front of us, a crenelated, oval-shaped plum about six and a half miles long, with mountains up to 2,000 feet. I knew the island was uninhabited, but I looked for smoke and houses anyway. Our chart, the best in existence, was poor and had a scale of about one million to one; on it Eiao measured less than an inch in length. The water was deep all around, however, and we sailed close to the shore for a good look.

We anchored in Vaitahu Bay on the northwest side. Since we had no chart of the bay we stopped a long way from shore. Margaret took the dinghy and the lead line and sounded the depths. I moved *Whisper* closer to shore as she waved me in. After I had veered lots of chain I put Fang, who was meowing loudly, in the dinghy, jumped in, and we all went ashore. The beach was stony, the swells were larger than I realized, and in maneuvering to get ashore I got crosswise to the swells. Before I knew what had happened, the dinghy was upside down, we were in the water, and Fang had disappeared.

We were only a few feet from shore and easily got to the beach, but we couldn't find Fang. We called and called, but the poor cat probably got frightened and ran into the woods. We looked a long time and finally went back to *Whisper*. I was a bit chastened at my poor dinghy handling. Margaret had sprained her ankle, I had wrenched my shoulder, and we had lost the rowlocks that I had neglected to tie to the dinghy.

Back on the ship, we found that the swells set up a steady, monotonous rolling, but our stomachs were well used to the motion and we were reasonably comfortable. I caught several red snappers for supper and we turned in early. The next day we searched everywhere for Fang and even left a dish of food on the beach. We walked through a grove of handsome gray-barked pisonia trees with large, light-green leaves and ate our lunch in the shade while in the tree-tops above us dozens of fairy terns fluttered about like butterflies. In the afternoon we walked up on a high ridge to the north. Wild goats clattered on the rocks ahead of us, and we soon got exhausted climbing up the forty degree slopes in the tropical heat. No wonder each tribe was isolated in the old days! On top we had a fresh breeze and we sat and rested while the clouds from the trade winds streamed seaward over our heads. About four miles to the northeast we could see the brown profile of the island of Hatutu.

On Sunday, May 28, after hours and hours of hunting for Fang, and sad at losing our dear little mascot, we headed for Taiohae Bay on Nuka Hiva. We arrived the next day at noon, the eighty miles taking twenty-six hours. Nuka Hiva, the principal island of the group, measured about ten by fourteen miles with mountains that ranged up to 3,890 feet. The cliffs of the island were high and green—a heavy green that seemed powerful and strong, perhaps from the contrast with the dark volcanic rock that was everywhere. As we slipped past the two rock sentinels guarding the entrance to Taiohae Bay we could see several small ships at the head.

"Good heavens," said Margaret, handing me the binoculars. "I do think one of the masts has a blue top. And only one ship has a mast with a blue top."

"*Escapee*," I said. "But she can't be here. Raith and Vivienne Sykes were bound for the West Indies when we last saw them in San Francisco."

"I know," said Margaret. "But the mast top is blue."

The bay was deep and calm, but a swell pushed in from the south. As we edged deeper into the long bay we got closer to the spurs of the mountains, which came right down to the water. Everything was green, too green, garish almost, and the impressions on my eye were as intense as a spray of colors from a prism. A native was fishing along the western shore, and I found myself looking at my first Marquesan. He smiled and waved. A puff of wind pushed us faster and suddenly we were next to the ship with the blue-topped mast, our friends from Canada, the Sykes in their heavy forty-foot cutter. Our anchor rattled down and we swung near them.

"How many days?" chorused the crew.

"Twenty-five days from California," we shouted.

We were soon aboard *Escapee* exchanging gossip. The Sykes, with two men and two women for crew, had come to Nuka Hiva from Mexico.

"We decided to follow the trade winds," said Raith, tall and handsome as always. "We had a wonderful crossing. But six people eat a phenomenal quantity of food in a month. I thought we had put enough on board in Acapulco for a small army, but we ate everything except the rice husks and the spinach."

The swells rumbled and smashed to spray on the beach near us, and when *Whisper* got parallel to the incoming rollers the motion flung the dishes off the saloon table. We noticed that the one other ship, a blue-green trimaran from Seattle, had a second anchor laid out from the stern to hold the hull at right angles to the swells. We did the same and life on board became easier.

We inflated our Avon rubber dinghy—which wouldn't capsize—
and rowed ashore, hopping out on the small stone pier between
waves. On the front of the warehouse was lettered KAOHANUI, the
Marquesan greeting. Half a dozen boats were pulled up on the beach
and others were stored in boathouses of native thatch. About 150
people, mostly Marquesan, lived in Taiohae, the main settlement in
the islands, and many of their small houses paralleled the beach,
fronting on a short road that I later found out was the only road in the
Marquesas. The government buildings had roofs of red sheet iron and
the style was early nineteenth-century colonial.[7]

When I walked around I thought I was looking at faded prints
in an old history book. The post office, for example, was quartered in
one corner of a large, squarish, two-story building with enormous
shuttered windows, surrounded with wide outside porches with white
railings. French and Marquesan were the languages. There was no air
transport (no airfields, no business) and people and goods came and
left on schooners that arrived from Tahiti once or twice a month. In
1967 the population of the Marquesas was 6,000.

We called on the local gendarme and showed him our passports,
French visas, and ship's papers. We told him that we planned a
brief visit in the Marquesas and a short cruise through the southeast
Tuamotus before heading for Tahiti, where we hoped to be on July 14,
Bastille Day.

"Ah yes, monsieur," nodded the French official courteously, "I will
radio Papeete of your plans and we will hear tomorrow."

During our interview the daylight faded and the office grew dark.
The gendarme called to a woman somewhere. A moment later a
small engine chugged into life. A tiny bulb over the desk flickered
and began to cast a feeble, yellowish light. The official smiled with
pride. We smiled too, but I realized how far from home we were and
how remote in time were these islands. I looked around and saw the
mustachioed Frenchman, the fading horse prints on the wall, the
tropical foliage through the window, the ancient typewriter, and the
carafe of wine on the lace tablecloth. Was I seeing this scene or had I
taken it from Paul Gauguin?

The next day we found the baker and for ten francs (11 cents
U.S.) bought delicious-smelling batards, long slim loaves of freshly
baked bread that tasted wonderful with butter (canned, from Australia, at 55 francs) and coffee early in the morning. We got papayas
from a Chinese-Marquesan family and took quiet walks along the

shore and up the valley. Next to the warehouse near the pier was a shower. You soaped up and then danced under the single pipe while the icy water rinsed you off.

We met Bob MacKetterick, a white-haired Englishman from Liverpool who had been a trader and a storekeeper among the islands for much of this century. A seaman on sailing ships in his youth, Bob was now old, half blind, and ailing, but his love of yarning was undimmed. We sat on his peaceful veranda, which looked south across the bay, and drank a glass of wine while his mind trailed back over a hundred subjects. But one subject he never mentioned was his son Maurice, now the main trader with his store and house only a little way down the road. Many years ago they had had an argument, and Maurice, who had been helping his father, had left to open his own store. From that day the father and son have not spoken.

In Maurice's store we saw our friends from *Escapee*. They were buying heavily. Maurice, cheerfully rushing around and chatting in three languages, sold everything: rice and sugar, globes for pressure kerosene lamps, Diesel oil, Hinano beer, soft drinks, cloth, sewing thread, canned goods. . . .

We walked to the end of the pier, one of the social centers of Taiohae, where people were always fishing. The fishing was in two parts. First the islanders caught silvery bait fish six or seven inches long on dry flies, two of which were pulled behind a short piece of bamboo dragged crosswise to the water. A bait fish was then hooked through the tail with a big hook and tossed out in hope of getting a big fish for dinner.

In the Marquesas there was no electricity for cold storage, so you could buy fresh meat only when an animal was slaughtered locally. Occasionally a beef was brought down from one of the plateaus and led out on the rocks along the shore. The animal was killed and the meat sold at so many francs per kilo. The butcher spoke only Marquesan, but from what we could make out, all parts of the animal cost the same, whether you got filet mignon or scraps for the cat. If a piece of meat was too big, you gestured to have it cut in half; you could have either part for the same price, no notice being made that one side was prime meat and the other side mostly gristle and bone.

If you wanted the best meat you had to get out on the rocks early and stand at the butcher's elbow while he hacked away. (If you were late, all that would be left would be hoofs, horns, and hide.) The butcher had no paper or bags and most people simply carried their bits of meat—bloody and dripping—away in their hands. All told it was a grisly scene, too much for my weak stomach, and though I enjoy a steak once in a while I preferred to eat from a tin rather than witness the slaughtering. Ugh!

The next morning the gendarme sent a message to come to his office.

"It is difficult now with the atomic affairs for us to give permission for you to travel to Hao," explained the official. "The trip would be dangerous. The southern Tuamotus are not possible these days."

We spent the afternoon rearranging our itinerary to visit the northern Tuamotus. The change turned out to be wise. So far as we had known, the last foreign sailors to have seen Hao were aboard the three-masted barkentine *Cap Pilar* in 1937 and the Brixham trawler *Arthur Rogers* in 1952. The crews of both ships had found the island primitive and unspoiled. Now we were told that the atoll had a long airstrip for jet aircraft, innumerable military facilities, and hundreds of French military men. For Hao the old ways were finished. For us the interest was gone.

In the afternoon we were surprised to see a small sailboat with a Japanese flag tacking up the bay. The ship was the *Pioneer*, a twenty-one-foot sloop with three excited fellows on board. They had come from Panama and were the first Japanese yachtsmen to visit the Marquesas. The skipper was Susumu Amao, an enthusiastic twenty-four-year-old navigator who wore a wristwatch chronometer large enough to be a sundial. We wondered about the language problems between Japanese and Marquesan, but the three fellows soon returned from shore holding up a fish and a stalk of bananas, trophies of smiles and gestures.

In company with *Escapee* we sailed to Taioa Bay, five miles to the west, where we found a perfectly sheltered anchorage, splendid in every way except for microscopic no-no flies, pestiferous insects that combined the qualities of biting ants with the cunning of mosquitoes.

Daniel and Antoinette Tikitohe paddled out to see us in a small canoe and brought us bananas and limes. They were glad to have visitors in their quiet valley, once peopled with perhaps a thousand human beings, and we showed them *Whisper* and told about our trip. Daniel took us and the crew from *Escapee* up the canyon through groves of coconut palms to a wonderful ribbon waterfall that poured down from the green mountains almost overhead. Daniel was an excellent woodcarver, and I bought a ceremonial lance incised with traditional Marquesan carving that we put up in *Whisper*'s saloon. Margaret made lunch and everyone sat around eating, except Daniel, who finally admitted that he had a toothache.

"There are no dentists in the islands," he said. "The French doctor at Taiohae will pull bad teeth but he is often away on rounds to isolated places. Sometimes he is short of local anesthetic."

I got out my dental kit and put a temporary filling in Daniel's tooth after explaining that it would be good for only one or two months. The next morning I found two freshly caught fish wrapped in a banana leaf in the cockpit.

A little before noon we headed for Ua Pu, whose warm gray skyline cut high above the horizon with a forest of stony peaks, spires, and pinnacles. The island would have been right at home in the Swiss Alps, and from twenty miles away you were certain the misty silhouette was a fanciful illustration in a book of fairy tales. But closer at hand the mirage firmed into reality, and we anchored near a rocky ledge in Hakahetau Bay on the northwest side of the island. While I did a few jobs on board, Margaret went ashore. Later I read her journal:

June 11. Yesterday I went ashore in the Avon dinghy with my washing. A group of young girls helped me land and lift the dinghy up on the rocks. I walked up the stream and was about to begin when some of the local women who were washing beckoned to me. They found me a nice place with running water, no leaves, and a good stone to pound on. "Do you know how to pound?" one asked. I nodded vaguely and slyly imitated the movements of the women. We chatted as we worked and pounded. "How old are you?" they asked. "How many children?" "Where was your boat built?" "How long did it take to get here?" "From what country do you come?"

I said that I was English but had lived in France and America. We talked about the nasty no-no flies that bit so viciously. "Do you have no-nos in America?" asked one of the women.

On the way home I picked up two loaves of bread that I had ordered from the baker. When I passed the store I saw half a dozen tipsy, red-eyed men outside and I was invited to have a drink with them. Red wine and beer seem big stuff here.

Too bad the men spend all their money on drink. God knows the women and children and houses are poor enough. I saw the Catholic priest with his prayer book pacing back and forth underneath a breadfruit tree outside the church. His hour of meditation,

*I suppose. Prayer, however, is not enough. What these people
need is less booze and something constructive to do.*[8]

Sometimes in the afternoons a few natives paddled out to *Whisper*
in a pirogue, tied astern, and climbed aboard for a look. Often they
brought fruit or coconuts. In return they were happy with a few
cigarettes and were delighted to look below, to inspect the compass,
to finger the sails, and to handle the tiller, when they always smiled
and got faraway looks in their brown eyes. For the Marquesans, however, the days of sail were finished except for an occasional yacht and
a few inter-island schooners. The horsepower of the islands was calculated not in terms of sail area but in Johnson and Evinrude outboard
motors, which the men always ran at full throttle. The natives often
went between the islands in outboard-powered runabouts, not a small
undertaking, and they liked to boast about their fast times.

Everyone we met was a good singer and enjoyed nothing better
than to play the ukulele or guitar. Their tunes had simplified chord
structures, but any lack of harmonic variations was compensated for
by fast-paced strumming. Some evenings we had a dozen people in
the cockpit strumming and singing and laughing. It was good fun for
all.

One Saturday morning at dawn we lay becalmed five miles off the
northwest coast of Hiva Oa. The leeward side of the island was
brown, and the parched volcanic tableland climbed slowly toward
distant clouds. It took four hours to sail five miles, but finally we
slipped past Grosse Tour, a 735-foot thumb of black rock, and into
the eastern bight of Hanamenu Bay, the prettiest small anchorage
that we had ever seen. Open to the north, the bay was about one
fourth of a mile wide and three fourths of a mile long, with high cliffs
of brown jutting up hundreds of feet almost from the water's edge on
the east and west.

But the head of the bay was its heart. Immediately above a long
beach of white sand rose a splendid grove of young and old coconut
palms whose bare trunks arched skyward into thick masses of bright
green foliage (I thought of a giraffe wearing an Easter bonnet). Our
eyes traveled to two huts above the beach and to several outrigger
canoes drawn up beyond the reach of high tide. In back somewhere
smoke puffed up from a cooking fire, and in the distance we were
vaguely aware of dun-colored cliffs. The warm sun beamed down and
I got a whiff of sweet scent. The only sound was the surf running up

on the beach as the small waves lapped on the white sand. Suddenly we were in the South Seas, the tropical islands of one's dreams.

As we looked, scarcely believing our eyes, one of the outriggers set out from the beach and three men waved to us as they paddled north to fish. We anchored in six fathoms near the other ship in the bay, a blue, thirty-three-foot Belgian cutter named *Procax*. We jumped into our dinghy and splashed ashore, where we found a fine stream of sparkling water at the end of the beach. Along the stream were lush growths of tropical foliage, dozens of small and large plants, and we saw a human hand in the cultivation of enormous shield-shaped leaves of taro, the serrated green of *épinard*, and the tall swordlike bunches of sugar cane. As the water tinkled along it some-times bore petals of red from hibiscus flowers. We sat in the stream with only our noses showing and let the wonderful water run over us.

The outrigger returned and the three men ran the canoe up on the beach and covered it with palm fronds. They waved us nearer. The youngest climbed a coconut palm and threw down drinking nuts, which the others husked, chopped open, and handed us. The liquid was cool, sweet, and refreshing.

We introduced ourselves to Lucien Rohi, his teenage son Ozanne, and to the old man, gray-haired Tuo Kaimuko, who was seventy-two. Lucien's father was French; his mother was Marquesan. He owned much of the land around Hanamenu and lived there with his Tahitian wife, Louise, and his son. The fourth resident of the valley was the old man. A bearded European appeared with a smiling, round-faced blonde woman, and we met Guy and Viviane Cappeliez, the owners of the Belgian yacht.

Suddenly we heard the snort of a motorboat and shortly were introduced to the French doctor from Atuona, his male nurse, and the driver of the launch. Lucien had planned a luncheon for the doctor and we were all invited.

"*Faîtes comme chez vous*," said Lucien. "My home is yours." He stood smiling as he welcomed us when we arrived at his small dining house up the valley. He led us to a table heaped with fresh *poisson cru* (raw fish marinated in lime juice), steaming bits of pork, savory fried goat, tart *épinard* (spinach) picked that morning, still-warm home-baked bread, large red plantains, and breadfruit that had been baked, sliced, and fried. After lunch a guitar and ukulele were soon going full blast. The launch driver was fat and toothless, but when he smiled his eyes laughed; his right hand was a blur on the guitar strings and he played song after song, each faster than the last, and soon everyone had a foot tapping to the Marquesan and Tahitian tunes. Dancing was inevitable, and we were soon all out under a big tree, clapping and shouting and trying new steps. It was a wonderful day.

The next morning we saw Lucien and Ozanne disappear around the corner of the bay in their canoe. A little later they appeared with the outrigger loaded with bananas and papayas, which they presented to us and the Belgian couple. Another morning we watched the men lay out a long gill net from shore and catch several dozen small fish; just before lunchtime we were given some of the fish, neatly cleaned. We walked up a mountain with the Rohi family on a coffee-picking expedition and on the weekend were invited to two meals and singing that lasted eight hours. We didn't know what hospitality was until we met Lucien. "I think the old Polynesian way," he said. "Everyone is my friend. If you're nice to people, they're good to you."

The old man, Tuo, lived by himself in one of the huts on the beach. Sometimes at night it was chilly and one morning he asked

Margaret for a blanket. "In the dark it is cold and I am so old," he said sadly. Tuo appeared to have only a ragged old cotton blanket, so we gave him a good woolen one. Not that it was an extra blanket, but Tuo seemed to need it more than we did.

When Lucien found out about the blanket he was furious. "That confounded old man has demons in his head," he snorted. "Tuo keeps asking for things he doesn't need. He already has seven blankets from seven yachts!"

The people at Hanamenu had been good to us. What could we do for them? I thought and thought and finally decided to ask them to lunch on *Whisper* and then to go for a little sail. From our supply of California foodstuffs Margaret fixed a meal of things the Rohis normally didn't get. Afterward we went out for a sail and we let each of our guests take the tiller for a bit. They loved it and told us that although yachts occasionally called at Hanamenu, no one had ever taken them sailing.

On the day we said goodbye we had real tears in our eyes. Lucien handed us a big sack of ripe mangoes and Tuo, still chuckling about the blanket, passed along a basket of oranges. A breeze ruffled the placid water of the bay, our sails billowed out, and we glided away from our friends.

4 /

The People of the Sea

AT 1745 ON JUNE 20 WE SAID GOODBYE TO THE MAR-
quesas and set a course to the west-southwest toward the Tuamotus,
500 miles away. As we sailed out from the lee of Tahuata the wind
freshened and I soon rolled a small reef in the mainsail. Astern the
scene was savage. The dark mountains were all mixed up with heavy
clouds that swirled upward in the brooding dusk. I wondered
whether the gloomy prospect had something to do with the tragic history of the place.

Our visit to the Marquesas had been crammed with interest, but
it was good to be at sea again. Heavy squalls hove *Whisper*'s rail
down to the sea, and I steered the ship with the tiller between my
knees while I played the mainsheet like a fisherman with a big catch
on his line. We had a fair wind, twenty knots from the southeast, and
as the islands slipped into the darkness behind us the squalls eased
and we were able to get the ship to steer herself.

Our destination was the Tuamotus, or the Dangerous Archipelago,
a name often found on charts. And a proper descriptive name it is,
for no appellation strikes more terror into the hearts of navigators than
these seventy-eight low islands spread across half a million square
miles of ocean. All but one of the islands are flat and low-lying atolls,
irregular rings of coral thirty feet above the sea at maximum and often
only ten or fifteen feet higher than the waves. Coconut palms increase
the height a little; however, from the deck of a small ship you can't

see the islands until you are within five or six miles—even when the conditions are ideal. Many of the reefs are hardly awash and extend a few feet below the surface for miles, especially on the southeast sides of the atolls. The coral is hard and unyielding, and a pinnacle of the flintlike stone can puncture a ship's bottom as easy as a hammer can smash a light bulb. Charts and surveys are imperfect, and unpredictable and often reversing currents flow strongly. It is easy to run onto an island at night or during thick weather, and many hundreds of ships have collided with reefs in this geographical jigsaw puzzle.

The combination of restricted visibility, treacherous currents, and poor charts are enough to give fainting spells to any navigator, especially when he reflects on the miserable history of ships among the Tuamotus. Marine insurance agents turn white at the mere mention of the name. A few navigational aids would help immensely, but the French government—which has spent billions of francs on its nuclear program in the southern Tuamotus—has failed totally to help the surface navigator. There are no buoys, no beacons, no lightships, no radio stations, no electronic aids—nothing. It is up to you. In the Tuamotus the captain of a ship *must* keep track of where he is.

On *Whisper* we relied on celestial navigation, and as we neared the Dangerous Archipelago we were up each dawn and dusk taking star sights. During the day we implemented the star sights with observations of the sun and moon. In fact we shot the sun so much I thought it would fall out of the sky.

On the morning of Wednesday, June 21, we were running hard, rolling along the tops of big waves, and had logged ninety miles in fifteen hours. The swells had increased from the southeast and at 0900 two heavy seas thundered over the port quarter and slammed on board. To slow the yacht we handed the mainsail and continued under the working jib alone. The motion was fairly severe, and the cooking stove got to swinging so violently in its gimbals that I had to lash it in place. That night we listened to some wonderful Latin jazz music and to a superb woman singer—with a voice like Sarah Vaughan—from Havana, Cuba, of all places. I always marveled at the short-wave reception on the Zenith radio.

The deck leaks were worse than ever. Everything in the forepeak was soaked again. In disgust I grabbed an armful of ruined sailing books and flung them over the side. Margaret held up a blanket saturated with salt water. "Ah, the joys of cruising," she said, shaking her head sadly.

After lunch the following day we bent on the storm trysail, which helped to steady us a bit. Later the wind veered to the east and increased to twenty-five knots, not so windy really, but the seas were large and lumpy. During the past two days we had seen some monsters. By noon on Saturday—the fourth day—we had logged 478 miles and the island of Ahe should have been in sight. At dawn that morning I thought I had a whiff of land—"some sort of sweet smell," I noted—and birds flew around the ship. The sky was overcast, half a dozen dark patches of rain were scattered around the horizon, and visibility was poor. We saw no land.

"According to the moon and sun sights we should be four miles from Ahe," I told Margaret at 1100. "I am sure the island is east of us and the easterly wind should continue to set us away. However, I don't want to be around here in the dark. I'm going to head for Rangiroa, which is about seventy miles away. We'll carry on for forty miles and then heave to until daylight. We should see the atoll tomorrow."

The wind was now behind us and the jib flogged and banged. It was held out with a pole to balance the mainsail, but when the ship yawed on a big sea the sail would get backwinded. Then when *Whisper* went the other way the sail would suddenly fill with wind and belly out with a tremendous bang. To keep the sail from blowing to pieces we replaced it with a smaller storm jib, which set much better for the sea conditions.

At 2100, an estimated thirty miles from Rangiroa, we hove to until 0400 the next morning, when we got under way with a bright moon lighting the sea. The wind had eased a little and we wanted plenty of sailing power in case we had to claw off land, so we put up the reefed mainsail in place of the trysail and hoisted the working jib. I sharpened the course up to windward to compensate for leeway and current and steered by hand since the vane couldn't cope with the big seas coming up on our port beam.

Shortly after lunch, as we rose on top of a swell, I saw something ahead. I rubbed my eyes and looked again. It was an atoll. What a thrill to see a long strip of green and a glistening ribbon of white coral stretching across the horizon. We were about five miles away and soon ran near enough to see the blue waves bursting into white spray on the barrier reef. How exciting it was to see the white sand and the palms close up!

Now a new game began. We were at an atoll—but which one?

They all looked the same, and with no navigational aids it was hard to identify particular islands. I was certain from my daily sights that the land in front of us was Rangiroa. The next question was which part of the island lay before us? The atoll was forty-four miles long and fourteen miles wide at one point and made up of a continuous reef about one half mile wide that went around in an oval to form a large lagoon. What we saw was only one section and all parts looked roughly identical. Of course my sights should have told me where I was located along the reef, but under the seas that had been running I didn't trust my position closer than ten or fifteen miles.

From our direction of approach I assumed that we had closed the northeast side of the atoll and that a distant point to port was the eastern corner of the island. Therefore we turned to starboard and ran in the lee of Rangiroa, reaching along at high speed in the calm water. The scenery was gorgeous. Close in we could see the reddish lip of the barrier reef that pushed above the surface. Generally the water was deep, but in a few places close in where the water shoaled over coral sand the color of the sea changed from purple to lighter blues. We could distinguish separate islets and groups of palms on the land and occasionally we passed large blocks of coral that had been thrown up on the beach. We saw no people.

Our course paralleled the land and we should have been steering 315 degrees; instead, our course was 200 degrees. I began to take bearings of different points of land with the hand-bearing compass. Nothing checked, and I soon realized that we had come upon the northwest side of the island instead of the northeast. We were going away from the passes instead of toward them! Now that I had a notion where we were we hove to in the calm water and I climbed the ratlines and sat on the spreaders. With the binoculars I looked carefully toward the west. Staring as hard as I could, I was just able to pick out the smudge of Tikehau atoll, ten miles away. This confirmed our position. The strong southeast current had set us northwest about twenty-five miles since the previous evening.

We retraced our steps quickly, for the sun was low. However, by the time we got to the northern tip of Rangiroa it was late in the afternoon, and around the corner of the island the seas, wind, and current were totally against us. We had eight miles to go before dark to locate one of the passes and finally to enter the lagoon. It was impossible.

We returned to the lee of Rangiroa and found a patch of coral sand about one fourth of a mile from the reef and anchored in six and a half fathoms. The anchorage was perfect as long as the winds continued south or east, for they held us away from the barrier reef. The anchorage outside the lagoon was not worryfree certainly, but it was calm and sheltered and gave us a place to spend the night. I put a blanket and pillow on the cockpit seat and stretched out, ready to put to sea at the first shift of wind. But the trades remained steady and I dozed through the night, wakening from time to time to see the black outline of the palms against the starry sky.

The next morning we sailed around the northeast corner of the atoll to Avatoru Pass, which we identified by the village on the southeast side toward the lagoon. We had calculated the time of slack water, and sure enough the water was calm in the pass. It was just before noon, the sun was high and in the east, and the light conditions were excellent for coral pilotage. I put on Polaroid sunglasses, climbed the ratlines, and waved Margaret ahead. She eased the sheets and we headed in.

It was my first passage through coral and I had a bit of stage fright. However, with the sun over my shoulder I found it easy to direct the ship from up the mast. Whenever the water shoaled over coral sand the color of the water changed to increasingly lighter shades of blue and finally to greens and whites. It was simple to watch for the heavy brown coral heads beneath the surface and to signal the helmsman accordingly. The pass was noisy from the roar of water, so I directed Margaret with hand signals that we had worked out beforehand.

In a minute we were at the pass, and the ship was even with the ends of the barrier reef which ran away on each side of us like great barricades of dull-red iron. As far as I could see on both sides the force of the ocean rose and fell on the reef, and I wondered how mere stone could stand such pounding. A big swell would hesitate for a moment, shudder, and then boom into fragments of white, sending thousands of tons of water cannonading against the reef. No ship, no mere structure of man, could stand *those* breaking waves for long!

We slipped inside the pass and into smoother water. The deep purple of the ocean depths was behind us. Now we saw lighter blues and greens and fish darting away from the yacht. The *U.S. Pilot* book had suggested anchoring behind Avatoru village, but as we neared a small concrete wharf where a group of people stood watching, an outrigger canoe came out and a man motioned us to stay in the pass and to anchor about 150 yards off the village. The man, a stocky, muscular Tuamotuan, paddled alongside, tied up, and hopped on board.

"My name is Rita Maruhi," he said in broken French. "Best to anchor in the shelter of the pass. Strong winds in the lagoon. Put one anchor out in front and one in back."

We tacked, sailed back to the place Rita indicated, and dropped the bower anchor in five fathoms. Rita carried out a stern anchor in his pirogue and then dived overboard to check it after I had hauled in on the warp. He climbed back aboard smiling.

"O.K. now," he said. "The current normally runs two to five knots in the pass. We find that two anchors keep a ship from swinging and fouling her ground tackle on patches of coral."

I gave Rita a cigarette and Margaret handed him a glass of lime drink. He was intrigued with our fiberglass hull and with a chart that showed our trip. He told us that he had worked as a deckhand on a large schooner and was madly in love with all sailing ships. He stayed a little while and then went to check his fish traps.

We rowed ashore and pulled the dinghy up on the white coral. Sometimes it was sandy, sometimes fine gravel or small lumps, and sometimes large blocks. But regardless of the form the coral was always underfoot and always hard and brilliantly white in the sun.

The village of Avatoru, one of two on Rangiroa, boasted 300 residents, several churches, half a dozen small stores, a light-generating plant, and a tiny refrigerated fish storage warehouse. The houses were mostly small, one-story clapboard homes with porches, glass windows, and tin roofs. Many were painted startling shades of pink and green and yellow. The doors and windows stood open, and bright, boldly patterned cotton curtains flapped in the wind. Inside we noticed strongly colored covers on the beds and chairs—often large flowered prints in heavy blues and reds. A few houses were old native style of plaited palm leaves over thin wooden frameworks. The streets were neatly laid out, and several children were busy raking yards and walks. Around a few of the larger houses a little stringy plant that served as grass was cultivated. The women with these "lawns" carefully raked them and we were amazed to see one woman pushing a lawn mower. Palms grew here and there along with a few hardy shade trees and shrubs. We stopped to admire some large hibiscus blossoms.

"*Ia ora na*," said a stout, elderly woman sitting crosslegged on a porch near the road. "*Ia ora na*." This was the melodious Polynesian greeting that we were to hear often. The lady was drilling tiny holes in a pile of small shells she had collected on the reef. She then strung the shells on a length of fishline. The woman beckoned to Margaret and put a shell necklace around her neck and kissed her gently on each cheek. She gave me a necklace also. It was a pleasant, friendly gesture, and the lady's smile showed that she enjoyed giving the necklaces as much as we liked getting them.

We saw children lugging pails of drinking and washing water from the cistern behind the main church, whose large metal roof was the principal catchment of rainwater for the village. In front of several houses small papaya trees grew in old gasoline drums that held a few precious bits of soil that were carefully covered with old leaves to make humus. When we passed the school we heard shrill shouts of a phrase we were soon to know well: "*Uatae mai te popaa*," which meant "Here come the white people." The youngsters scampered around us, laughing and shouting. Some were flying kites. We were startled by a battered truck that rattled past us on the hard coral road. We crossed to a Chinese store, where we bought stout pandanus sun hats, and we finished our long walk by circling back to the dinghy, where we met Rita, who gave us a fish for dinner.

In the three weeks we stayed at Rangiroa we found the Tuamotuans completely generous, fun-loving, remarkably gentle with children, hopeless drinkers, and totally unconcerned with money and possessions. Their lives and language reflected the openness of their sea environment, their attachment to the atoll, and their dependence on fish and the coconut palm.

The Tuamotuans required no clocks and calendars. A native only had to look up, and we heard a moon or sun or star name that defined the very minute. In some mysterious way Rita always knew the exact state of the ingoing and outgoing tidal stream in the pass; he could instantly tell me the time of the next period of slack water, which I could approximate only after calculations with the tide tables. The men would cock their heads and listen to the roar on the reef for a moment and let you know whether the sea was angry or troubled or sleeping and whether the reef was dry or swept by foaming seas. You had to sing an American song to them only once and they could sing it back to you.

The men were masters at fishing and could quickly catch what they wanted from the bountiful lagoon, along the reef, or in the open sea. Every fish had three or four names, depending on its stage of development and its suitability for eating. Before going out the men

would earnestly talk over not only which fish to catch but how many and at what stage of growth.

Our English word *coconut* meant nothing in the South Pacific. The Polynesians recognized at least five stages of nut growth and three types of nut coloration that combined to make fifteen or more names in everyday use. For example, the common drinking nut was called *viavia kekeho*. *Viavia* was the third stage of nut growth, a full-size nut with thin coconut meat and nicely flavored water. *Kekeho* referred to the color of the nut—light yellowish brown—and denoted certain aspects of taste and quality. To have asked a Tuamotuan for a *coconut* would have been as puzzling to him as for an American to have asked a New York automobile salesman for a *vehicle* instead of a Ford convertible or a Chevrolet station wagon.

The main method of earning hard cash in the South Pacific is from the sale of copra, the meat of mature *ngora* coconuts, split away from the shells and dried, and sent away for its oil, which is used in soap, lard, and glycerine. But generally the natives make only enough copra to satisfy their whims for luxury goods. On the average a man might cut copra four or five days a month. Why do more? There are always fish and coconuts. The house is already there and one can play with the children, sing with friends, or just sleep—in the shadow of the coconut palms, of course.

Not only did the palms supply the wonderful coconut—eaten in a dozen ways—but the trees were used for everything. Palm trunks made good house posts. The hard outer part of the trunk was excellent for furniture and canoe paddles. Palm leaves were plaited into mats for wall coverings, roofs, sleeping mats, handbags, and fans. Split leaves could be woven into hats and slippers. The women could plait a small basket to carry food or goods in one or two minutes. Coconut shells served as cups, boat bailers, dishes, scrapers, and made excellent buckles, buttons, and first-rate charcoal. Coconut fiber was burned in cooking fires, stuffed into pillows and bed sacking, and the fiber could be rolled into stout lashing twine. Three tough green strips could be ripped from a central leaf stalk and braided together for a canoe anchor line. Coir fibers made first-class floating rope, and fine dance skirts were fashioned from dry root fiber. Yes, the coconut palm was wonderful![9]

During our visit we sailed across the big lagoon to see the wreck of the ninety-eight-foot San Francisco schooner *Wanderer* that had piled up on the southern tip of the atoll in November 1964 while trying to sail between Arutua and Rangiroa at night. We stumbled through the deserted village of Otepipi, once a busy place; now we saw only old stone foundations and a few huts used by fishermen. In the middle of the dead village we walked through a large Catholic church in perfect condition. It looked ready for a Sunday service and was neat and tidy with a deep-blue ceiling and pretty panes of colored glass. It needed only a pastor and people, but no one was there. It was spooky.

We crossed to the northeast shore and anchored seventy-five yards from tall coconut palms in the perfect calm of the lagoon, dozens of miles from any human beings. The trade wind blew in our faces and the tops of the palms rustled and swayed. A half mile across the narrow islet we could see whitecaps curling up on a nervous ocean, but we were sheltered and safe.

The lagoon shoaled over clear white sand and we sat over the shadow of the ship and watched the colors of the pellucid water change from cobalt blue to milky green. The colors were so real and strong that I almost felt the *texture* of the blue water. What words could I use? Viridian? Agate? Turquoise? Emerald? Amethystine? Indigo? I was at the blue and green ribbon counter in a Paris silk shop and all the ribbons were unwound in front of me. I saw a blue rainbow with a hundred separate colors of sheeted flame all intensified by the searing rays of the sun that bounced up from the floor of white sand. *Whisper* seemed to float on a dream of color, a shining essence of bottled sunlight.

At night I looked out and saw the same scene under the quiet light of the full moon. The blues had softened to delicate purples; the greens had been drawn out to gentle grays. The glare of the noon light had eased to a whisper and a touch. Maybe the whole thing was a dream. . . .

A big advantage of cruising in a small ship was that we had our home with us, lots to eat, comfortable beds, and plenty of reading. We had letters to write and a dozen small jobs to do on the yacht. We took long walks on the beaches and out on the reef. We put on face masks and swam a dozen times a day, paddling around the coral heads to watch the tropical fish. At one place we saw hundreds of tiny blue fish with yellow tails and big white eyes. Margaret pointed to an orange diamond-shaped fish marked on its sides with black cones underlined with white. We saw angel fish, both black with white stripes and white with black stripes. But as soon as you would exclaim at the coloration or shape of one fish, it would get topped by another fish that darted in front of your mask.

Rita had invited us to go fishing with him, so we sailed back to

Avatoru and went out in his canoe. We anchored in a depth of thirty feet near a small islet or motu. The current was racing out of the pass and when we got into the water we needed to hold onto the anchor line. We all wore face masks and could look down through the clear water to the bottom, where there were gray sharks three to five feet long and dozens of fat blue-gray fish with wavy blue-striped fins. Rita smacked the water with the flat of his hand several times and then quickly dove down to the bottom with his spear gun. He never missed, and in fifteen minutes he had a dozen meaty eighteen-inch fish in the canoe.

"The sharks won't harm you as long as you can see them," Rita explained to us later. "We don't like to swim at night, though."

That night we were to eat at Rita's house. Since we had never been there, the arrangement was to meet at the post office at 1800. Rita had gone off to the other village on an errand but was supposed to have returned in the late afternoon. At 1800 we were at the post office. At 1900 we shrugged and returned to *Whisper* and made dinner, feeling that perhaps we had misunderstood the hour. At 0200 the next morning I heard a knocking on the hull and peered out sleepily to see a bleary, red-eyed Rita alongside in his canoe. He was very apologetic and also very drunk. I thought I heard him say that his wife had had dinner ready. However, we didn't know where his house was and we didn't want to go there without Rita.

"Another time," I said and went back to sleep.

We found out the next day that it was just as well we didn't go to dinner, for at 2000 the previous evening Rita's wife had given birth to a child! Rita, no doubt feeling the strain of fatherhood, had gone out for a few beers with his friends.

The next evening we went to Rita's house to meet his wife Pare (pronounced Pa-ray), to see the new baby, and to have a glass of wine. Pare was sitting up in bed. She was a tiny, pretty woman from Raevavae in the Tubuai islands south of Tahiti. She had wonderful white teeth, and when she smiled the whole world seemed to glow. She gave us more shell necklaces and Rita presented us with a dried shark's jaw.

A few days later we returned to the house for dinner. Pare was up and rushing around and we had a splendid dinner of hour-old *poisson cru*, baked fish with coconut cream, fried fish, boiled fish, big fish, little fish, skinny fish, drinking nuts, coconut pudding—all delicious and all eaten at breakneck speed. No wonder the Polynesians have to sleep after eating.

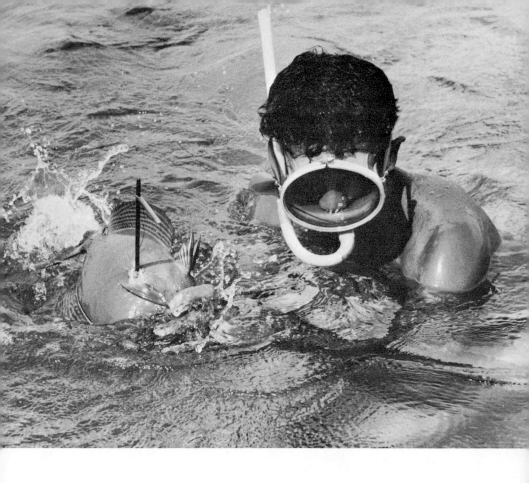

When we rowed back to *Whisper* the air was sweet with the smell of tiare Tahiti blossoms. The spell of the South Seas was truly on us and I felt totally rested and at peace. I hadn't a care in the world.

The next night, the evening before we left, we invited Rita and his family to dinner on *Whisper*. At 1800 the whole family appeared alongside in the canoe. Rita helped up his two young boys, a girl of eight, the new baby, and Pare, all smiles as usual, who wore a new pareu and a crown of freshly picked and woven flowers. She had made fragrant head leis (called *heis*) for Margaret and me and she kissed us on each cheek when she placed them on our heads.

The water in the pass was smooth and I noticed only the slightest rocking motion. I thought it was soothing, but it alarmed Pare who was worried that she might get ill. Her daughter copied her mother's actions exactly and neither ate much of the good meal that Margaret handed up to the cockpit on plates from the galley. Rita and I paid no attention, but Pare and her daughter were soon doubled up over the rail, much to the disgust of Rita. Without much ceremony he bundled his family into his canoe.

"Goodbye," we said.

"Not goodbye yet," said Rita. "I take family home and then come back to finish enjoying the evening. Polynesian women on board ships! Bah!"

The distance to Tahiti was 198 miles, and the next morning—Sunday, July 9—we slipped out of Avatoru pass and headed southeast between Tikehau and Rangiroa. At lunchtime on Monday our feet were tapping to the lilting music from Papeete that was coming in clearly over the radio. At 1500 Margaret ducked below and shouted, "Wake up! Wake up! I can see the green mountains of Tahiti ahead."

5 /

Everybody's Paradise

ONCE IN A FARAWAY PORT SOMEWHERE I WAS APPROACHED by a well-dressed young man about seventeen years old.

"Excuse me," he said cautiously. "But have you been to Tahiti?"

"Yes," I answered. "I have just come from Papeete, where I had a good long visit."

"Did you see the girls dance?" he asked eagerly.

"Why, yes, I did," I answered.

"Did any of them dance nnnnnaked?" he said, glancing over his shoulder to see if anyone was listening. "I mean with bbbbbare breasts and aaaaall?" He blushed when he asked the last question and I had the feeling that although he knew the words he had never pronounced them before.

"Perhaps," I told the young man without answering his question. "I saw lots of lively dancing to spirited drum music. I met a slim Chinese-Tahitian girl with golden skin and lovely black hair that reached to her waist. She wore a trim red-and-white pareu and kept fresh hibiscus flowers in her hair. Her eyes were big and brown and as soft as butterfly wings. She wore fragrant tiare Tahiti blossoms that she had woven into a necklace, and she played the guitar and sang in a low husky voice. . . ."

"Oh, mmmmmy!" said the young man. "And did you go out sailing in outrigger canoes?"

"Oh yes. In the big lagoons under the shadows of the blue mountains. We fished and swam and . . ."

"Could you pick fruit off the trees and eat it free?"

"At an owner's invitation you could have bananas, papayas, oranges, limes, mangoes, coconuts...."

"I wish I could go," said the young man. "I'm going to save hard and maybe someday...."

I don't recall whether my questioner was from Japan, Canada, the United States, New Zealand, or where, because I have heard the same inquiry in many places. But the one thing I do know is that the young man had a typical case of the *romantic dream*, the infectious idiocy that obscures, weakens, and otherwise dilutes any realistic appraisal of Tahiti. *Everybody everywhere* has heard about Tahiti. *Everyone* plans to go.

When we headed for Tahiti in *Whisper* I didn't know what to expect. I had read half a dozen books about the island, thumbed through perhaps fifty magazine pieces over the years, and talked to a few—not very many—people who had actually been there. All the opinions added up to a general impression that the good old days

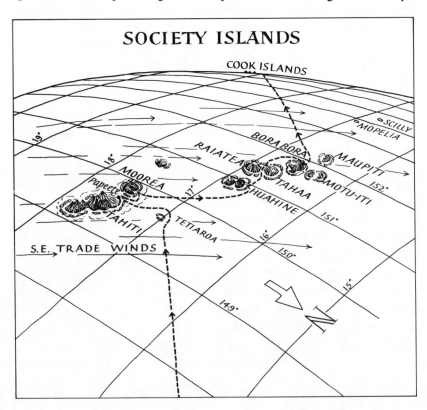

were gone, that most of the flowering beauties had been picked off by the French Navy, that Papeete was crowded and dirty, that prices were out of sight, and that every year the French authorities added a few more sticky rules about visas and length of stay. I knew that jets were now winging in tourists by the hundreds, that new hotels were growing faster than palm trees, and that, in 1968, for example, seventy-two cruise ships put 46,574 excursionists ashore. Mr. Geraud Gilloteaux, the capable director of the tourist bureau, told me that 72 percent of the 28,402 tourists were from North America, stayed one week, and spent $32.25 a day. I knew also that most tourists met only one another and stayed pleasantly isolated in their deluxe hotels and that their impressions of Tahiti were utterly superficial and deceiving.

Yet we had been told that the Bastille Day celebrations were fun, the island itself was high, verdant, and particularly lovely, and that nearby Moorea was a dream. We enjoyed the spirited Tahitian music and we had already met a few Tahitians who were hospitable, mercurial, and endless fun. In Papeete we would see yachts from all over the world, and we knew that if we stayed away from the tourist circuit we might sample a little of the real Tahiti.

It was true, both the good and the bad, the old and the new. The island lay in front of us with its hovering clouds, green mountains, and coconut palms. A noisy bumblebee turned into a jet aircraft that swooped low over the airstrip at Faaa to the southwest. Across the foaming reef we could see the tops of the warehouses, the masts of ships, and the acacia trees along the red-roofed waterfront of Papeete.

It was mandatory for foreign ships to take a French pilot, so at 0600 we were outside the harbor entrance with flags requesting a pilot and *pratique*—the clearance granted to a ship after compliance with port regulations. I felt very correct and proper, but no pilot appeared. Suddenly we heard the deep boom of a ship's horn and we turned to see an enormous white high-sided cruise ship slide past us and disappear into the harbor without stopping for a pilot, waiting her turn, or anything else. As the ship passed us a Chinese messboy emptied a big garbage bucket over the side and we rolled in the swells along with orange peels and grapefruit rinds. "What a way to begin!" I said. Several fishing boats chugged past us on their way out for tuna and a little later a small ferryboat hurried toward Moorea.

Finally at 0700 a fiberglass launch with two outboard motors came churning out of the pass, made a high-speed sweeping turn in front of us, and a man in a purple-flowered shirt—who I had to assume was the pilot—waved impatiently for us to follow him. He led us to a quay where we tied up with fifteen other yachts, and in a few minutes the agriculture, immigration, customs, and quarantine officials had cleared us. The golden rule to easy entry was the French visas we had gotten in California.

After three months of Pacific solitude the noise and bustle of Papeete astonished us. In a way we were eager for a change, but it came too quickly. Cars, large and small trucks, and crowded open buses clattered and snorted along Quai Bir-Hacheim, the waterfront road. Women and children, often two together, one behind the other, hurried past on wheezing motor scooters. One official wanted me to sign a form, so we hopped on his motor scooter and bounced off to an office somewhere. Everyone was well informed and courteous, but the pace was double-quick. Sign this! Do that! Go there! Step up! Fill this out! Fast! Quick! Hurry! Maybe I had been away from civilization too long.

Back at the ship, Margaret was still adjusting our lines to the seawall, for we had dropped a bow anchor and twenty-five fathoms of chain and had backed stern to the quay. It was exciting to see flags from all over and such home ports as Paris, Juneau, Zeebrugge, Mooloolaba, Vancouver, Southampton, Toulon, Plymouth, Basel, Glasgow, and Vlaardingen neatly lettered on the yachts. Some of their crews took a lively interest in our arrival. We looked over the sloops and schooners, the cutters and ketches, squaresail yards, awnings— everything. We met the Belgian yacht *Procax* again, saw our friends the Sykes on *Escapee*, and were tied up next to *Eryx*, Jean de Vogué's handsome eighty-three-foot topsail staysail schooner that we had met in the Marquesas.

In the harbor to the north we looked over to several big cruise ships and toward half a dozen small, work-worn motor vessels. Across the way we noticed what seemed to be a whole fleet of French naval ships with hundreds of uniformed sailors rushing around. To the west were four or five trading schooners, one of which was hoisting a new canvas mainsail. Another schooner was discharging a load of outer islanders who were all laughing and shouting.

Almost the first story we heard was of *Skunda*, a thirty-two-foot schooner from San Francisco owned by Bruce and Suzanne Lamb. A few days earlier the ship had been on course between the Tuamotus and Tahiti when a strong current pushed by the southeast trades had set the ship far to the northwest. At 0330 one morning, while the owner was below ill, the little ship struck the reef on Tetiaroa, a four-mile-long atoll thirty miles north of Tahiti. The schooner was holed but not badly and she hung on the edge of the coral. The owner summoned a tug from Tahiti which pulled the ship off the reef. Unfortunately the high-capacity pumps on the tug failed to work, and the schooner sank in 120 feet of water while the horrified owners watched all their worldly possessions get swallowed by Davy Jones. It was a dreadful incident.

Bruce Lamb reckoned he had been exposed to a two-knot current on his port beam which had set him to leeward about fifty miles in twenty-four hours. Both Eric Hall on *Manuma* and we in *Whisper* had experienced similar currents. At noon on July 10 I figured I was thirty-six miles from the northwest corner of Tahiti. I had taken morning and noon sights, but foolishly I hadn't worked them out, since I thought we would see Tahiti in a few hours. I had expected the atoll of Tetiaroa, the island on which *Skunda* had foundered, to be out of my sight to *starboard*. Imagine my surprise at 1400 when I saw Tetiaroa to *port*. What a current!

Now we were safe in port once more. Above us on the Papeete waterfront trucks kept unloading piles of plywood and lumber. The sound of hammering pounded through the air. Workmen covered light framing with plywood and palm-frond mats, and stalls and temporary buildings began to fill the mall along Quai Bir-Hacheim. As soon as a building was completed it was decorated with crepe paper, cardboard flowers, and palm fronds and filled with cases of Hinano and Manuia beer. Signs advertising this bar and that went up, and gambling games, sideshows, restaurants, cafés, chance boards, dance floors, sidewalk bingo, and all the highlights of a midway fair blossomed on the waterfront. It was as if we were outside the main tent at a circus.

The next day—July 13—people converged on the waterfront and soon filled all the streets. At 1000 a cannon was fired from a French warship and the *fête*—one day early—was on. One man got so carried away—no doubt taken in wine—that he celebrated the start of the two-week Bastille Day holiday by jumping into the water, clothes and all. We heard drumbeats of a parade and turned to see high-stepping dancing teams rush past. On the following day we watched the race of the fruit carriers, men who staggered under poles laden with giant stalks of bananas, long strings of breadfruit, and heavy stems of plantains. We took photographs at a spear-throwing contest where expert Polynesian men hurled javelins at a coconut target thirty feet up on a pole. During the week we saw a speed contest between native women to find the fastest weaver of palm-frond baskets. How their fingers flew! We stood on the shore of the lagoon and admired the skill and strength of both men and women paddlers in the outrigger canoe races. One morning we took turns using the binoculars to pinpoint action in a race between sail-driven outrigger canoes. With the gray-blue mountains of Moorea in the distance, we held our breath as an outrigger with a colossal spritsail from the island of Anaa inched past a gaff-rigged sloop with a huge jib from Raiatea. How quickly the outrigger canoes, with their big sails to hurry them along, glided on the smooth lagoon.

Every night for a week we attended the native dance competitions, which were superb. Expert teams from all over Polynesia competed for cash prizes. Each team had a percussion orchestra and generally about twenty men and twenty women, although one of the best teams was all male. Prizes were awarded for dancing, for the orchestra, and for the costumes.

The men and women wore finely combed grass skirts that were accented with elaborate waistbands decorated with shells and tassels. Everyone sported high headdresses—often with colored feathers— and many had pretty circlets of woven flowers around their necks and wrists. The sharp staccato of drumming started, a spirited *otea* perhaps, and the women's hips gyrated smoothly and quickly. The men took fast steps to the right and left while bowing each way, perhaps acting out the beginning of a song. Forty pairs of bare feet stepped neatly together, and the words the dancers sang blended into a splendid melody. How fast and exciting it all was! How much fun it must have been to do, for the dancers loved to perform. Happiness seemed to flow from every movement.

No matter how complicated the dances were they always included a tamure. But words to describe a tamure! A man faced and stood close to a girl. The drumbeats were quick and strong. Her hips pulsated and her long grass skirt followed in an oscillating, swishing blur. He danced in a bit of a crouch with his bent knees rapidly opening and coming together like scissors. The two performers were close together and soon their bronzed bodies gleamed with sweat. The drumming was loud and the steps were quick, sexy, and wild. The limbs of the dancers flashed faster and faster. The drumming crackled

like spring thunder, and we edged forward to catch a blur of flesh and costume.

Suddenly it was over and we saw the partners smiling and laughing as they crumpled from exhaustion after the dance. How abruptly the Pacific dancing stopped! A troupe would be going full tilt and then bang! Not a sound. Not a movement. You felt that someone had pulled an unseen electric switch.

Some of our greatest fun was going around Tahiti on the public buses, which were open along the sides and back. A ride was a good way to get the feel of the lush and uncrowded countryside and to travel to the beaches. *Le truck*, as one was called, ran out to the various districts from the central market in Papeete, where you pushed from one to another to find a bus that was going to Papara or Taravao or wherever. Almost everything was transported by bus, and the driver or several passengers would always turn to help a woman with three pigs or a small boy with a big tuna. Bicycles, cases of beer, battered foot lockers, pieces of iron pipe, and stalks of bananas were piled loosely on the roof, and the whole topload threatened to roll off with every frequent lurch.

A delightful habit of the Society islanders was their quickness to laugh at anything. One day we were on a bus going to Mataiea when a front tire exploded with a tremendous bang. The wounded bus slumped to the side of the road and the men and women laughed until their eyes brimmed with tears and they almost fell from the side benches. Their laughter ranged from deep earth-rumbling belly laughs to squeaky soprano giggles, with a whole cacophony of in-between chuckles and guffaws. When the Tahitians laughed, every bone and fiber of them laughed. You felt happy just watching them and you had to join in.

We found it easy to meet people on the buses and we got acquainted with several Tahitian and French families who took us for rides, invited us out for meals, and visited us on the ship. But we had lists of stores to buy and it was imperative to repair the forward deck leaks on *Whisper*. Since deck leaks were common and fifteen world-circling yacht captains were nearby, I asked three of them to inspect my problem.

"I think your trouble is from leaking front ports," said Ron Mitchell, owner of the Australian ketch *Calypso*. "I suggest that you put new sealing compound under each port."

"From my study of your leak I think you need a waterproof canvas boot to cover the joint between the mast and the mast step on the coachroof," counseled Dr. Guy Cappeliez, the bearded skipper of the Belgian cutter *Procax.*

Edward Allcard, the merry master of the British ketch *Sea Wanderer,* had other ideas. "Deck leaks are troublesome but the results are worse," he said. "For your peace of mind you should remove all the important stored goods in the area that gets wet and place them in sealed plastic boxes."

Since we were anxious to stop the forward deck leaks that had plagued us all the way from California, we followed all three suggestions.

Practically all the commerce in the Society Islands was in the hands of the Chinese. Instead of stores that specialized in ship's goods, sportswear, tools, lumber, or rubber products, however, the tiny Chinese shops carried a hodgepodge of items that defied classification. A typical store that measured twenty by thirty feet might have anchors, butter, radios, swim suits, bicycle fenders, plastic buckets, ice cream, welding rods, and stationery. You started out in the morning with your list and went from store to store and felt victorious if you captured two items in five.

In one shop I entered, the Chinese owner shook his head as I advanced with my list.

"Why are you shaking your head already?" I asked. "I haven't even told you what I want yet."

"That's O.K.," he said glumly. "I won't have it."

Finally the rush of the people, the noise of the *fête,* the congestion in the harbor, the expense associated with the city—all these things made us yearn for peace and quiet. We put two sailing friends —Tony and Anne Carter, who lived in Papeete—on board *Whisper* and slipped out of the harbor. We headed across to Moorea, a lofty, dark-green island about ten miles northwest of Tahiti, and entered Papetoai Bay. Tareu Pass was easy and we glided southward on the tranquil, perfectly protected bay into the very heart of the island itself. Tall volcanic peaks rose on three sides and the high skyline of the wooded mountains was complete somehow and soothing to the eye. We handed the jib and ghosted along on the dark water with the mainsail scarcely pushing us. There were a few houses but we saw no one. We didn't hear a sound until I pulled the windlass pin and the anchor splashed down in eight fathoms. Margaret swam ashore with a long line that she tied around a coconut palm, and we warped the ship shoreward almost under the branches.

Here again was the romantic dream of the South Seas: the calm blue-black water, the green palm branches shimmering in the warm sunlight, the towering, swordlike mountains, and the trade winds softly brushing the palm fronds together. Fragrance from a flowering tree drifted out from shore and its odor almost became legendary incense.

All of a sudden two Tahitian girls clad in yellow pareus and riding bicycles wavered around a bend in the road along the edge of the bay. What a fine sight they made!

"*Ia ora na*," they called, waving at us and blowing us kisses and almost falling off their bicycles with laughter.

"*Ia ora na* yourself," we shouted back, waving and smiling as the girls disappeared along the shore.

Two generations of small-boat sailors had agreed that Papetoai Bay was the most beautiful anchorage in the world. We concurred

fully and were content to sit and look, to walk around the shores, to swim half a dozen times a day, and to do easy jobs such as varnishing the tiller and scrubbing weed from the waterline. It was good to unwind from the fast life of Papeete. When Tony and Anne Carter left us they wrote in our guest book, "The most restful weekend ever."

From Moorea we headed to the leeward islands of the Society group. Huahine was the first, eighty-five miles to the northwest, a night and a day away. We arrived at the small village of Fare, where the French schooner *Eryx* was already tied up. Her skipper, Jean de Vogué, kindly met us in his dinghy, invited us to dinner, and took a stern warp ashore. It soon began to rain hard while a gray beat-up motor vessel unloaded drums of gasoline and kerosene and took on copra from a large tin-roofed warehouse on the cement wharf. The quayside was filled with scampering children, elders sitting and chatting, and vendors selling drinking nuts, mangoes, and ice cream from hand freezers. Above us stevedores slung thick rope nets around greasy bags of copra. The men and women wore wide-brimmed hats woven from pandanus, and when they walked you heard the soft flip-flop of their sandals.

Late that night we had to shift our anchorage twice because of strong currents charging through Avamoa pass and swirling around the lagoon. The weather worsened. *Eryx* left the dock and steamed up and down inside the reef until dawn. I didn't want to take a chance with coral patches, so we tied up alongside the quay, put out four automobile tires to protect the hull, and laid out an anchor abeam to keep us from bashing into the dock. Even so we bent most of the lifeline stanchions on the starboard side. At first light we cleared out and went to a nearby small bay, suggested by local fishermen. We dropped two heavy anchors on long cables and a light stern anchor to keep us from swinging, and we lay stormbound for three days while a southeast gale—locally called a *maraamu*—whistled overhead.

At 0300 one morning during the height of the storm I heard a car horn frantically beeping. I looked out to see a pair of yellow headlights rapidly flashing on and off at us.

"Halloo . . ." came the windswept voice of the local gendarme. "A . . . tidal . . . wave . . . warning," he shouted. "Take . . . any . . . action . . . you . . . need . . . to . . . take," he said.

I took an aspirin and went back to sleep.

On the third morning the gray motor ship—in spite of warnings of heavy head seas—left for Papeete, her passengers and crew confident of a quick trip. That afternoon the ship limped back to Fare, her passengers gray and pale, her crew ashen and weak, her main cargo hatch damaged, and much of her cargo wet.

When the storm blew out we walked up to the north end of the island to Maeva, an old village partially built on stilts along an inland arm of the lagoon. The village looked a bit battered, but it still had one old-style Polynesian meeting house, a large structure that looked like an enormous upside-down plaited basket. A number of *maraes*—ancient stone platforms once used for religious purposes—were being restored by archaeologists. The area had obviously been inhabited for hundreds, perhaps thousands, of years, and we looked at the remains of extensive stone fish traps.

The next day we left Fare and sailed inside the lagoon to the southwest corner of Huahine, where we tied up at Haapu, the most remote village we had seen. All the houses were of native materials, and several dwellings were on stilts over the water. Transport was still entirely by outrigger canoes, and along the shores we saw many new canoes under construction. Each hull was shaped from a single log that was hollowed out with a curved ax blade.

We were a great attraction, and soon half the adults and all the children seemed to be on board. In a short time the decks were black from the dirty feet of the youngsters who spent hours looking in on us through the ports. The Tahitians were on the ship early in the morning and late at night, with short breaks for meals. In the evening the women would come down to look in. Everything we did seemed fascinating to the people.

We met Tetuanue Nanua, who took us off to see the new church. The village had only 218 residents, and we were puzzled when we saw several other reasonably sound churches standing unused. Generations of competing missionaries had formed groups that favored first one religious sect, then another. Each had built its own church, made its converts, and then faded from prominence. No traveler to the South Pacific can fail to observe the idiocy of such squabbling.

"Is the new church Catholic?"

"No."

"Protestant?"

"No."

"Mormon?" (Very big in the South Pacific.)

"No."

"Seventh-Day Adventist?" (Also very big.)

"No. The new church is Christian."

"Christian?"

"Yes, Christian. We worship God, sing hymns, read the Bible, and conduct services. So many of the white preachers have come and fought with one another and gone that this time we decided to have our own church.

"Do you like our new building?" Tetuanue was proud and his face beamed with satisfaction as he looked up at the high ceiling. "We have worked hard and soon the building will be finished."

The volunteer labor of the untutored Tahitian builders had resulted in a sturdy, crudely constructed church that completely lacked any sort of unified design. A journeyman American carpenter would have cried at the waste. How foolish it was to spend so much energy and money to duplicate existing structures. How much copra was cut to pay to import the cement, the boards for the pews, the glass windows, and the metalwork! How much more useful a new dispensary, a small hospital, or a school might have been. All through the Pacific we were to see the dreary results of futile squabbling among shortsighted missionary groups whose measure of success was not the general good of the people but the number of supposed converts whose devotion was often bought with gifts.

The local Tahitian chief, Nanua Mai, visited us on *Whisper* and asked us to his home for a meal. It turned out to be a colossal affair. We had steaming pig from the earth oven, crisply fried slices of breadfruit, *épinard* with coconut cream, baked reef fish caught that morning, juicy chunks of spicy *poisson cru*, hour-old drinking nuts, and fresh mangoes and oranges. We ate until we were ready to burst.

"Eat more!" urged the chief.

"Full up absolutely!" we chorused.

The chief disappeared in the direction of the cookhouse.

"I hope he's bringing coffee," Margaret whispered. "I'm so stuffed."

In a few minutes the chief returned, smiling broadly and bearing a platter with twelve fried eggs.

"A special treat for our guests," he said triumphantly.

I groaned when the eggs were put in front of me. All the guests stopped to watch. What could I, the visiting captain, do but try? I managed two, and passed the platter to Margaret who somehow ate three more before she gave up.

We didn't eat again for two days.

One night we stopped at the home of Tetuanue to hear

hymn singing, known in the Society Islands as a *himine*. Polynesians are born singers, with a natural ability to harmonize and to use counterpoint. While their children slept on the floor and a pressure kerosene lamp cast flickering shadows over their faces, seven women and six men sang powerfully and well, a chorus that breathed gusto and spirit and took your breath away with its intensity. The woman in charge sang a strident, high-pitched counterpoint that was a bit screeching at times, but it added a depth to vocal music that I hadn't known before. We went back several nights. I will always remember Haapu as the singing village.

On August 18 we sailed from Huahine, touched briefly at Raiatea, skirted Tahaa, and slipped through Teavanui pass into the big lagoon at Bora Bora. The island was high, with steep, craggy mountains up to 2,386 feet. Bora Bora looked something like Moorea except that the lagoon was larger and the mountainous interior seemed more open and less wooded.

We were just in time to see a big stone fishing party, a kind of super fish drive. Whether the stone fishing was an excuse for a happy social occasion or put on by the need for fish I don't know, but it was certainly a joyous time. About 400 people gathered on the west side of a peninsula that jutted into the south lagoon. The Tahitians began to weave palm fronds into a long bushy net about three feet wide and maybe 1,000 or 1,500 feet long. The net was carried and pulled into the water and positioned in the shape of a large V with its fingers open to the west. The net holders—mostly women—stood every few feet and held the net out as far as they could, the tallest woman out farthest.

The women all wore bright pareus, the men colorful loin cloths, and everybody had crowns of flowers. We stood on the white sand beach above the shining azure of the shallow lagoon and looked at the rainbowed clothing, the bronzed bodies, the shining black hair of the women, and the dark green leaves in the long net.

Meanwhile 100 men in fifty outrigger canoes spaced about 150 feet apart had formed a long line far out across the lagoon. As I looked the fleet began to advance. At a signal from the leader of the fleet, a man standing in the bow of each canoe tossed a stone tied to a short line into the lagoon. He then retrieved the stone and at the next signal threw the stone again, chasing any fish ahead of the canoes. The canoes at the ends of the advancing fleet moved faster to make a curved line that gradually moved toward the open net. The stones

continued to fall like beats of a drum, and the canoes moved both ahead and closer together.

Everybody was shouting and yelling when the line of canoes arrived at the net. The Tahitians began to close the ends of the trap, and most of the boatmen jumped in the water to help the women. Little by little the perimeter of the now unbroken net began to shrink and the forest of legs of the net tenders blocked and scared the fish. An excited ring of people grew closer and we began to see fish jumping and splashing. The net was drawn near the beach—the legs were solid now—and the fish were speared or seized and tossed up on the beach, where they flopped around until a head man made a general distribution. Everyone was laughing and the general glee made your heart sing. The fish were of all kinds: green, yard-long spotted fish with jutting lower jaws, fat red snappers, blue parrot fish, round yellow fish with gray stripes, funny-looking skinny white fish with sad eyes, orange fish shaped like dinner plates—heavens! All kinds and all aimed for the evening dinner pot. The stone fishing was wonderful and we were amazed at the spectacle.

We had a good time in French Polynesia. In spite of all the talk that "paradise was finished," we found the Marquesas, Tuamotus, and Society Islands lovely beyond hope. We admired the people, enjoyed their customs, and had the fun of sharing many experiences. We wish we could have spoken their language, but except for a few words their three tongues were impossible to learn in three months. Marquesan is as distinct from Tahitian as Italian is from Spanish. Maybe next time we could learn more.

Now it was goodbye. The course was 220° M. and the distance to Rarotonga was 540 miles.

6 / ～～～～～～～～
～～～～～～～～
～～～～～～

Where Are the Cooks?

WE KNEW RIGHT AWAY WE WERE BACK AT SEA, FOR A
strong blast of wind hove *Whisper*'s starboard rail down to the water.
Bora Bora rapidly fell astern, and in less than two hours I was up on
the foredeck reefing the mainsail. Margaret was sick, King Kong, our
new Tahitian cat, was sick, and even I—old iron stomach—lost my
lunch. The rot had set in.

At dusk we saw the 700-foot mountain on the small island of
Maupiti a few miles off to starboard. Fortunately the east-southeast
wind was fair over our port beam or a little aft, a reaching wind, but
it continued to freshen. At 1815 I put on my safety harness and began
to steer by hand because the vane could no longer cope with the
seas, which pushed the ship first to the right and then to the left. Our
course was good, our speed excellent, and I hesitated to slow the
yacht because we were making such good time. However, I soon had
my hands full steering, and an hour before midnight I realized that
more sail would have to come off.

While I was thinking about the sail changes there was a sudden
roar and everything turned white. A big sea had broken over the port
side and had filled the cockpit up to the tops of the coamings. The
rush of water had swept me onto the side decks and against the lifeline stanchions. The next thing I knew I was spitting water like a
civic fountain and thinking that an airplane had crashed on top of
me. In the cabin the floor was swept by an avalanche of books that

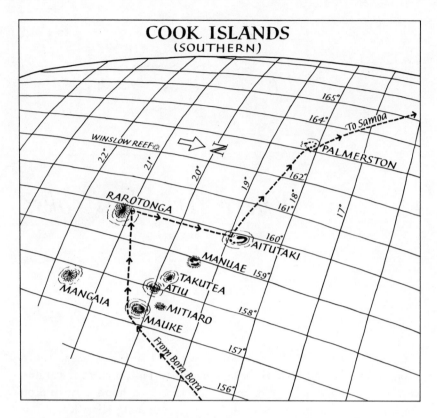

COOK ISLANDS
(SOUTHERN)

was well sprayed with water and tapioca pudding from pans that were flung off the gimballed stove.

I climbed back in the water-filled cockpit and watched motes of phosphorescence swirl round and round as the water slowly drained back into the sea. Some of the water slopped out when the ship rolled, but it still took fifteen minutes for the cockpit to empty. At that moment I lost all interest in large cockpits. I later calculated that up to the tops of the coamings the cockpit had a volume of about sixty-four square feet or a water capacity of two tons, an astonishing weight for a ship that displaced only six tons.

After the wave we took the hint that we were moving too fast. I hauled down the working jib and we hove to until 0700 the next morning, when we bent on the storm jib. The wind was still thirty knots—a moderate gale—from the east-southeast with large seas. After we got under way again we steered carefully and bore off whenever we saw a big swell approaching. Finally at 1430, after a squall, the wind abated somewhat and we managed to get the self-steering working by sheeting the jib flat. When we had hove to during the night I had forgotten to pull in the line and rotator of the Walker log, our distance recorder. The log line had gotten around the rudder, and the rotator continued to turn until the line was in an awful tangle. Margaret made some heroic stabs with a boat hook, triumphantly retrieved the horribly snarled line, and retreated below to untwist the mess.

Obviously we weren't used to being at sea again, for in the afternoon Margaret wrote in the logbook: "I have been having hallucinations of palm trees alongside the ship. Hal keeps hearing cars start up."

A little later the wind increased again, so we pulled down the mainsail completely and continued at hull speed under the storm jib alone.

At noon on August 27, the third day, the sky cleared and we had bright sunlight. The ocean seemed calmer and we hoped the gale force winds were over. We hoisted the reefed mainsail, which lessened our rolling, and celebrated the end of the storm with a substantial hot meal. The improvement was a false alarm and at 2100 the wind increased again. *Whisper* began to race through the water. Two waves thumped over the port side and broke heavily on board before we could hand the mainsail. We continued under the storm jib alone.

Ever since we had left Bora Bora, water had been flying everywhere. There seemed to be as much below as outside. Heavy spray drummed on the coachroof with every roll of the ship, and the water worked under the main hatch and dribbled into the quarter berth and galley. The forepeak deck leaks began to run as usual. Altogether the situation below decks was more suited to tropical orchid growing than to sailing. "Where oh where can I hide the ship's logbook to keep it dry?" I said.

August 28. 0400. Reset steering vane after squalls. Still running under storm jib alone. Wind from the port quarter. Heavy rolling. Bad ventilation with everything shut. Need more Dorade vents. A bit cooler 1200 miles south of the equator and a wool shirt feels good at night. Boy am I tired! What I want more than anything else is sleep.

At 0830, after a series of squalls, the wind decreased. While I was hoisting the reefed mainsail the clouds opened up a bit and I saw both the sun and the moon. Margaret quickly handed up the sextant and wrote down the time while I measured the angles. The observations put us ninety-seven miles from Mauke and 245 miles from Rarotonga.

We had shaped our course to pass slightly south of Mitiaro and Mauke because we had been warned of a strong current near the two small islands.

We were going through the southern limits of the southeast trades and the squally weather continued. At noon the next day we had both the full mainsail up and the working jib set, but later we pulled down one third of the main again. On the evening of August 29, star sights of Betelgeuse, Canopus, Achernar, and Capella put us thirty-one miles from our destination.

We kept a careful lookout because Rarotonga was only a few miles long and would have been easy to have passed in the dark, which would have meant beating back. At 0300 I stood in the companion-way looking around while I drank a cup of hot chocolate. Suddenly I saw two lights, a red and a white, off to port. By staring hard under the weak glow of the new moon I was just able to make out the shadowy profile of an island to the southwest. It was wonderful to see navigational lights for mariners after the slim pickings in French Polynesia. My heart was full of thanks.

We immediately came about and put *Whisper* on the starboard tack to work north of the island. As dawn broke across the sea the green bulk of Rarotonga hove into the yellowish sky. From a distance the island appeared as a triangular stone fortress that seemed strong and enduring but somehow terribly alone and isolated. The island had such *clarity* in the early light. It was almost as if you had removed a pair of dirty glasses from in front of your eyes and saw the scene now sharp and clear and brilliant all in a twinkling.

It probably sounds silly, but as I watched Rarotonga grow bigger and its distant pyramid change into a miniature range of mountains and valleys I felt a little tinge of achievement at having found the island. Not that it was hard particularly, but I suppose somewhere there is a bit of Columbus or Captain Cook in all of us, and though today we only play at discovery, the game is still thrilling.

How exciting it is to sail to a new island! Suddenly all those hours —watching the compass, the eyestrain over the charts, the celestial observations, the calculations, the sail changes at night, the wet clothes—suddenly all those things are behind you and mean nothing, for the prize is at your feet.

The island stands before you, green and golden in the early-morning light. The mountains rise boldly, soaring up to rocky sum-mits and descending in wrinkled ridges and swooping escarpments.

On the lowland the ever-waving palms look familiar and you wonder what is growing on the cultivated fields. Closer still a blue wave booms once on the fringing reef and in a magical instant is split into a million fragments of white. A red building, a steep-roofed church, and a flag stiff in the trade wind appear from behind a headland.

You check the chart for rocks and depths and ease in toward the shore. Now you can see houses in the village and a white-fronted store. A fisherman in a canoe outside the reef smiles and waves his arm in greeting as you glide in close to the land.

Now is the moment to go in. Down with the mainsail. Hard around on the tiller. Change the jib sheets. You work the tiller with one foot as you stand on the cockpit seat to judge distances. You run in through the pass, nervously watching the claws of coral on each side. Now down comes the jib, its white folds fluttering to the deck. As you round up into the wind the ship loses way and you fling a line to a pair of arms that materializes from the crowd on the pier head. The yacht swings for a moment and then settles down as her dock lines are made fast.

"How long 'de trip take, capt'n," calls out a friendly voice.

"Four and a half days from Bora Bora," you reply.

"Good time, capt'n."

You have arrived.

Tiny Rarotonga, a mere twenty-five square miles in area, is one of the fairest islands in the Pacific and easily ranks with Tahiti, Moorea, and the Marquesas. The administrative center and largest of New Zealand's Cook Islands, Rarotonga is formed of an oval-shaped cluster of mountains seven miles long and five miles wide that pushes grandly above the sea. The highest peak is Te Manga, 2,110 feet, but there are half a dozen more only a little lower. Below the skyline of wrinkled green, the island slopes off into ridges heavily wooded with banyan, breadfruit, tamanu, chestnut, and candlenut trees. In the higher valleys you can pick tiny orchids and walk beneath enormous tree ferns. Downslope you see thousands of orange trees, thriving fields of tomatoes, and lush swamps of taro whose leaves look like giant dark-green butterfly wings at rest.

The climate is one of the best in the world. During the day the temperature is always between 76 and 84 degrees. At night it ranges between 66 and 74. The island has a small fringing reef but no lagoon to speak of, and the only shelters for ships are at Avarua and Avatiu on the north shore. Both places are mere cracks in the reef, although Avatiu is being continuously improved to give modest protection to vessels up to about 100 feet over-all, the length of the motor ships used for inter-island transport.

Before *Whisper*'s dock lines had stopped swinging at Avatiu, two little cars squeaked to a stop on the jetty. Four young men, who represented the departments of agriculture, health, customs, and immigration, pushed through the crowd of onlookers and jumped on board. All were neatly groomed and immaculately dressed in white shirts, white shorts, and high white stockings. We shook hands and filed below.

"How long do you want to stay?"

"Clearance papers from your last port, please."

"Have you any guns aboard?"

"What do you have in the way of spirits?"

"Your smallpox vaccination certificates expired in California. How did you get through French Polynesia? Come to the hospital for shots, please."

"What fruit have you on board?" (A grapefruit, three or four papayas, two dozen limes, and the fruit basket were whisked away and never seen again.)

The men were good-looking Polynesians—called Maori in New Zealand—who spoke excellent English. They obviously liked to come aboard the ship and were pleased to look around. But they seemed so efficient and formal and unbending that I was somewhat awed by their white-starched presence. (Maybe it was because things were so casual in French Polynesia.) I thought of offering the men a drink, but I wondered whether I would be arrested and carted off to jail if I produced a bottle of California brandy. I thought I had better not. I asked a few questions, promised to go to the hospital, handed over the fruit, and went forward to lower the yellow Q flag. As I watched the men drive off I was breathless from their efficiency, which seemed to belong more to a rifle drill team than to dockside formalities.

The first thing that surprised us when we went ashore was the general feeling of orderliness. Everything appeared to be arranged and planned somehow. The men wore trousers and shirts and the women European-style cotton dresses. No longer did you hear a gentle *ia ora na* but a snappy *good morning*. The people walked quietly along the sides of the neatly paved asphalt roads, and although it was a Wednesday morning I had the feeling that church was just out. The New Zealand government—which did furnish good medical and dental care—was more paternalistic and rule-conscious than the French, who ran things without interfering with the natives so much. Or if you changed the words you might say there was a certain gusto and spirit in the Tahitians that was dampened and ironed flat—or almost flat—in the Cooks. We were to learn that only occasionally would the inner quicksilver of the Cook Islanders show itself.

I went to cross the paved road along the shore and looked first to my left and then to my right as I stepped across, something I had done a million times before. A horn beeped and brakes screeched and I leaped out of the way and turned to see a Land Rover automobile coming toward me on the right-hand side of the road. Yipes! I was back in England, where the traffic runs opposite to the rest of the world.

After I recovered from almost getting run over we walked three fourths of a mile to Avarua, the main village of Rarotonga and the government center of the Cook Islands. Dozens of small Honda motorcycles buzzed past us, usually with two people aboard, and life seemed to be prosperous around the busy stores and trading companies. The government buildings, neatly constructed and painted, with metal roofs, were the featureless, one-story offices you might see anywhere. Tall, pale New Zealanders and stocky, somewhat darker Maori dressed in the shorts and immaculate white stockings that we saw everywhere hurried from office to office with papers and briefcases. Signs read H.M. CUSTOMS, H.M. POLICE, H.M. IMMIGRATION, and so on. I thought the Gothic churches of the London Missionary Society (LMS) might have been appropriate in England, but on a tropical island they were monstrous, ugly, and singularly out of place. I was appalled at the waste of good land for the LMS cemeteries, which were marked by acres of hideous gravestones.

On the Union Steamship Company dock hundreds of cases of orange juice were on their way out to a freighter anchored off the reef. Dozens of jovial stevedores loaded the boxes on a tiny railroad system that took them to the end of the pier, where they were passed from hand to hand to whaleboats and lightered to the ship and the world market beyond.

We knew that three of the Cook Islands had airfields, but we were surprised when we found out there was no regular air transport and no airmail service. We had asked our bank to send us funds, but we discovered there was no bank in the Cook Islands. Our mail was no doubt in Wellington, New Zealand, waiting for the monthly steamship. Without money our stay looked bleak, but the government treasurer, Tom Overhoff, understood our problem and kindly advanced us funds.

We found the government freezer in Avarua a wonderful place to shop. Friendly girls in white were delighted to gossip about our trip and to sell us fresh vegetables, eggs, and delicious frozen meat from New Zealand. The prices were low, the variety excellent, and the quality high. After a sea passage and visits to islands where the diet was mostly fish, taro, coconuts, and tinned meat, we doubly enjoyed the fresh food.

Everyone kept inviting us to go dancing, so the next night we walked along the shore, past the rusting wreck of the 100-ton schooner *Yankee*, to the dance hall, where I paid our admission charge of thirty cents each. The dancing was sensational, and the din from three guitars, a tambourine player who sang, and a determined drummer was incredible. You had to talk by sign language, for all you could hear was music blasting out of a bank of shoulder-high electric amplifiers turned to full volume.

The dance hall was packed. Most of the girls and many of the men wore flower garlands of frangipani called *ei*. Everybody seemed to be there—not only the young and the old, but the very young and the very old. *Everyone* danced *every* dance. The music was mostly modern, and the steps were a helter-skelter combination of the twist, frug, rock and roll, jitterbug, tamure, and any quick step you care to name. To call the dancing spirited hardly describes it at all. When the music started the scene was like a volcanic explosion, and the energy burned up on the dance floor was enough to blow a hole in the sky. Two hundred couples shook, lurched, swayed, quivered, seesawed, wriggled, staggered, zigzagged, and squirmed. I thought 400 firecrackers had exploded.

The dancing was such fun! If you tried to sit out a number and to feebly fan yourself back to normal, a girl would appear and drag you off to the floor. On one turn near the stage I looked up at the orchestra. I almost fainted when I saw that the leader, clad in a chartreuse-and-magenta shirt, with a big flower garland around his neck and a crown of blossoms circling his head, was the staid immigration official who had been on *Whisper* the day before. He had a big smile on his face and he was frantically strumming away on his amplified guitar and hugely enjoying himself.

Part way through the evening a troupe of twenty teenagers put on a special exhibition of traditional dancing. Such a show was called an "item" in the Cooks, and the young performers were led by an older, expert dancer. This night the leader was a woman from Aitutaki who was a superb dancer and who shepherded and prodded her grass-skirted charges through their intricate steps. Afterward the leader did a slow solo number. Her dancing was astonishingly graceful and sensuous. Her face beamed, her hips talked, and her hand movements literally sang. The dancing was earthy, and radiated voluptuousness and life. In no way was the effect prurient or lustful. The dancing was the essence of shining beauty. It is impossible to describe art with words, but I might be able to suggest a measure of her skill when I say that no one applauded when she finished. Everyone in the hall leaped to his feet and cheered spontaneously.

On the way back to *Whisper* I kept humming the new tunes I had heard and the next morning I caught Margaret trying out a few dance steps on the foredeck.

Next to us in the little harbor were two small yachts that we had seen in Papeete. Ed Boden from California was genial and handsome, a forty-year-old civil engineer who had purchased a twenty-five-foot *Vertue*-class cutter named *Kittiwake* in England. He had thrown away the engine, stoutly rerigged the ship as a masthead sloop, and was having a wonderful time sailing leisurely around the world. Though he was by himself he was by no means a loner, for he made dozens of friends wherever he went. The Polynesians were

hopeless at mechanical repairs, something that Ed was particularly good at, and he fixed dozens of motorcycles and outboard engines wherever he went. His small sloop was always a social center, and—though he made big disclaimers—when the pretty girls were around I am sure he liked to see them. Ed was a good sailor and he taught me many tricks of sail handling.

"My ambition is to be the first person to sail around the world and not write a book about it," he said.

Our other neighbor was Eric Hall, who sailed by himself on *Manuma*, a Nicholson 32 fiberglass sloop built in England. Eric was an ingenious fellow, and one day he showed me a rope ladder he had made that he could hoist to his masthead in case he had to go aloft while at sea. Eric was older, a retired naval engineer, who—though always willing to lend a hand or to give advice—kept more to himself and liked to go for long walks. He was taking his ship from England to New Zealand.

The contrast between the two captains was astonishing. There were always several motorcycles or bicycles parked on the dock above Ed Boden's ship, with people coming and going and half a dozen adults and children on board. Someone would be strumming a guitar and Ed would be tinkering with an outboard engine or playing his tape recorder. His ship was loaded with gifts of fruit and fish and we always wondered when he slept. On the other side of us Eric Hall would be reading or cooking a solitary meal. I don't think he was lonely. He preferred a quiet kind of existence. Perhaps we saw the races personified: the gregarious American and the retiring Englishman. Certainly you could choose the sort of life you wished when you were on a small yacht.

While we were in Rarotonga we met all the island characters, or at least the prototypes. We bicycled out to Rutaki and called on Andy Thomson, the legendary South Seas schooner captain who had skippered trading vessels in the Cook and Society islands for forty years without an accident. Andy had retired and was energetically tending an enormous vegetable garden behind his house.

"I'm over eighty now," said Andy with a big smile. "My health is quite good but my wife suffers a bit from arthritis. My only problem is a continuing thirst for alcoholic spirits."

We exchanged visits with Andy several times and he told us yarn after yarn while he consumed glass after glass of whisky. ("The hurricane was a double one and with the lee shore only five miles away I took over the wheel myself . . .")

We shook hands with Father George, a sympathetic, cigar-smoking, old-time Dutch priest who taught us a few phrases of Maori and gave us rides on his powerful motorcycle. He proudly showed us his small church near Titikaveka, where he made us coffee and played opera records on his gramophone. Father George was keen on sailing ships. He kept a large logbook and asked each visiting skipper to fill in a page with details of his ship and trip. You could scarcely read some of the entries without your eyes getting a little misty, for life and death was down in black on white.

The book recounted that in 1966 a Canadian yacht had struck the reef on the northwest side of Rarotonga in the middle of the night. A large number of local men worked four days to free the ship.

"The sight of the *Trendaway* sliding into the boat passage and to the sea along with the roar of over one hundred helpers will live in my memory forever," wrote the captain.

We got acquainted with Walter Hambüchen, an American who spoke bitterly about his homeland. Walter, once an ecologist, edited the island newspaper. "Rarotonga is my home now," he said. "I will never go back to the nervous confusion of the United States."

The local fishing expert, Peter Nelson, came aboard *Whisper* and explained how he used the Japanese long line method to catch tuna. Peter was a quiet, curly-headed New Zealander who described the different islands with soft-spoken precision.

"You see, on Puka Puka the men have plenty of time," said Peter. "When they buy a box of matches they carefully split each matchstick down the middle. That way they get two boxes of matches and pay for only one."

We had dinner with Graeme and Rosemary Wallis, two schoolteachers from New Zealand who were experts on local history and who took us hiking in the mountains. Later they loaned us a Honda motorcycle. We inspected a forty-foot catamaran being built by Brian White, the shipping manager of the Cook Islands Trading Company. We met Maori families and were often invited into their homes when out for walks, especially on the weekends, when we were sometimes given a glass of bush beer, vile stuff made from oranges.

We attended the dedication of a new community hall at Titikaveka and got involved in a Maori feast with chicken, pig, noodles, taro, breadfruit, yams, eggs, rice, orange juice, and various salads and desserts whose Maori names I never managed to sort out. Everyone ate with his fingers, quite an adventure in slippery eating, especially when you tried a dish that was a kind of jello . . . oops—there it goes. The food was laid out on tables, and flies were a problem that was solved by young girls who stood behind you all through the meal and kept long fly whisks moving back and forth.

Officially there was no racial discrimination in the Cook Islands and many white men had Maori wives. I was surprised to discover that few of the men taught their wives to speak English. It seemed a pity, for it cut the wives out of so much of the social life that the men enjoyed. English was taught in school, but in the past—especially on the outer islands—not all the young people attended. Perhaps as schooling is improved the problem will ease. I can't imagine being married to someone and not to speak his principal tongue.

Everyone was kind to us. We had hot showers at the little government hotel, the laundry did our work free, and the head of the woodworking department at H.M. Public Works, Malcom McQuarry, helped us with several repairs to the ship. All throughout the Pacific, people assisted us and freely gave us goods and services. Though we were ordinary people we were on a great adventure, the kind that many men and women dream of and with which they can identify. Perhaps by helping us they participated a little in our journey.

Whisper's deck leak was no better. The next suspect was the forward coachroof portlight. It was poorly made and had always leaked a little. After some deliberation I removed it and fiberglassed the opening with twelve layers of cloth. I backed up the repair with a piece of plywood and laid a piece of teak—a gift from the local coffinmaker —across the inside to match the paneling. Certainly the leak would have to stop soon!

Almost every night during the fifteen days we were in Rarotonga we heard drums and the sharp crack of sticks on wood blocks in the packing shed above the little harbor. Twenty or thirty teenagers would gather to practice traditional dances, and we often watched an older expert lead his pupils through intricate steps and songs again and again as a beautiful bit of island culture was passed on. The young people liked to gang together every night and to work at their steps. We thought it was a good way to grow up.

On September 14 we sailed from Rarotonga. We had reached the southernmost point of our trip and henceforth we would head north and west until we got to Japan. Our first destination was Aitutaki, 140 miles north.

A stranger to the Cooks might consider the islands a unified group like Hawaii or the Azores. The truth, however, is that the Cooks are fifteen tiny bits of land scattered over 750,000 square miles of the

Pacific between French Polynesia on the east and Samoa and Tonga on the west. The Cooks—whose land totals less than 100 square miles—are really two groups of islands 500 to 750 miles apart. Aside from their name and flag they bear little relation to each other. Tops of extinct volcanoes form most of the southern islands, while coral atolls make up the northern group. Transport is by ship and usually slow and infrequent.

Captain James Cook discovered five of the southern islands in the 1770s and the rest of the islands gradually became known. Beginning in 1822 the London Missionary Society (LMS) moved in and quickly converted the natives to Christianity. Soon the islands were controlled by the missionaries, who meant well but imposed unreasonably burdensome moral laws on the easy-living Maori. The rules were based on Calvinism and directed by zealous evangelists who worked from grim, thick-walled churches that looked more like fortresses than places of worship. On Sunday, to take just one example, no work, sport, or relaxation was permitted. No fires were allowed, not even a cooking fire. The entire day and evening were devoted to scripture reading, prayers, sermons, studying gospel messages, and catechizing. The missionaries on each island worked hard to get funds and goods from their converts to extend the church work elsewhere.

During the nineteenth century, France, England, Germany, and the United States were busy claiming islands in the Pacific, but no one paid much attention to the Cooks. It wasn't until 1901 that the islands were placed under British sovereignty. Constitutional government was gradually introduced, and the excesses of the Protestant church were whittled down. We had heard that the Blue Laws—the LMS rules—had been especially strong in Aitutaki. Now the island was on our skyline and we would find out.

The sail from Rarotonga had been delightful. High aloft a few soft smears of cirrus had floated like swirls of whitewash on blue paper. The wind was from ahead, about ten knots, the seas were slight, and with all our sails set we had glided along like a feather on a quiet pond. We arrived at night and hove to until morning.

I had been told to sail back and forth in front of the Arutanga anchorage on the northwest side of Aitutaki. We did so and soon a small government launch came out of a narrow pass that led from the lagoon, which was studded with coral patches. The launch chugged alongside and a short man clad in a white shirt and white shorts stepped on board.

"Welcome to Aitutaki," he said with a smile and a warm handshake.

"My name is John James MacCauley, but everyone calls me Jock. I'm the resident agent and I'll give you a few directions as we go in."

Jock helped us furl the sails and then took a towline from the launch which was guided by a native helmsman who expertly piloted us to the tiny anchorage at the main village of Arutanga. We dropped an anchor and put out two stern lines to trees on shore. *Whisper* was well protected by land on three sides and had three miles of shallow lagoon on the fourth. Unlike Rarotonga, there was no surge. Eight big whaleboats, two power launches, and two other yachts lay nearby. Our friend Ed Boden in the twenty-five-foot *Vertue* sloop *Kittiwake* had sailed ahead of us and was waiting with a pot of coffee.

"Would you like some bananas?" he said as he poured. "I have already fixed eleven outboard motors and I just happen to have five stalks. Also I can let you have twenty giant papayas. Would you like a fish for dinner?"

On the other side of us we looked at *Clarinda*, a straight-stemmed, twenty-nine-foot gaff cutter, surely built before World War I. She was a Plymouth hooker, a converted fishing boat with a long bowsprit, and had been sailed from England by Colin Iles and Martin Mitchell. A third crewman, Peter Harrison, had joined later. Colin planned to settle in New Zealand and take up farming. However, there was a slight delay because the three fellows had made a wonderful discovery in the Cook Islands: girls!

Aitutaki was four miles long and one and a half miles wide, a fertile summit land of volcanic origin that was surrounded by a much larger triangular-shaped lagoon that measured twenty-seven miles in circumference. The highest point on the island was Maungapu, 390 feet, from whose windy summit you could look down on a lagoon of sparkling green, across to palm-topped patches of white coral sand along the barrier reef, and to the purplish ocean beyond. The 2,500 people raised oranges and bananas and made copra, but after Rarotonga the pace of things seemed slow.

Like all the outer islands, Aitutaki suffered from the exodus of its young people, who were attracted by the bright lights and money of Rarotonga and New Zealand. Unfortunately the smartest often went first and tended to leave the less talented behind. We were to see few people between fifteen and forty. With an official policy of discouraging tourism, poor transport, and the flight of its vigorous youth, the future of the outer islands was doubtful.

During our 16 days at Aitutaki we became good friends with the
resident agent, Jock, and his wife, Mate (MAH-tēy), a delightful New
Zealand Maori woman. We had many meals with local people, watched
native dancing, toured the island, and even played tennis. One day
Jock and a few friends took us on a picnic and shell hunt to Akaiami, a
small motu of white sand and utter peacefulness on the eastern barrier
reef. Once the motu had been a stopover point for inter-island seaplanes,
but the traces of man were almost gone. Now above the untouched
sand the leaves of the palms, tamanu, and hibiscus trees swayed and
dipped before the fresh wind of the southeast trades as they always
had, and when I walked on the dazzling beach and felt the warm
Pacific water wash across my feet I thought how transient and puny
man was.

A Maori friend, Dora Harrington, taught me the words of a local
folk song. Sometimes we went to the dance hall, where—as in Rarotonga but on a smaller scale—the people managed to burn up a few
million calories. We learned to eat *uto*, the fibrous filling of a sprouting
coconut which some people compared to ice cream. Somewhere I
picked up a bug and spent a few days in my bunk feeling unhappy

until the local native doctor paddled out and gave me a bottle of sulfa tablets which soon cured me.

Because of the LMS Blue Laws, now modified but still not to be ignored, it was improper for a man and woman—young or old—to be seen walking together. In a group, O.K., but two alone was severely frowned on. Affairs of the heart had to be carried on with extreme discretion. You met someone miles out in the bush, each party having arrived from the opposite direction. All the people in a village knew of the meeting but no one saw anything.

The three fellows on the yacht next to us, *Clarinda*, had made friends with girls but unfortunately had carried on too openly. Gossip started that the girls were common. The mothers lost face and became resentful. To regain prestige one mother went to the police and swore out a complaint against one of the *Clarinda* crewmen. The charge was serious and dealt with the rape of a girl under fifteen. After the resident agent initialed the charge a chief judge would have to come from Rarotonga to hear the case.

Jock was an old hand at such problems. He managed to delay initialing the complaint while he ordered the yacht to leave.

"I won't be sorry to see the boys go," he said, shaking his head. "You see, if the woman could have publicly vilified the man in question— 'Pig! Pig! Miserable pig!'—her standing with her peers would have reverted to normal. Now there is trouble for me, the police, the woman, other yachts—it's a mess."

The captain of *Clarinda* promptly hunted up the indignant mother, apologized profusely, and somehow got her to drop the charge. People were disgruntled but everyone was able to breathe again.

While this was going on we had our own problems. During the gentle sail from Rarotonga, Margaret had appeared in tears one morning. "It's the deck leak," she wailed. "Everything is wet again. We've spent so much time for nothing. If the ship leaks under these easy conditions what is it going to do in a really bad storm?"

Jock offered to have one of the local boat experts look for the leak. "However, if that doesn't work, you should memorize a Maori chant to Tangaroa, the god of the sea," he said. "Whenever you see a big wave coming you shout '*Tangaroa i te Tiitii. Tangaroa i te Taataa.*'"

I took pains to learn the chant, but I also decided to remove four feet of toerail on the starboard side, to plug some of the bolt holes, and to see what happened on the run to Samoa. We did several other small jobs, spent a morning filling our water tanks, and gave a little party for our friends.

On Sunday, October 1, the day before we left, the pastors in each of the Aitutaki churches made the following announcement: "The black yacht *Whisper* will leave for Palmerston Island tomorrow morning. The captain has offered to take any mail, citrus fruit, flour, sugar, cabin biscuits, and small packages. No chickens or pigs or lumber."

The Smallest Island

PALMERSTON WAS 219 MILES WEST OF AITUTAKI, AND with a fair southeasterly wind I reckoned the trip would take two days. However, the weather was unsettled and overcast, and the trade winds were stronger than I had anticipated. By 1700 the second day we had logged 157 miles plus an estimated twenty-four additional miles for the current swept up by the prevailing wind. Because of cloud cover and rain I was unable to get sights, so I hove to on the port tack since I didn't want to pass Palmerston in the dark and have to beat back.

We *had* to find Palmerston, the westernmost island of the southern Cooks, for *Whisper*'s saloon was piled high with mail, flour, sugar, shiny tins of cabin biscuits, burlap sacks stuffed with oranges, unwieldy stalks of bananas, and large and small packages. At 0630 on the third morning I let the backed headsail draw again and we resumed our course of 270° M. Half an hour later, as a rain shower cleared, I was pleased to see a sliver of land ahead. At first I thought the land was a long way off, but the tiny islet on the north side of Palmerston was only four miles away. It *was* tiny.

When I looked ahead and saw the small atoll in the middle of the turbulent ocean it seemed a miracle of existence. How could such an insignificance of land, a mere scrap of nothing, survive when the sea was angry? Before me was a rudimentary piece of the universe, a shadowy outline without real dimensions, a collection of earth fragments like those a small boy would use to build a sand castle on a beach.

Yet—unlike the small boy's handiwork that always washed away—the land had risen from the bottomless deeps of the Pacific, a wheel of life that had somehow endured and grown and had finally flowered in plants and birds and fish and man himself.[10]

In factual terms I could write that Palmerston was an uneven, almost submerged thin oval of brown and reddish coral seven and a half miles long and five and three quarters miles wide on which six lumps of sand, each holding a bouquet of palms, were scattered like white beads on a dark string. Fifty miles from Palmerston the ocean was over 16,000 feet deep; not until you were within nine miles did the tiny atoll begin to climb from the floor of the ocean. There was no central land mass at all. From my perch up the mast I could see directly across the shallow lagoon, past the short whitecaps, to the far reef. Under the gray sky the diamond greens of the shallow lagoon were muted to soft emerald and quiet cobalt.[11]

The island was uninhabited until 1860, when an Englishman named William Marsters settled on the remote atoll. Marsters, born in Birmingham in 1821 and brought up by his grandmother in Leicestershire, went to sea at fourteen as an apprentice and eventually became a mate on a whaling ship. He changed jobs during the gold rush in California and worked at mining for a while, but later went to sea again until he jumped ship at Penrhyn in the northern Cook Islands. Penrhyn was a wild place in 1850, but Marsters got along well and even married the daughter of the chief. He traveled among the Cooks, visited Samoa, and in 1860 sailed to Palmerston with a labor force of islanders to establish a coconut plantation for a Tahitian businessman named Brander, who owned the little atoll.

In addition to one wife from Penrhyn, Marsters married a second woman, who was his first wife's cousin. The labor force on Palmerston had been recruited for one year but no one from Tahiti appeared until 1866, when Brander's son-in-law came with the news that Brander had died. Marsters promptly gave Brander's relative a bill for the labor and for necessary supplies that he had bought from passing whalers and had paid for with gold nuggets he had gotten in California. Brander's relation responded by giving Marsters the island in lieu of payment. The new owner pondered his future and must have wondered what his grandmother in Leicestershire would have said.

The lagoon was filled with fish, there were always coconuts, and the people made copra and collected a few supplies for whaling ships. Marsters acquired another wife, a woman from Manihiki, and eventually had a family by each of his three wives. The virile Marsters had seventeen children in all. The number grew to fifty-four in the second generation and to more than 1,000 in the fifth generation, now spread far over the Cooks and New Zealand.[12]

According to Christian ethics, old white-bearded Marsters' sins were manifold. However, he was a practical man with a good deal of common sense and he ran the island reasonably well. He taught his children to worship God carefully and insisted on a rigorous upbringing of all the young people.

"The boys were frequently made to row to the other side of the lagoon and back—nine miles—before breakfast, and had learned to battle with the elements in boat and canoe, to fish with spear, rod and line, and net, to catch birds, to work with tools, build houses, and a score of other crafts before they were in their teens," wrote Commander Victor Clark, who spent eleven months on the island in recent years.[13]

A test of manhood was to build one's own boat, which had to pass the scrutiny of the other islanders and to stand up to the rigors of the sea.

Many stories have been circulated about inbreeding on Palmerston. According to Commander Clark, such tales are myths. You need only to meet the present-day Marsters to see how healthy and alert they are. Old William did not allow a brother and sister to marry. Half-brothers and sisters could, but only one couple did. The others took Maori wives and husbands from elsewhere in the Cooks. In more recent generations the Marsters have married within the family but no closer than cousins. More often they have chosen mates from distant islands, and new blood has flowed into the family.

In the early days the atoll developed somewhat as Pitcairn Island did, with little contact with the outside world. Old William taught his descendants to speak the English of his native Leicestershire, but over the years the phrases became strange and hard to understand. It wasn't until the present days of radio, the influx of a few outsiders, and occasional travel to the other islands that the accent of the English got back to normal. Many of the young people of each generation have gone to other islands where there has been more opportunity. But in spite of the emigration, a colony of eighty to one hundred has remained, interwoven in a giant family of three main branches with incredibly complex relationships.

A visitor in 1929 who called on the son of old William (who—like his father—had also married several times) discovered that the island magistrate had a very young wife, a daughter a good deal older than the wife, and a granddaughter older than both his wife and daughter.[14]

When England assumed control of the Cook Islands at the end of the nineteenth century, Palmerston was run under a lease from the British government. In 1953 the island was given to the inhabitants, who largely run their own affairs. An acknowledged head of the family keeps order and any disputes are settled by a family council.[15]

If you look at a map you might think that Palmerston would be visited by vessels from Samoa, Tonga, or Fiji, but the reality of island commerce is that an island group tends to be served by its vessels alone which voyage for definite commercial reasons. Palmerston's main cash crop is twenty to thirty tons of copra annually, not very much really, and trading ships call only about twice a year.

I put *Whisper*'s helm down and hauled in the mainsheet as we rounded the north point of the atoll and headed toward the principal islet. Our sails had been sighted, and four boats and a dozen men came out. They were a healthy-looking lot, dark from the sun, with heavily calloused feet. They wore shorts or trousers, a mixed-up collection of tattered sweaters, and well-mended jackets. Most had on hats or caps of some kind. Though we were only 1,100 miles from the equator, the wind was cool under the gray sky. Warm garments were clearly valued possessions.

"Welcome to Palmerston," said Bob, who was first on board and handed us four drinking nuts. He was a tall, handsome, thick-set man in his fifties whom I liked at once. The way he smiled and moved around the decks put me at ease.

The passes into the lagoon were shallow and encumbered with coral, so Bob directed us to an anchorage on a sand patch about 200 feet outside the barrier reef some three fourths of a mile from the village. The trade wind was steady, and it held us away from the reef. We unloaded all the packages and fruit.

"You and Margaret come ashore with me," said Bob. "Joe will stay on the ship until you return. If the wind or current shifts and the ship swings toward the reef, he can slip the anchor and sail away from the island."

I had never left *Whisper* with a stranger before, certainly not in such a hazardous position. But the Marsters had excellent reputations as boatmen and the condition of the boat that Joe had built and come out in indicated a good deal of knowledge. *Whisper* was in the lee of the island, so there was no sea swell, but the twenty-knot trade wind kept a heavy strain on the anchor chain. Before we left I put out a second anchor, also buoyed, and went over the details of the anchor winch and sail handling with Joe.

The small village was on the lagoon side of the westernmost islet and, like most atolls, was composed of sand and gravel and small lumps of coral. The beaches were white and sandy, and the shallow water felt warm when we waded ashore. Young palm trees, perhaps fifty feet high, were everywhere, and their leafy top-hamper rattled noisily in the wind. We walked past a row of small palm-thatch boathouses near the shore to Bob's house, where his family was waiting to greet us. When we shook hands, each person held onto our hands and smiled and said a few words of special greeting that made us feel particularly welcome. Two chairs were put out for us and we had tea and cookies. Bob's wife was a big woman who sat crosslegged on a pandanus mat on the floor, a position she was obviously well used to. Another woman was about to have a baby, and several youngsters frolicked around the room.

Bob's house had a tin roof, but many roofs were made of plaited palm leaves. The floor was concrete and the crossbeams and rafters were shaped from coconut wood. A kerosene pressure lamp was suspended overhead, and a splendid pandanus hat trimmed in red hung on one wall. In a corner stood a sea chest and the inevitable foot-operated sewing machine. Every bit of fresh water on Palmerston was rainwater. There was enough, but I noticed that when Margaret finished washing, her bowl of soapy water was carefully poured on a young lime bush that Bob was trying to grow in the coral.

A little later a stout young girl named Tupou appeared. "Compliments of Mr. Ned Marsters," she said. "Please come to tea."

Ned Marsters, the magistrate, was the grandson of old William, the first settler, and though Ned was hospitable and remarkably courteous, there was no nonsense about him. You soon learned that he was in charge of the island and that was that. Ned must have been in his mid-sixties, a serious, stocky, clean-shaven man with white hair, bushy gray eyebrows, and the healthy bronzed skin of all the Marsters.

"We had better eat now," said Ned as soon as we entered his house and met his family. Ned's place was a sort of island headquarters that included the medical station, a water catchment storage system, and various rooms. "We can talk at the table."

We sat down to a first-class meal of chicken in curry sauce, taro, rice, and a dish called po-ke, a mixture of pumpkin and arrowroot. There were lots of flies around the food, but Tupou stood opposite us and fanned them away with an elaborate fly whisk made of six long bosun-bird tail feathers.

Margaret asked Ned about the weather. "Do you think it will get worse?" she said.

"No, not just yet," said Ned thoughtfully. "Let's see. . . . Today is October fourth. The strong winds don't generally come until January and February, although in 1883 a December storm destroyed all our coconut palms. In January 1914 our houses and crops were wrecked by a hurricane which swept many islands in the South Pacific. In 1923 most of our houses were leveled and the crops destroyed, and at the end of March in 1926 the atoll was completely devastated. Early in 1931 we had much damage by heavy gales, and in February 1935 practically all the coconut palms and ground crops were swept away. Another bad one came in 1942.[16]

"We used to have eight islands on Palmerston, but two of them washed away in the storms."

He spoke with a mixture of pride and resentment in recounting how the people of Palmerston had resurrected themselves with little help from the outside after the major storms of 1926 and 1942. "The incentive for schooners to call is copra," he said. "After the hurricanes had destroyed all the coconut palms we had no copra to sell and hence no schooners came.

"It was a difficult time," said Ned. "I had many young mouths to feed and all we could eat was fish. I fished all day every day and slept little at night worrying about getting enough to eat. The women dug in the center of the island and made several small taro plots. We scarcely had any tools to move coral and earth and had to construct wheelbarrows from wood. No schooners came for a very long time and we had no sugar or flour or matches or coffee. As soon as possible we got a thousand sprouting coconuts from Manihiki and planted them.

"But I don't want to scare you with all this talk of hurricanes. A bad one comes only every dozen years or so. Most of the time the weather is good."

We got on the subject of music and I mentioned how good the people of the South Pacific were at playing ukuleles and guitars.

Ned shook his head. "Both of those instruments are new to these parts," he said. "When I was in Tahiti in 1912, neither was known. But a few years later—in 1917—the ukulele and guitar had reached Rarotonga by way of Tahiti, and in 1925 we got them here. Before that we played the accordion and the mouth organ."

After we had eaten, Ned sent Tupou with us on a tour of the island, which didn't take long because the atoll was only one half mile wide. The houses of the eighty people were neatly arranged and built either of wood or thatch. Each had a separate cookhouse, a washing shelter, a toilet, and often a fenced enclosure for small black pigs. The lanes between the houses were swept clear of leaves, and here and there was a bed of flowers. We admired several fine breadfruit trees, walked along underneath the rustling palms whose slender brown trunks arched before the wind, and had a look at the taro and arrowroot patches.

We passed the cricket pitch and stopped at the school, where we talked briefly with the teacher and the eighteen pupils and shook hands with each one. In spite of the occasional hurricanes the island seemed reasonably prosperous. We walked beneath a few small banana and papaya trees and noticed many chickens strutting around. In the center of the atoll we were surprised to see a few large tamanu trees, thick-trunked heavyweights that might be compared to the oak trees of the temperate zones. The wood is hard and is used for canoe hulls, boat frames, cabinet work, and wooden bowls.

The occupants of almost every home we passed rushed out to see us, to shake hands enthusiastically (an island passion), and to invite us in for a visit. Palmerston is a low island, without navigation lights, and is hard to spot from the sea, especially at night. In the past a number of ships were wrecked on its reef. Among the houses we saw ships' cabin doors, bits of staircases, paneling, and stoutly built bunks with sets of drawers underneath.

We were tired and returned to Ned's house, where we met Ben Samuel, a lively, wide-awake chap who was the "dresser," the first-aid man. Ben had just come in from the reef with four big blue-green parrot fish. We were invited to spend the night on the island, but I elected to return to *Whisper*. Ben gave us one of his fish for dinner and we looked forward to eating the tasty, thick, boneless meat. Bob took us back to the ship and returned home with Joe.

During the night the wind increased a little, and when Joe came out at 0700 the next morning we winched in the main anchor and chain and hung on a light Danforth anchor and a nylon warp which was easier to cast off in case of trouble. I bent on a smaller jib and tied a deep reef in the main. Joe seemed happy to stay on board and look after *Whisper*, so we went ashore.

We walked around the island, met the radio operator, and had a look at the church—a dark, weather-stained, incredibly decrepit structure that was built of salvaged wood and bits of old ships. The steps to the pulpit were fashioned from a companionway whose shiny brass rail and brass treads had surely rolled across many a seaway.

During the last hurricane the church was blown some distance away, but the men of Palmerston salvaged the remains and patiently rebuilt it, although the building lists to port. Ned showed us a special stormproof house whose timbers were eighteen inches square and sunk deeply into the coral. The massive beams and stout planks were salvaged from a wrecked ship that was hauling bridge timbers from America to Australia.[17]

We looked at photographs of Commander Victor Clark, an English sailor whose yacht *Solace*, in the same position that *Whisper* now occupied, swung onto the reef and was wrecked in 1954. With the help of the islanders in an epic effort, the thirty-four-foot ketch was hauled across the reef to the village, where she was rebuilt to continue her voyage around the world.

At our request dinner that day was curry chicken again plus rice, taro, coconut and arrowroot pudding, small crispy-fried fish, and coffee. As before, Tupou stood opposite us with her fly whisk and chased away the flies. Ned muttered about political troubles and how outsiders were trying to get control away from the people of Palmerston, but I didn't think he had much to worry about.

We heard the bang of a gun and Ben rushed past with an old rifle. "A nice fat bosun bird is flying around," he shouted as he ran toward the beach.

Margaret walked over to visit Joe's wife, and a little later Ben—he had missed getting the bosun bird—and I went fishing on the reef. We put on stout plastic shoes to protect our feet from the sharp coral and waded west from the village to the edge of the fringing reef, where the raging seas thumped and thundered as they crashed on the reddish-brown coral. You couldn't watch without wondering how the reef could withstand the endless cannonading of those tons of furious water. A ship wouldn't last ten minutes on such a reef, I thought to myself. A steel hull was the only hope. I looked nervously to the north where *Whisper* lay anchored a little offshore. She was safe and her position unchanged.

Ben used a heavy three-pronged spear about fifteen feet long with remarkable success. We stood together and peered into the deep pools. I saw nothing. Ben, his eyes glinting with delight, pointed excitedly at a fish, raised his spear, held it for a moment, and flung the javelin. About half the time when he pulled back the spear there was a fish impaled on its tip. He then strung the fish on a length of tough fiber stripped from the central leaf stalk of a palm frond. With so much fishing on Palmerston I thought such expeditions would be old stuff to Ben, but he beamed with delight the whole time we were out. In forty-five minutes Ben had four parrot fish from eighteen to thirty inches long and half a dozen smaller ones.

I happened to glance to the north toward *Whisper* and stood horror-struck when I saw the ship spin around and head away from the island. Ben and I rushed back to the village, wading through the shallows as fast as we could. As we neared the beach, people began to appear from everywhere.

Those who live close to the sea realize that when there is trouble everyone must work together, smoothly and quickly. There is no time for arguments, only time for cooperation and help. Long-practiced plans go into operation and emergency measures take precedence over everything. We had to get to *Whisper*, which was getting smaller and smaller, both to retrieve the ship and to bring back Joe, who without knowledge of celestial navigation would be unable to find the island once it got out of his sight.

The Palmerston boats, twenty feet long, were stoutly built, with closely spaced frames and thick planking. The open boats were very heavy, but when the order went out to put one in the water, the nearest four people—men or women—picked one up at once on a sort of double-yoke arrangement and quickly carried it from its boathouse to the water. Willing hands loaded the rudder, sails, spars, oars, containers of fresh water, line, tarpaulins, and a small outboard engine.

Then I was in the boat with Ben at the tiller and Ned, Tupou, Margaret, and a young boy. We poled through the pass and chased *Whisper*, which was several miles away, drifting slowly, while Joe, without sails, steered across the wind toward the southeast. We made good time in the trim Palmerston boat and soon got alongside the yacht.

"The ship started to swing toward the coral," said Joe when I climbed aboard. "There was barely time to slip the anchor."

With the boat in tow we sailed back to our anchor off the reef. The wind was still over twenty knots and its change from the southeast to the east was probably responsible for the vagrant current that had swung *Whisper* toward the reef. The unsettled weather was worsening.

Clearly it was time to go. By now four other boats had come out from the village. Everyone climbed on board and we tied the boats astern.

"I had hoped to stay a few days so we could have gotten to know you a little," I said. "To leave now simply tears the heart out of me."

"Don't worry," said Ned. "We understand."

We gave the assembled people two pieces of line, a sack of fresh limes, and some requested tubing fittings and valves and bits of hose and clamps. Ned had asked us for Vaseline. Fortunately we had a large can that I was glad to give him. We passed up all our old clothing and what few cigarettes we had. I gave Joe a knife and several hand tools along with some canned and powdered milk for a new baby.

The people began to press letters and packages on me, along with greasy coins and well-creased New Zealand dollar bills for the postage. I took the mail but refused the money. A man I had not seen before gave Margaret a lovely bowl of tamanu wood. A girl handed me a fresh loaf of warm bread. Margaret held up two rare seashells. Suddenly I had a fish, a piece of exotic wood, two coconut bowls, a crown of fragrant flowers. . . .

"We had planned a feast in your honor," said someone. "We're sorry that your hat's not ready. After you admired the hat in Bob's house we wanted to make one for you."

We all shook hands one last time, and the many Marsters climbed into their brightly painted boats and headed toward the lagoon. Margaret sailed slowly ahead with the mainsail while I hauled in the nylon warp. Finally I reached the fathom of one half inch chain at the end and with a mightly heave flipped the anchor on board. As Margaret bore off I winched up the jib and with both the wind and current behind us we were quickly carried away from Palmerston.

I could hardly look back for the tears in my eyes.

An epilogue to our visit to Palmerston came more than a year later. When we were on the island, Ben Samuel, the first-aid man, had an ailing Seagull outboard engine that needed a vital part. The engine meant a lot to his family, and I told Ben that I would try to get the part in Samoa and send it to him.

"But I need it now," he said. "By ship it will be a year or more."

Three or four times a year a plane of the Royal New Zealand Air Force flew from American Samoa to Aitutaki to calibrate the radio direction-finding equipment of the airport. I knew the plane flew over

Palmerston during its flight, and I thought I might be able to arrange an air drop.

When we got to Apia in Western Samoa a friendly mechanic found the part, which I wrapped in a rag and stuffed into a large coffee can together with a dozen ball-point pens the Marsters had asked for. I put a note inside, wrote the destination outside, taped the can shut, and attached a long yellow ribbon streamer. A pilot at Polynesian Airlines kindly agreed to take the can to Pago Pago and leave it for the next New Zealand plane. I had done what I could. Now it was up to others.

More than a year later I received the following letter:

Palmerston Island
December 20, 1968

Dear Hal:

Thanks very much for the part of the Seagull that you sent on the calibration aircraft. It was dropped down on the water catchment roof. Now I have confidence in you because I didn't trust you when you told me you were going to send the part on the calibration plane. When the plane circled around the island several times I knew the plane was going to drop something. I remembered what you told me. So thanks for your kindness. I send you greetings from Ned, Bob, and the other people on Palmerston. I passed on your best wishes and love to all the people here.

Now I would like to give my greetings to you both for Christmas and the New Year. Also I convey my greetings to your families.

Thank you for the ball-point pens that you sent. I have been in Rarotonga for two months and have just returned to Palmerston. So Hal please would you send some of the pictures. I would like to have some to remember you in the future. Also send some old clothing for the families here on Palmerston. If you need any local things please let me know.

I conclude my short letter here with Thanks to God for all your best. I wish to hear from you and Margaret.

Cordially
Ben Samuel
Dresser, Palmerston

8 / 〜〜〜〜〜〜〜〜〜〜〜〜〜〜〜〜〜〜

The Heart of Polynesia

"SOMETHING IS AHEAD," I SAID TO MYSELF ON THE MORN-ing of October 10. "Tall mountains seem to be mixed up with those clouds. It must be Samoa."

"*Land ho!*" I shouted.

Margaret came on deck and studied the horizon ahead. "Oh no," she said, shaking her head. "I don't agree at all. You're dreaming. Those are only clouds with bluish tops."

It was hard to pick out land when a cumulus build-up towered in the distance. I knew we were close to Tutuila, but were those 2,000-foot mountains ahead or not? How easy it is to wish things in front of your eyes and to lose arguments with yourself when you want to see something! We continued to the west-northwest for another four hours before a dark line on the horizon thickened slowly into green and blue mountains fronted by bold cliffs with necklaces of white where the ocean broke on the fringing reef.

Whisper had logged 466 miles between Palmerston and Samoa, a five-day run with mostly heavy stuff from the southeast, gale-force winds and seas that had whipped us down to a solitary storm jib. ("All shipping in Tonga, Fiji, and Samoa is in port because of storm force easterly winds and heavy, disturbed seas," croaked the radio between bursts of static.) On October 8 we had made a run of 121 miles with only 103 square feet of canvas flying. Fortunately the steering vane had worked to perfection, and we scarcely touched the mechanism except to change the wind-blade adjustment a few degrees one way or the other.

The seas rose up big and irregular and lots of water slammed on board. The forward deck leak was worse than ever, and for several days we mopped up a bucket of sea water from the lee side of the cabin sole every two hours or so. Boarding seas filled the cockpit to overflowing several times, and plenty of water squirted in around the main cabin hatch.

The most insulting deluge came through the Dorade vents, the special coachroof ventilators with water traps that usually stopped everything but air. I was asleep when the top of a wave rolled on board, cunningly filled the ventilator above the head of my berth, and suddenly poured in on me. I was asleep one moment and spouting water and cursing the next. Margaret couldn't keep from laughing, and I had to smile to myself when I realized what had happened.

October 7. 1600. Speeding along under headsail alone. Cloud cover gray and dark but not thick and I can see blue sky in places. Waves

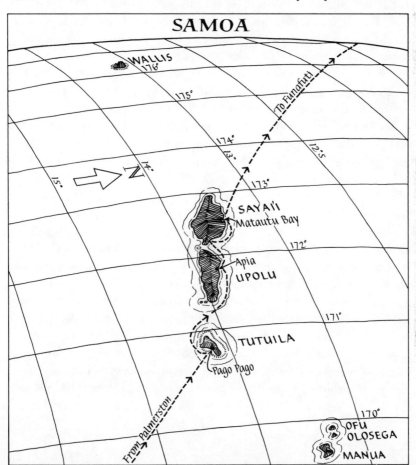

large and the yacht skims forward on big rollers several times a minute. About every 30 minutes or so the top of a wave slops on board with a noise that is a little unnerving. Surprising how chilly it is without the sun. Good to have on oilskins and a stout safety harness when I go on deck. I have been sitting in the cockpit chuckling over a book by Nancy Mitford called The Blessing, *a paperback that is completely soaked through. As I read I tear off the pages and watch them flutter away. . . .*

The wind, the irregular up-and-down motion, and the leaks combined to make the passage damned unpleasant for four days. We had the ship's hatches and ports mostly closed because of all the water flying around, and the ventilation below was poor. The air was hot and stuffy and it was too rough to cook much. But on the morning of the fifth day the wind eased, the sun came out, and no longer were we on a roller-coaster ride. Maybe a little adversity heightens beauty, for after the storm the sky seemed bluer, the sun warmer, and the sea had a quality of magnificent gentleness. I stood in the companionway for hours, filled with delight at the sparkling ocean and the too blue sky. The air was as clear as the rays of a star, and I felt that I could see all the way to eternity. My uncluttered life was indeed sweet, and it seemed—as it always does—that the simplest pleasures were best.

Not only is the sea unspoiled and without artificiality, there is a primeval quality, a *purity* surrounding its environment. Maybe you appreciate the sea because when you are lost upon its vastness your life is not jammed up with the trivia, the meaningless detail, and the foolish stuff of civilization. Somehow a fundamental strength—a mysterious and independent energy—seems to flow from the wild and undisciplined ocean. Perhaps on some level we recognize an affinity with the ultimate powerhouse of nature.

Samoa consists of three large islands plus a handful of smaller ones. The islands are high, bluish-green, and wooded, their rounded summits sticking up from a great submerged range of volcanic mountains that surfaces from the deeps of the Pacific. Tutuila, owned by the United States, is the smallest of the big three islands but has the best natural harbor in the South Pacific. The highest peak on the fifty-four-square-mile island is 2,141-foot Matafao which rises above a 1,200-foot ridge that runs along much of Tutuila's nineteen-mile length. The opening to the great harbor of Pago Pago (pronounced Pango Pango) faces south,

and as we approached we had to watch out for breaking seas that were sometimes kicked up by heavy swells that erupted on off-lying banks of coral a few miles south of the island.

The weather was light and we sailed shoreward, close-reaching with a gentle northeast wind while we glided up and down on big swells. Through the binoculars I picked out radio towers, and soon we were even with the red-and-white entrance marker on Breaker Point. The *Pilot* books warned of Whale Rock in the middle of the fairway, and as I looked ahead off to port there was a tremendous whoosh and rush of white water as a swell broke on the rock. We saw a red bus creeping along the shore and we began to pick out a rusty roof, a slab-sided warehouse, a wisp of smoke. Tall cliffs and mountains rose on three sides of us and it seemed that we had reached the end of the bay and that the charts were wrong. But as we drifted slowly northward the main harbor magically unfolded to our left, and we headed into a quiet bay where we were totally protected from ocean storms. An aerial tramway spanned the harbor overhead and a few small ships were tied up to docks along the south shore. Across the way on the north side I saw dozens of large fishing ships with high prows and sharply curved sides. The yellow sun hung low in the sky and the long shadows of the jutting mountains cast shimmering patterns on the still dark water. Altogether the scene was beautiful and we were thrilled to sail into American Samoa.

My reverie was short-lived.

"Hey, buddy, you can't tie up here," bellowed a hoarse voice when I approached a dock near the main settlement. We continued a little farther and saw a car drive up, a man get out and motion us toward an old pier, where we went alongside. The pier was particularly rickety and the edge toward the water bristled with enormous nails and spikes. We quickly put out tires to protect the hull. Several more cars drove up with Samoans who were customs and health officials, but the immigration and agriculture officers were busy at the airport and weren't able to come for several hours. I wanted to go out and anchor, but we had to stay at the terrible dock until our incoming clearance was finished. *Whisper*'s hull got badly scratched by several fiendishly long spikes that stuck out from the old pier. Finally we were ready to go.

"You can tie to a mooring in the harbor without charge for four days," said one of the officials. "After that you have to pay port dues. For your thirty-five-foot length the charges are twenty-five dollars for the first month, fifty dollars for the second month, and seventy-five dollars for the third."

The charges seemed enormous.

"I'll anchor then," I said. "This is an American ship and I have good ground tackle and—"

"You still have to pay," said the man. "It's no good to anchor because the bottom of the harbor is foul with pieces of old ships and cars and trucks and whatnot dumped in by the Navy. You had better tie to a mooring and think about it."

We did as he suggested and went to bed.

The next morning I was awakened by a squeaking noise and I suddenly realized that I was listening to birds. I climbed on deck and sat in the warm sun and looked at the magnificent harbor which lay under the green bulk of Rainmaker Mountain. A big Australian ship had docked at the main pier, and we heard the shouts of the stevedores as they unloaded cargo. Near us half a dozen other yachts—including several trimarans that I later found out were abandoned—lazily circled their moorings. The motor ship *Dick* of Apia, flying the red-and-blue ensign of Western Samoa, chugged past with a load of waving Samoans and a deck cargo of giant taro. *Dick* was a funny old ship about fifty-five feet long, painted many shades of blue and white and red, with a toilet perched aft above the water on two timbers that stuck over the stern.

Margaret and I went ashore in the dinghy and walked to the post office, where we found a long line of people in front of the windows. We collected a bundle of letters and several parcels and mailed all the letters and packages that we had brought from Palmerston. The little post office was a popular place, for the Samoans not only received and posted letters, but they sat around reading their mail and industriously penning long letters. The women tended to be large, often with broad shoulders ("Good football players," I said), and generally wore bright cotton print dresses. The men were stocky, dressed mostly in shirts and trousers, and often rode bicycles or motor scooters. Outside the post office a Samoan policeman directed traffic with a lot of fancy hand signals that used up so much energy he had to be relieved every few minutes.

Margaret went shopping for fresh food while I hobbled off to the hospital. On Aitutaki I had gotten coral cuts on the Achilles' tendons of both ankles and the wounds had steadfastly refused to heal, probably because they were always wet when sailing. The hospital was a large, impressive-looking, old-fashioned series of buildings with busy departments and plenty of patients.

The doctor sucked his breath in sharply when he pulled the bandages off the backs of my ankles and uncovered horrible festered wounds. He prescribed gentian violet ("never lime juice") and antibiotic ointment. "You must keep your ankles dry," he admonished, an order I dutifully followed for the next three weeks until the coral cuts healed.

When I returned to *Whisper* I had to look twice to find her, for Margaret had all the wet things from the forepeak hanging out in the sun to dry. The ship was festooned with sheets, trousers, cushions, charts, sails, and things I'd forgotten we had. I took drastic action to solve the forward-deck leak and removed five feet of toerail on each side and filled the bolt holes and hull-deck joint with epoxy resin. The appearance of *Whisper* suffered a little, but I was quite ready to trade beauty for dryness.

On the next mooring was the thirty-six-foot Carol ketch *Myonie*, an American yacht registered in Ashland, Wisconsin, of all places. Al and Helen Gehrman were on their way around the world for the second time. Al was a podiatrist, a foot doctor, and from time to time the voyaging would stop while he repaired a few feet to raise further cruising funds. Al was in the midst of a big job. The casing of the reduction gear on his auxiliary engine had broken so he removed the engine, extracted and repaired the broken part, and put the units back —all by himself while on a mooring.

It was possible to rent an automobile, but we found bus rides much cheaper and more fun. As in Tahiti, the buses were the main transport, and everything was hauled in the ancient vehicles, often castoffs from Kansas City or New Orleans. There were long benches down each side of the buses and the sides were windowless and open. The scenery along the south shore of Tutuila was spectacular. We often climbed high above a beach or a bit of dazzling shoreline lagoon as our old bus groaned along the steep and bumpy roads.

We passed many Samoan villages, collections of thatched huts that looked like brown cupcakes amidst the tall trunks of the coconut palms. A Samoan house is called a fale (FAH-lee) and consists of a high, dome-like roof that rests on inner and outer posts of breadfruit wood ranged around in a circle. The supporting posts—set on a raised stone or concrete foundation—entirely replace the usual walls and partitions of a house. The high thatched roof is particularly effective against the heat of the sun, and the absence of any walls means that cooling breezes can blow right through the house. Privacy doesn't seem to be a problem, since everyone can see everyone else. In case of windswept rain a series of woven screens, something like venetian blinds, can be let down from the roof. Pandanus mats are put on the floor for sitting and sleeping, and the fales are usually free from Western-style furniture except for a foot-operated Singer or White sewing machine. Cooking is done in a smaller shelter in back.

The native structures near Pago Pago were quite junky in appearance, with pieces of rusty iron sheeting in place of thatched roofs. But farther away the villages were more unspoiled and prettier, with swept paths and flowers growing around the fales. In the outer districts the men wore wrap-around skirts called lava-lavas and the women dressed in pulatasies, ankle-length skirts with fitted tunics—usually of contrasting colors—that extended down to the thighs.

Each village had an extra-large fale in the center, a sort of meeting-house, and we often saw a group of men sitting around in a circle crosslegged on mats in the traditional Samoan manner while they discussed some problem or other. As they talked they made sennit, coconut fibers that were twisted and rolled into a twinelike cordage that was used to lash things together.

On the way back to the harbor a young boy hailed the bus, indicated that someone in a nearby fale wanted a ride, and said something in Samoan. I was surprised when a number of the passengers got off and walked to the fale. Each reappeared with a case of beer, which he stacked down the main aisle of the bus. Soon there were twelve cases of beer on board. Finally the passenger appeared, an older man with a tailored lava-lava who was carrying a briefcase and seemed to be someone of consequence. We continued along for a few miles to another village, where the scene was repeated, except that the beer was off-loaded. The passengers lent a hand as a matter of course, and the bus waited until the delivery work was completed. I found out later that if you had an errand in a store the bus driver would wait for you if you asked him. Never mind the schedule!

The ultimate in bus assistance came a few days later when we rode westward along the south shore. Evidently a woman was building an addition to her house, for the bus left the main road and stopped at a lumber yard. Everyone got out and helped load long two-by-fours, unwieldy pieces of plywood, and heavy iron pipe—not a little but a lot. The loading took a long time. The springs of the bus were bent way down, and Margaret and I wondered whether we had gotten into a work detail by mistake. Finally the driver indicated that we were ready to go, and everyone got on, climbing around the enormous load down the middle. The bus staggered off, never daring to leave first gear.

In Tahiti we had met several officers from large Korean fishing ships because the men had stopped at all the yachts to ask for foreign postage stamps for their collections. Their calls were clever, since the yachts received mail from many places and usually could give the Koreans a few new stamps. The Koreans also liked to practice speaking English. In Pago Pago the two large tuna canneries—Star Kist and Van Camp— were supplied by big fishing fleets from Japan, Taiwan, and Korea, and we soon met a Korean officer ("Stamps, please, for my collection"), Captain Myung Ki Moon of the Nam Hae fleet ship #270. Captain Moon was a short man, about five feet tall, with a round face, long black hair, a rumpled blue suit, and endless enthusiasm.

"Come to my ship, please, for a little visit," he said with a bow.

The following afternoon we took the bus to the north side of the harbor. At the shipyard next to the canneries we found an amazing scene, one that must have made the old Polynesian gods up above shake their heads. Fifty or sixty motor fishing ships from the Far East lay rafted together in long rows as they underwent repairs and painting. The ships from Japan and Korea were modern steel vessels, but those from Taiwan were wooden with high, amazingly curved sides, the sort of sheer you might expect to find on the emperor's launch in an old Chinese scroll. Without the weight of tons of fish in their holds the Taiwan ships lay at odd angles, their decks canted and the masts leaning way over.

Hundreds of energetic Oriental crewmen swarmed over the ships, hammering, wire-brushing, sawing, riveting, and painting. Japanese welders knelt on the decks, their hoods masklike and their sparking welding rods blue and ghostly. Sweating Formosans threw fishing floats into shore boats while gangs of begrimed Koreans sat balanced on crude rafts on the water while they scraped on the sides of the hulls. Some ships were diseased with rust. Others gleamed in antiseptic white. Laundry fluttered from a dozen decks, and loudspeakers shook with the tremulous vibrato of Cantonese singers from Hong Kong, squeaky flutes from Taipei, and scratchy violins from Pusan. The water was streaked with heavy oil, putrid with fish waste, and stinking from garbage and sewage. A ship out of the water had new bottom paint and was about ready to skid down the ways while the crew madly polished the bronze propeller. In front of us a Chinese carpenter shaped a curved plank with a long chisel and a leather mallet. On the side of the quay a dozen Orientals hurried around measuring out new fishing lines which lay in long, starkly white rows on the oily earth.

We found Captain Moon buttoning his trousers in the wheelhouse.

"Ah, postage-stamp people," he said, waving us in. Captain Moon's 160-ton steel vessel was one of sixty-one identical ships that had been built in Le Havre, powered with Fiat Diesels with German reduction gears, and outfitted with radios from England, fishing tackle from Japan, and hardware from the United States. "A truly international ship," said Captain Moon, chuckling at his little joke.

Ship #270 had been laid up for months waiting for a new engine part from Germany. In the meantime the vessel had been painted inside and out. We saw that half the deck space was filled with fishing floats, buoys, and lines, and that most of the space below was taken up by the large engine and refrigerated hold. The quarters of the officers and crew were tiny, but the men seemed well used to climbing over one another and were cheerful and busy although perhaps weary of the long stay in port. After having seen Polynesians for so long the energetic and fast-moving Koreans seemed nervous and high-strung to us.

Most of the Far East Samoan fleet practiced the long line method of deep sea fishing in which a stout main line about 1,000 feet long is attached to flag buoys and is paid out overboard. From this main horizontal line, five to thirteen branch lines hang vertically downward and are provided with hooks baited with eight-inch frozen fish from Japan.[18]

"This assembly is called a basket," explained Captain Moon. "When we are on the fishing grounds my men put out about 375 such baskets which means that we have some 3,375 hooks strung out on fifty to seventy-five miles of line. We adjust the buoy lines to control the depth of the hooks to meet the bluefin tuna or albacore which generally swim thirty-five to 120 feet below the surface."

The men fished for albacore, yellowfin, big eye, and marlin. The albacore ran ten to forty pounds, the big eye 100 to 400 pounds, and the marlin 140 to 600 pounds. The capacity of the refrigerated ship was seventy-five tons which hopefully had been reached after a trip that was sixty days long and included forty-five days of fishing. The twenty-four crew members worked on a share basis of thirty-five percent of the catch, with the rest going to the Korean government which provided the ship and took care of its expenses.

In 1967, the Star Kist cannery paid $380 for one ton of albacore, $280 for yellowfin, and $180 for big eye. A little arithmetic told us that the contents of the refrigerated hold were exchanged for about $21,000. The crew shared $7,350, or an average of $360 if the catch was good and of high quality. It seems that commercial fishing—no matter where practiced—is a tough life, with long hours of drudgery at low pay. "Of course our life would be better if it weren't for the sharks, which take twenty to twenty-five percent of all the fish we catch," said Captain Moon.

Before we left we had a drink of iced pink punch and were given a few fish hooks and a dried shark's jaw. "Save for me all postage stamps from foreign countries, please," said Captain Moon.

We gave him our promise.

One day a sailing enthusiast named Grant Masland came down to *Whisper*. Grant was a director at the television station and he took us on a tour of the station and of several elementary schools. Since Tutuila was small and the schooling had been widely criticized in the U.S. press, a major island project was the transmission of lessons by television. A master teacher working under ideal conditions in Pago Pago could prepare an arithmetic or language lesson that could be beamed all over the island together with expensive artwork and teaching aids that could never be justified for one teacher alone. It seemed a good scheme until we learned that $6,000,000 had been spent on the station and its equipment (six video tape recorders at $60,000 each), money that could have trained perhaps several hundred Samoan women to be teachers or have established a small teachers' college. In the schools we visited we felt that the television lessons were presented as *a substitute for* a teacher rather than as *a supplement to* a teacher. It seemed to us that the young people spent entirely too much time passively watching television. The pupils were bored, unchallenged, and quite outside active participation in the lessons.

We met Don Farrell, the capable and talented principal at Pavi'e'i, a fine new school in a village on the south coast. Don was in love with his job, thoroughly happy to work with his Samoan pupils and teachers, and he thanked his lucky stars at having such a fortunate opportunity. Don was a good amateur painter, he liked to play the valve trombone in his spare time, and he was keen on gardening which showed up in the borders around the school buildings which were bursting with flowers and decorative shrubs. But Don was not typical. Too many of the Americans I met were interested only in high overseas pay, extra allowances, travel, and U.S.-type housing. They tended to erect exclusive enclaves ("Samoans keep out") where they sat around drinking and complaining about their sacrifices at leaving home. "I am here for only one reason," an American schoolteacher from Oklahoma told me.

"I want the money and when my thirteen months and twelve days are up I will leave here forever."

I have no respect for such people, for in turning away from those around them—in this case the interesting Samoan people—they cheat themselves dreadfully. Certainly they could learn a few words of Samoan, if for no other reason than to impress the people back in the United States!

Although I met some good people in American Samoa I did not enjoy the visit. The Samoans were well aware of the position and money of the Americans, and I often felt tension and hostility in the air. The Americans got stateside wages; the Samoan women at the canneries received 60 cents an hour. Yet the prices in the stores were not significantly different from those in San Francisco. The ramshackle native housing around Pago Pago, the rundown shops, the rickety stores, the polluted bay, and the greedy merchants around the harbor were an absolute disgrace. I failed to see how a jet airstrip and a luxury hotel would help the average Samoan on Tutuila.

We paid our harbor dues, fivefold more than anywhere else on our Pacific trip,[19] and with Grant and Lynne Masland on board for the overnight sail to Apia we slipped seaward under the lofty brow of Rainmaker Mountain.

9 / ~~~~~~~~~~~~~~~

Twice Adopted

WHEN I LEFT PAGO PAGO IN AMERICAN SAMOA AND sailed the eighty miles to Apia, the capital of independent Western Samoa, it was like going from a dark closet into a large, well-lighted room. The ghosts from the dark were gone. The room was filled with relaxed, hospitable people. A big bowl of fruit sat in front of me and I found that the coins in my pocket were worth three times as much.

We liked Western Samoa at once. We arrived on a Sunday evening, usually a time when clearance officials are away and return grumbling to charge overtime. But the first official who stepped on board smiled pleasantly.

"Welcome to Western Samoa," he said as he stamped our passports. "How long would you like to stay with us?"

It took only a few minutes to clear and we tied to a large mooring buoy in the harbor. The amazing thing about anchoring in a harbor at night is how different the appearance becomes at first light. Mysterious shapes turn into ordinary buildings; a shadowy hull becomes a whale boat on a mooring; from the sound of the surf you worry that you've anchored almost on the beach, yet in the morning you're half a mile away. Screams in the dark are only shore birds scrapping over a piece of fish. The red winking light that seemed so close is really on top of a radio tower two miles away.

We were on the north coast of Upolu, anchored in the middle of the harbor of Apia, a city of 25,000, about one fifth of the country's people. Western Samoa is made up of two main islands, Upolu and Savai'i (sah-VYE-ee), both forty-eight miles long and up to twenty-five miles wide. The islands have mountains from 3,000 to over 6,000 feet, but the high places are usually hidden in clouds, and from the ocean the main view is of swelling hills of green that roll gently upward until they disappear into wispy layers of white.

The last land of any consequence that we had visited was Tahiti. The islands of Upolu and Savai'i were of comparable size but immeasurably more fertile, with large coastal lowlands of deep rich soil. There was plenty of rainfall and a big local population that was both friendly and would work cheaply. It was no wonder that white planters and entrepreneurs had cast covetous eyes on this fair land a century ago, and that Germany, England, and the United States had sent warships to look after the interests of each country's greedy nationals. Indeed the ships might have fought and begun a war if a hurricane hadn't wiped out the competing warships in Apia harbor in 1889. Germany ran Western Samoa until World War I, when New Zealand assumed charge. In 1962, Western Samoa became independent, although she still leans heavily on New Zealand aid and British-trained leadership.[20]

We took the dinghy and rowed ashore. Apia harbor is roughly semicircular in shape, about one mile across, and open to the north, with the entrance somewhat encumbered by reefs. A new wharf and warehouse have been built on the eastern side. Landward of this is a long, tree-shaded beach on which the local tugs and ferries are dragged up on crude marine ways for repairs and painting. We left the dinghy under a breadfruit tree and headed along the main road, which circled the bay.

An English Austin chugged slowly along and we passed many Samoans walking. The men wore lava-lavas and were generally big and full-fleshed. We passed a hotel, half a dozen small churches, a noisy bus depot, various shops, and the big trading stores of Burns Philp and Morris Hedstrom. Many of the women were dressed in pulatasies, the long Samoan skirts that seemed to impart such a graceful motion to their walk.

Where Main Beach Road intersected Vaea Street we watched a Samoan policeman direct traffic. He was dressed in a gray lava-lava with a Sam Browne belt and stood on a small platform under a large square umbrella. He controlled the pedestrians and vehicles with an amazing display of arm, hand, and elbow motions. His white gloves pointed up, then down, sideways, together, his arms crossed, uncrossed,

spread apart, stood at right angles. He was an artist with his hands, a conductor of movements and motion. No one could describe his gestures, but everyone understood them. The people and cars and trucks followed his directions and flowed smoothly through town with hardly a stop.

The Samoan women sold fruit and vegetables along the main street. The produce was exhibited in palm-thatch baskets behind which the women sat on mats holding aloft black umbrellas to shade them from the hot sun. You could buy such things as cucumbers, pineapples, limes, mangoes, passion fruit, and green beans very cheaply. In American Samoa one or two papayas cost twenty-five cents; in Apia you could buy a whole basket of enormous papayas—a load you could scarcely lift—for the same price.

All the produce was big, well-formed, and beautifully ripe. The people too were healthy and vigorous, with sturdy, muscular bodies, glistening skin, and shiny white teeth. The abundant land gave them an excellent diet—though they often ate too much. It was a local joke that a beefy Samoan could destroy an enemy by merely sitting on him.

The next afternoon we stopped at Aggie Grey's Hotel. In Rarotonga, Captain Andy Thomson had told us to call on Aggie. "I once did her a small favor and at Christmas time she always sends me a bottle of whisky, which helps me get over New Year's Day, a troublesome holiday," Andy had told us.

Many years ago Aggie started a small hotel with beds for twenty-two people. Now she could take 160 in a jumble of modern buildings and gardens next to the Vaisigano River on the east side of Apia. One took it for granted that her rooms were clean, her formally served set meals good, and her people dependable. It was the depth of her welcome, the people you met, the happy way her dining-room girls danced the siva-siva, and the fact that she served an honest drink and managed to straighten out your jumbled currency that made you remember. And a generation did and passed the word, and Aggie became famous.

I found myself face to face with a tall, dignified woman perhaps in her late sixties. Half Samoan, the daughter of an English pharmacist, the widow of a New Zealand businessman, and the mother of five well-educated children, Aggie was unlike anyone I had ever met. She wore a long red mumu with a white flower print that, together with her gray hair and erect carriage, gave her a thoroughly commanding appearance.

She spoke softly and slowly, almost as if she were choosing the best word from a list of many, and I found myself listening intently. She told about her early days, her house in the Bay of Islands in New Zealand, the problems over money and transport, and how she had put up the passengers from the flying boats during the seventeen years they had flown to Apia. We talked for only a little while, but it seemed that I had known her always. From time to time an aide would whisper some problem in Aggie's ear. She would make a decision, utter a few commands in Samoan, and return to the conversation with hardly a break in her delivery. She was a completely gracious woman who radiated poise and character and had the stuff and substance of royalty. I hoped that all queens were like Aggie.

She chuckled when I told her that Andy Thomson said he often dreamed about her and thought she was the most beautiful woman in the world.

"That goddamned old liar hasn't changed a bit," she said. "He always was full of hot air and whisky. I guess that's why I love him so. . . . Now I know you're off the little black yacht and I want you to have dinner with us."

I protested that I hadn't come to cadge meals and that we generally ate on board.

"Young man," said Aggie imperiously, suddenly standing huge and tall above my chair, "you're my guest. One of the girls will tell you when your table is ready."

The following day I went to see Captain Benson, the harbormaster. It was now the end of October, and the South Pacific hurricane season would begin in a few weeks. Samoa was along the northern edge of the danger area, but our planned course was northwest and hopefully would take us rapidly away from the hurricane danger.

"Stay with us here in Apia until March," urged Captain Benson. "If a hurricane comes, we'll take care of you. My boys will haul you up on the beach over in the corner. It's the only way a small ship can survive.

"If you remain here until the southeast trades return in March, you can continue with a fair wind," said the harbormaster. "It's pleasant here in Apia. The people are good, the water in the bay is reasonably clean, and there are no harbor dues."

Benson was right. Apia was pleasant and I thought hard about the invitation to stay. However, if we waited five months our sailing schedule would be completely upset. It was important for us to time our passages to miss the typhoon season in Japan and the winter gales in the Aleutians. Benson's invitation was tempting, but I decided to continue.

For a long time I had considered putting canvas weather cloths around *Whisper*'s cockpit to cut down the amount of spray that flew up on the helmsman. We inquired about a sailmaker and were told to see the local expert, a man named Tapasu who lived in back of Main Beach Road. The principal streets of Apia had European type buildings—the usual stores and shops and offices and schools—along with several notable structures left over from the days of German rule. But once away from the waterfront area you rapidly left most of these buildings behind. You were back among trees and fales, cooking huts, and paths in the woods. In a twinkling you were in *fa'a* Samoa, the Samoa of tradition and antiquity.

Tapasu welcomed us at once and the women spread mats for us to sit crosslegged on. I thought our visit would be only a few minutes, but I didn't know much about Samoa.

Tapasu was an alert, slim man in his late forties who was delighted, simply delighted, to see foreigners and to talk about ships. In his earlier days he had sewn sails, worked on inter-island schooners, and had even survived a shipwreck.

Tapasu's fale was surprisingly large inside, about forty feet across, and with its high airy roof and lack of furniture had lots of room. We met several of Tapasu's married children and said hello to his younger children and grandchildren. Various women were cooking out back, and Tapasu's immense wife, Sivaiala, a skilled seamstress, was busy sewing on her foot-operated machine. We began to get a notion of the Samoans' love of oratory from all the questions. How old were we? When was the ship built? How tall was the mast? Did we have oars or an engine? Where had we gone to school? How much did it rain in San Francisco? What was snow like? And so forth. We sat so long that our crossed legs ached terribly.

The next day Tapasu paddled out to *Whisper* in a handsome green-and-white bonito canoe to measure the ship for the canvas weather cloths. He spent an hour looking over *Whisper*, pronounced her O.K., and told us more about his experiences on schooners. "You had better come to tea at four o'clock," he said as he left. "The women will have something nice and I might cook a steamed pudding myself."

That evening we had steak, pig, green beans, fish, drinking nuts, and taro. The Samoans are very fond of taro, a root crop something like a giant turnip, and were continually munching on the big white tubers. I thought taro tasted like library paste and ate as little as possible.

During dinner I noticed Sivaiala looking critically at my shirt.

"That's poor material and the shirt doesn't fit very well," she said. "Go down to the store tomorrow and pick out a few fathoms of nice cloth and I'll run off some shirts for you."

During the next few days we spent a great deal of time with Tapasu's family. Sivaiala made shirts for me and dresses for Margaret, marveling at M's slim figure and at the small amount of material needed for a dress. "No Samoan in her," said Sivaiala wistfully.

We took half a dozen of the women from Tapasu's family out to *Whisper* for a visit. After the ladies had looked around the ship and played with the cat they sat in the cockpit under the broad awning and sang Samoan songs, clapping and laughing like young children, their voices carrying far over the still water.

I would hate to get in a fight with a Samoan, for they are generally powerful men and in addition are expert rock throwers. For supper one night Tipeni, Tapasu's fourteen-year-old son, was told to kill a certain chicken that was strutting around outside the fale. Tipeni was with me at the time and while he went on talking he picked up two rocks. He casually threw the first rock, which knocked the chicken down. The second rock hit the chicken's head and killed it. When I commented on his prowess at throwing, Tipeni shrugged, picked up another rock, and pointed at a flower on a distant hibiscus bush. A moment later a shower of red petals floated down.

A few nights later when Tapasu, Margaret, and I were out for a walk along the waterfront I happened to mention Captain Benson's invitation to anchor in the harbor until March. "A good idea," said Tapasu. "You can stay with us. We're your family now. You can move right in and live in the fale as long as you want."

At first we were flattered at the invitation, but we soon realized that Samoan hospitality was overpowering. You were expected for every meal and if you were late or missed a meal the family would be quite distressed. There would be a knock on the hull and a sad-faced member of the Tapasu family would hand up a warm fish and some goodies wrapped in a banana leaf. We enjoyed the family and liked them, but we wished to look around the island on our own sometimes.

We got acquainted with an American family from Hawaii, Charlie and Mary Judd and their three children. Charlie was the chief surgeon at the main hospital in Apia. He had given up a flourishing practice in Honolulu and had traded an income of several thousand dollars a week for one of a few hundred dollars a month. Charlie was a gentle man, a tall rangy fellow with glasses, balding gray hair, and a soft voice full of confidence. He had come to Apia for three years and liked his job immensely.

"I have the chance to do a whole range of surgical work," he said, beaming with satisfaction. "Back in the U.S. you are termed a specialist of some kind and usually do a limited type of work. Here I am called on to do everything. The job is difficult and challenging and I love it. And the Samoans are so appreciative of what I do."

One morning we went to the main station for a bus to the eastern part of Upolu. The driver waited until his vehicle was bursting with people, hand-cranked the engine into life, and started off. Soon it began to rain and the Samoans commenced to close the windows, which weren't glass but pieces of old plywood that you pulled up from slots down along the side of your seat. Soon all the shutters were up and the interior of the bus was as dark as the inside of a cave. The tropical rain thundered on the windshield and wooden roof and I wondered how the driver could see.

Inside we were all snug and the talk was animated and lively. We got into conversation with several men but politely declined their invitations, for we were determined to walk around a bit and not to spend the day sitting crosslegged on mats answering questions. The rain stopped, the shutters descended into their slots, and we looked out on a narrow track that cut through the leafy jungle of tall trees and shrubs. To our left the trees fell away toward the sea, and here and there we saw clusters of dark-brown oval-shaped fales and strings of fluttering laundry.

"Let's get off and walk," said Margaret.

The bus groaned away from us and we were alone at a place called Lufilufi. Below the road were half a dozen small fales spaced around a stream that coursed along beneath palms and breadfruit trees. The air was heavy with moisture from the rain, and fragrance from frangipani and tiare Tahiti blossoms. We walked for a while, worked around several hills, and then cut down a path toward the sea. Suddenly we were face to face with a startled Samoan girl.

"My name is Rosita," she volunteered after she recovered from her surprise. "Come—come to my fale and meet my aunt." Since we were a little tired from walking in the heat we followed Rosita and soon met Mrs. Taialii Alafaga, who quickly produced mats for us to sit on. We met her husband and mother and over a cup of tea found Mrs. Alafaga a relaxed woman who, though interested in us and our trip, didn't press us with too many questions.

We were a long way from the tempo of Apia. The little cluster of fales among the dark-green trees on the edge of the quiet sea was enchanting. Rosita took us on a little tour of some nearby caves with fresh-water pools. We watched Mrs. Alafaga grate coconuts for a sauce for a fish that was to be steamed for supper. Rosita wrapped the fish in a banana leaf, placed it parallel to and on top of the central mid-rib of a palm leaf, and then deftly plaited the leaves across the fish to enclose it in its own special basket, which then went on the hot coals.

Mrs. Alafaga discovered that she was the same age as Margaret, and the two women gossiped like old friends. She asked if she could see *Whisper*. The next morning she and Rosita took the bus to Apia and waved their handkerchiefs from the shore to attract our attention so we could gather our visitors in the dinghy. Another day her husband came to see us and we all went back to Lufilufi for the evening.

"You're part of my family now," announced Mrs. Alafaga during supper. "Come and stay with us. Forget the ship for a while."

I smiled acquiescence but my heart sank, for Tapasu had been urging us to quit the yacht and to move in with him. Two families had adopted us! Clearly our social life had become too much. The next day Mrs. Alafaga sent Rosita with a basket of taro and a message inviting us to tea. At the moment Rosita arrived, Tapasu's son was asking us to dinner.

According to the coconut radio a man with a long red beard had been towed into the next island in a dismasted yacht. We had thought of visiting Savai'i briefly, so we left at once in the hope of helping the disabled ship. Margaret sent Mrs. Alafaga a small present and wrote her a letter explaining why we were leaving. We walked up to Tapasu's fale to say goodbye in person. We didn't realize what would happen.

Farewells in Polynesia are bad news. As soon as we said that we were leaving everyone in the Tapasu household started to cry. It was terrible. All the women and children began to moan and weep and the men's faces were as long as yardsticks. Margaret gave Sivaiala a little present to thank her for her expert sewing and she burst into uncontrollable sobs, her big body trembling while she dabbed at her red eyes with a lace handkerchief. We thought we were only casual friends, but according to Tapasu we were important members of his family and would be sorely missed. Finally we left after much handshaking, many embraces, and more weeping. We promised to return, to write, and to exchange packages.

We were so depressed at the farewell that I swore never to do it again but to write a letter and to sail off quietly.

While we were tacking across Apolima Strait to Savai'i we caught a four-foot dorado on our trailing lure. When we arrived at Salelologa after the twenty-five-mile trip a crowd of several hundred Samoans collected to watch us sail in. A little later I hoisted the gold-colored dorado up on the main boom. The people on the dock wanted to buy the fish, but we had planned to have it for dinner. Several women demanded to buy the fish. Since Margaret was in charge of the money, what there was, I turned the problem over to her. The women on the wharf held up coins. Margaret shook her head. More coins. No! Still more coins. No! Finally one of the Samoan women jumped on *Whisper*, seized the fish, gave Margaret a whole handful of small silver coins, hopped back on shore, and triumphantly disappeared into the crowd with her fish while Margaret—in her new role of commercial fisherman—sat down to count her hoard.

Next to us on the dock we saw our old friend John Cotton sitting dejectedly on the deck of *El Viajero*, a crudely built, forty-foot, ferro-cement ketch. John had been engaged to ferry the ship from Villa in the New Hebrides to San Francisco. It was an ambitious trip for a single-hander, especially in an ill-equipped ship that sailed poorly to windward and whose engine would not run. North of Savai'i a spreader in the rigging had carried away. The mast crashed to the deck and John narrowly missed going on a reef. A local ship had towed him to Salelologa, where John had made arrangements for a tug to take him to Apia. We heard later that it took months for John to get the mast repaired. He finally delivered the ship to San Francisco from Apia after a seventy-six-day, nonstop voyage.

We found Savai'i a good deal more primitive than Upolu. The island was steeply mountainous, with recent lava flows, few roads, and even fewer white visitors. The villages were quite unspoiled and many of the men had extensive body tattoos. But it was hard for us to walk around because a crowd tended to gather wherever we appeared. The local police inspector put a guard on the ship at once, for Samoans—especially in remote places—have a different sense of values and tend to help themselves to what they want. In former times—and still today in some places—a Samoan could take the food or personal property of others for his own use.[21]

According to Western notions we would call many Samoans petty thieves, but the traditional Samoan concept is that everything should be shared. This modified communism may be O.K. for Samoans, but it is hard on visitors and I dreaded to leave *Whisper*. We heard a story that when a Samoan wants to grow beans he plants one seed for himself and a second for the thief who will certainly appear in the night at harvest time.

In Apia we had talked with several schoolteachers from New Zealand and they had asked us to call on them at Avao on the north coast of Savai'i. Since the charts were poor we made inquiries about Matautu Bay on which Avao fronted. We were assured that it was well sheltered with a sandy bottom in which our anchors would hold well. Late in the afternoon of November 21 we eased *Whisper*'s sheets and glided into Matautu Bay. The anchorage, however, was open to the north, and where the water shoaled over the white sand, big swells formed that thundered into white spray on the fringing reef farther inshore. The weather was settled and the barometer remained high, so we anchored the ship, tidied up her gear, and prepared to go ashore in the dinghy.

"Look what's coming," said Margaret, looking shoreward. "I hope they're friendly."

A fleet of thirty outrigger canoes had set out through the surf and was rapidly closing in on our little ship. I thought that if we pulled away in the dinghy the fleet might follow us and leave the ship alone. But as I rowed toward the reef the canoes converged on *Whisper*. I felt that my little ship was Captain Cook's *Endeavour* in Matavai Bay in Tahiti in 1769, for while she rolled merrily at anchor the primitive canoes surrounded the ship and the husky, dark-skinned natives swarmed on board. The scene would have made a wonderful photograph, but of course I had no camera.

I turned to look at the swells bursting on the fringing reef and realized we would have to ride a wave across the coral barrier. In the twilight the approach seemed quite hazardous and we would not be able to get back to the ship until morning. I looked back at *Whisper* and saw one of the Samoans dancing up and down the decks with a life ring around his neck. I wondered whether someone had sliced off the mainsheet. I swung the dinghy sharply around.

"Sorry," ⁙ said, "but this is one place we're leaving." As soon as we got aboard I began to winch up the anchor while Margaret hoisted the mainsail. As we began to move seaward the canoes gradually left us. Savai'i faded into the dark.

10 / 〜〜〜〜〜〜〜

The Back Door to Yesterday

So FAR ON OUR TRIP WE HAD VOYAGED OVER ROUTES reasonably well known. Now we left the paths of the round-the-world sailors and headed northwest toward the British crown colony of the Ellice and Gilbert islands. It was in these seas a century ago that Yankee brigs and barks from Nantucket and New Bedford had come to search for the elusive whale. A generation ago mighty fleets of Japanese and U.S. warships had fought grievous battles. But now the equatorial ocean highways ahead of us were silent and empty except for an occasional inter-island schooner whose masts we might not spy once in a dozen years.

We had decided on the route but our charts were sketchy, the *Pilot* books vague, and authors had seldom found these seas. I counted sixteen islands in the Gilberts and nine in the Ellice group. But where to stop? It was the travelers' old dilemma: At which stations on the train trip should we get off? There was no conductor to ask and no Baedeker to consult. A good anchorage was equal to a travelers' hotel for us, so we looked for a lagoon where we could safely drop an anchor. The choice became name picking based on passable lagoons. Should we go to Nukufetau or Nanumea? Nukulaelae or Funafuti? We took pot luck and shaped our course toward Funafuti.[22]

The distance was 659 miles, the course 290° M., and the passage took seven days—no, six days, or was it seven? We had crossed 180° W. longitude and lost one day when we passed the International

Date Line. This always confused me and I let Margaret sort out whether Sunday was now Monday. Was Tuesday really Tuesday or was it Wednesday?

The trip to the Ellice Islands was easy, with mostly light following winds and periods of calms and variables. As we neared the equator the sun burned down and obliged us to wear shoes when we walked on the hot decks. The hesitant wind flickered between north-northeast and south-southeast and brought us half a dozen squalls every day, which cooled off the ship and gave us delightful fresh-water showers.

November 23. 0630. A little while ago I watched the light strengthen as the new day rose from the depths of the night. The colors were marvelous to see as they grew from the black that little by little became gray and then blue and pink. But not one shade of color formed before my eyes; there were a dozen, perhaps 50 separate grays and blues and pinks. The ineffable delicacies were far beyond any mere words. The experience of seeing whole civilizations of color was almost beyond human comprehension.

Combined with the colors were the cloud shapes: Trade wind clouds that stretched long and thin; clouds that towered high and reached low; streamers of white scudding east at one level while feather-edged ribbons of gray floated southward higher up. An enormous cumulus blocked the rising sun but soon the dark cloud was rimmed with pink that shimmered into gold before it became the white of day. All around me the colors changed, grew, combined, and disappeared. Dawn was finished. The new day had begun.

The wind picked up from the east and the next day our noon-to-noon run was 133 miles. Before supper I discovered that a jib sheet had slipped over the side and had gotten around something below the waterline. No amount of tugging would free the line, so we hove to. I put on a face mask and dived over the side to recover the line, which had somehow managed to knot itself into a loop and to lasso the rudder. That night at 0210 I looked out to see the exploding crimson of a meteor flash in the sky off to starboard. It was the biggest I had ever seen and, while I watched, the meteor burned out and its curving glow died like a spent firework.

On a certain point of sailing when the wind was not quite behind us and not quite abeam, we couldn't hold the headsail out to windward with a pole (our usual running arrangement) because when the ship rolled on a wave and skidded toward the wind, the breeze would get behind the headsail and backwind it. The drive of the mainsail then soon put the ship way off course. Conversely, if we set the headsail behind the mainsail, the headsail tended to be largely useless because it was shielded from the wind by the mainsail. This also put us off course.

With both arrangements the headsail was forever filling and emptying with bangs that threatened to blow the sail to shreds. The self-steering gear was quite unable to cope with this problem, which we usually solved by altering course a little. One day we tried running under a headsail alone when the wind came from this troublesome direction. The wind vane then steered the ship perfectly, but without the support of the mainsail *Whisper* rolled and rolled—even on a relatively placid ocean.

I was soon aware that Margaret was hoisting the mainsail and changing the course. "I'm tired of all this rolling," she said angrily. "You would think with a calm sea we could manage some comfort. I would rather take a day longer and arrive in one piece. I feel like pepper in a salt shaker."

November 26 was a tiring day, with little wind, two tremendous squalls, and heavy rain showers. At noon the fiddle rail on the stove broke and several dishes launched themselves to destruction. It was very chilly during the second squall and I blessed my oilskins. While I was on deck lashing the handle of the faulty roller reefing gear in place a small gray bird with pointed, sweptback wings suddenly fluttered to the deck. I carried it below and got out the bird books. With a bird in your lap the identification is positive. Length? Let's see—eight inches. White rump? Yes. Notched tail? Yes. Dangling webbed feet? Yes. Nostrils in tube on bill? Yes. The bird was a Leach's storm petrel, a delicate little fellow who stayed with us for several hours before continuing his flitting flight just above the waves over the open ocean.

At 2035 our position was an estimated seventeen miles from Funafuti. We hove to until dawn, when we got under way again with dark clouds frowning across the horizon from west to north, just the direction we were headed. I wondered whether we would be able to see the low atoll, but at 0740 Funafuti showed up ahead. Rain plummeted on deck and it was too gusty to use the vane. The wind worked from dead aft to the starboard beam as a rain squall passed going northward. Goonies, shearwaters, and a bosun bird flew around the ship. We headed for a tower structure of some kind and held our course until we were about half a mile from a point of land where we suddenly noticed a small group of people watching us. One man waved a large red flag. Red flag! Was landing prohibited? Was there a danger of some sort? Had I broken a rule? It later developed that he was just waving it for fun.

We gybed and ran southwest along the island for five miles to Te Puapua pass. Opposite the pass two more squalls bore down on us and erased all visibility more than 200 yards. While Margaret stood out to sea on a compass course I went below to check the engine. However, the little Diesel would only splutter and sneeze. It was the first time I had tried the engine since Samoa, and I found the fuel system choked with dirt and water from contaminated oil. While Margaret dodged squalls and tacked back and forth I spent a sweat-filled hour cursing and smashing my knuckles on the greasy monster. Again and again I took apart the three filters, cleaned them, and tried to get fuel through the lines, which were plugged with sludge.

It was hopeless. The fuel system needed major work. I emerged from the hell-hole covered with sweat and oil and fuming with rage at myself for not having personally strained every drop of oil I had bought in Apia. The cat meowed. Margaret said nothing. I cooled off by pouring buckets of sea water over me to clean up. We headed across the pass by sail. "The devil take his machinery," I muttered blackly.

Funafuti lies 510 miles south of the equator, almost astride the International Date Line, and is about 2,300 miles southwest of the Hawaiian Islands. The atoll measures eleven by fourteen miles and is shaped something like a man's head facing west, his profile outlined with the dot-dash pattern of a broken reef surmounted here and there by palm-topped islets which total about thirty in all. During World War II, Funafuti was a U.S. naval base and I have seen a photograph with twenty capital ships at anchor. The cautious directions in the *U.S. Pilot* had evidently been written for these battleships and heavy cruisers, for we had no trouble at all entering the large lagoon. The *Pilot* glibly spoke of rows of buoys, leading marks, and beacons, but except for a stone marker on Funamanu Island all were gone. World War II was a long time ago.

Inside, the weather improved, and in the calm lagoon we tacked back and forth up to the village of Fongafale where we anchored in the early afternoon while the Ellice Islanders lined the shore.

The village was along the center of the largest islet, a boomerang-shaped thread of coral six miles long which varied in width from a third of a mile to only sixty yards. The atoll land was so narrow! If you faced the green water of the lagoon and then turned around, you could always see the purplish seas of the open ocean gleaming between the palm trunks. During World War II a small airstrip was carved out of the widest place, and two or three times a month a small plane from Suva landed with mail and a few passengers. There were 685 natives and five New Zealanders on Funafuti.

After the flamboyance of the Samoans we found the Ellice people quiet and unobtrusive. Life on the atoll was fairly close to subsistence. The men fished every day and the women were experts at preparing coconuts, chickens, small pigs, bananas, and taro. The houses were open and built of pandanus-thatch roofs set on posts that stuck above foundations of lime or concrete. Sometimes a sheet of rusty iron was tacked on the roof or a few old boards were nailed across the sides. In general the houses were featureless and drab.

The people conversed in Ellice, a Samoan offshoot, but many of them knew some English and a few spoke excellent English from having worked at the phosphate diggings on Ocean Island. When the men fished they sailed in small outrigger canoes with spritsails of an inverted triangular pattern.

Like most places in the Pacific outback, the people were not only short of cash but had little chance to earn it. A new London Missionary Society church (LMS) was under construction at Fongafale, and when the foundation had been poured, a large amount of sand was needed, which was available at the south end of the main island. There were two automobiles and a truck on Funafuti. The local officials offered to rent the truck to the construction workers for one day for $1.50 so the sand could be hauled to the site of the church. The islanders had other ideas. The women plaited baskets of palm thatch, which the men put in their canoes and paddled south to the sandy beach. There the baskets were filled with sand and loaded into the canoes, which were paddled back to near the church site. Moving several tons of sand took many trips and much paddling over a number of days, but the job required no cash at all.

"Why spend money?" said one of the men. "We have plenty of time. Hauling sand by hand costs nothing at all. Besides, it's fun." He chuckled with glee.

Now the church was partially finished, and one day while we were walking around we happened to go past the new structure during a time of great excitement. That morning the roof had been completed, which signaled the start of a feast. As we walked in front of a nearby meetinghouse a woman darted out and put crowns of freshly woven flowers on our heads. We were invited to enter the meetinghouse, and a fine mat was spread for us to sit on. While I looked around I felt something and was astonished to see a woman sprinkling talcum powder on my shoulders. This, we found out later, signified that we could sing and dance, and we saw that all the other people—perhaps a hundred—had talcum powder on their shoulders too.

We ate with our fingers from a mound of island food that was placed in front of us on a banana leaf. A young girl sat before us as we ate and fanned the food to keep the flies away. Then the elders gave short speeches. Since I was a visitor I was called on to talk, and someone translated my English into Ellice. I told how glad I was to be on the island and how fortunate the people were to live on such a beautiful place. I said I was pleased to see so many happy people and to be at the feast. I complimented everyone on the new church and thanked them for their hospitality.

After the speeches the women ate. Then came singing and dancing. The women had powerful, low-pitched voices and were good at harmonizing. They loved to sing and their faces beamed with pleasure as the notes came out. The men sang in short, strident phrases and almost shouted at times. The women dancers dressed in white or patterned sleeveless blouses crisscrossed with bright bands of orange-and-red cloth and paper and wore short, very full grass skirts decorated with more strips of color. Around their necks and heads were garlands of tightly woven flowers, and tied to each arm between the hand and shoulder were four or five circlets of bright flowers made of colored paper.

The dancers didn't perform like Tahitians or Cook Islanders at all. Six of the Ellice women stood in line in front of a group of singers and acted as if they were in a stylized trance. They looked straight ahead or to one side or the other without smiling, purposely grim, sometimes holding their arms rigidly ahead or sideways and moving slowly in a formation of six. Meanwhile the men sat packed around a low wooden platform about six feet square that was covered with a mat on which they drummed with the flats of their hands. At the beginning of a song the drumming was light and intermittent, but at the climax twenty fellows pounded the drum for all they were worth while they sang at the tops of their voices.

It was quite a lunch, and afterward I reflected on how much

pleasure and happiness these people achieved on their tiny, primitive island.

I looked up from the village and noticed that the palm branches had begun to blow in a different direction. The wind had changed from the southeast to the west, which put *Whisper* on a lee shore with a coral reef only 100 feet behind the ship. We returned to the yacht at once.

A problem with calling at atolls and anchoring in lagoons is that if a strong adverse wind comes up, you really have no place to go except to head out to sea. But the new wind or the tidal stream conditions during the storm may make the pass impossible to use. Furthermore, if the pass is intricate you can leave only during daylight when you can see. Sometimes an atoll will have a few small islets or motus that you can work around to gain shelter, but generally your only defense is heavy anchors and stout chain. You have to stand and take it.

In extremes a ship can begin motoring into the wind to relieve some of the pressure on the anchors. Captain Andy Thomson told me that once when the *Tiare Taporo* was threatened by hurricane winds in the Suvarov lagoon in the Cook Islands he had full power on steaming into the storm. "We stood regular watches hoping to go nowhere," said Andy. "On the second day the storm passed over."

Within the eleven-mile sweep of the Funafuti lagoon the west wind soon raised choppy waves. However, the barometer was high and we had no intelligence of a major weather disturbance, so I elected to keep *Whisper* where she was. We let out more chain on our main anchor and I laid out a second anchor on a 200-foot nylon line. Putting out the second anchor in the dinghy was hard work, and as I rowed into the wind and waves my arms felt as if they would fall off. Our little drama went quite unnoticed on shore, but it was important to us and we did everything we could to anchor *Whisper* securely. Margaret sewed strips of canvas around the second anchor line to prevent chafe where the nylon ran over the bow fairlead. I put on a face mask and swam out to the anchor buoys to check that both anchors were properly dug into the coral sand and that the chain and line were not fouled on coral patches. We took down the awning and various lines aloft to reduce windage. The storm increased, and soon the lagoon was a froth of whitecaps, but after twelve hours the wind went back to the east and dropped to nothing.

The New Zealanders worked at the airstrip and both families had been amazed to see *Whisper* sail in. ("Nobody comes here. In fact nobody ever heard of Funafuti. How did you ever find us?") One quiet evening they all came out to the ship for drinks and a look around. ("Bloody amazing how you live on this little thing.")

We ate with both families, took showers, got ice, did our laundry, and were freely invited into their homes. Norman Jones was the works officer at the airstrip and Chris Rogers was the meteorologist. We liked them both, though the men were totally different. I almost wished Somerset Maugham could have met them.

Rogers was a quiet and reserved professional weatherman who was perhaps a little on the stuffy side, although certainly generous and helpful. He was closemouthed and wasted no time at all on social small talk. His pretty wife, Jocelyn, kept their house neat and perfect, and when we ate it was punctually at seven. Each course was served on gleaming, unchipped china with the correct spoons and forks. Jocelyn was clever at making small Christmas gifts for her people back home, and Chris showed us his immense shell collection, which he had catalogued with mathematical exactitude. We heard a lot of words, but I felt there were layers and layers of protective coatings surrounding their isolated lives.

Norman Jones, the affable works officer at the little airstrip, kept no secrets at all and soon told us all his problems, his hopes and fears, his worries and joys. He was only in fair health—pale and sallow in spite of the tropical sun—but he ran his house as an open establishment, dispensing ice to the hotel next door, beer to the Ellice men, and hospitality to all, including Saturday night bingo. He insisted on giving me tools from his home workshop and stores from the family kitchen. Norman and his wife had a Fijian man and an Ellice woman who were newlyweds staying with them and, together with Norman's six-year-old daughter and the house girl and various others, generally had ten or twelve for meals. Their screen door was always banging open or shut, the gossip and jokes never stopped, and the coffee pot percolated from morning till midnight.

We hoped to get a few loaves of bread before we left, but there were too few customers on Funafuti to support a regular baker. However, when I inquired, the assistant executive officer of the island, an Ellice man named Sapoa Nitz, said his wife would be glad to bake for us. Sapoa's wife offered to leave the loaves at the hotel.

The hotel was a funny little place that opened when the island had official visitors or when the plane from Suva was late and had to stay for the night. An Ellice man ran the hotel, but he showed enthusiasm only when it was time to close up. In theory the hotel was open one hour each evening, but in practice you had to make an appointment to buy a bottle of beer, which you were supposed to drink on the premises. Meanwhile, the manager stood around and made it very plain that he wanted to close up. When I asked him whether his closed-door policy didn't work against good receipts for the hotel he smiled impatiently. "Time to close up now," he replied. "Sometimes I don't open for weeks."

Sapoa Nitz's wife appeared with two giant loaves of bread, beautifully shaped and baked to a delicate golden brown. "Splendid," I said, handing her the two shillings. But when she gave me the loaves I almost dropped them, for each loaf seemed to weigh twenty pounds. They had been made with coconut-palm yeast and, instead of being light and airy, the bread was as hard as flint and as heavy as blocks of lead ballast.

We of course said nothing but thanked Mrs. Nitz profusely, and as we rowed out to *Whisper* for the last time Margaret sat in the stern holding the two loaves like golden trophies. We found out later that the bread was totally indigestible, and when we finally jettisoned it over the side, each loaf sank like a cannonball!

11 /

Close to Shipwreck

THE GILBERT ISLANDS ARE ROUGHLY 700 MILES NORTH-west of the Ellice group, and with the rainy season well advanced I wondered how long the trip would take. The fair southeast trades had weakened into unsettled weather from every direction, with a prospect of westerly gales and a remote chance of a hurricane.

On *Whisper* we found light headwinds as we worked toward the equator. The trip was slow and easy and my recollections are of gentle winds across a smooth, silvery, untroubled ocean. How lovely it was! Sometimes we were becalmed for twelve or fifteen hours until a little wind would ripple the enormous, very long and gently lifting swells that moved with a wonderful steadiness. If you closed your eyes you could scarcely feel them. It was only when you watched the horizon that you could gauge the rise and fall of the water. Sometimes I felt that I was on the hump of the earth and that the movement was not the sea but the earth herself, a throbbing pulse that came from the heart of the universe.

Whisper was at her best in these conditions. We had all our sails set, of course, and the ship went along incredibly well. The vane steered perfectly, far better than any helmsman who would have been cooked on deck.

On December 4 we passed Vaitupu, the last of the Ellice Islands. Vaitupu was a densely wooded atoll a mile and a half wide and three miles long, a shimmering ribbon of green stitched to a delicate thread of golden yarn. It seemed a very dream on top of the horizon. People on shore watched us as we crept past and we could see the palms, pandanus, and the oaklike fetau trees behind the long beaches of white sand. It was amazing to think that 900 people lived on the little island. We had barely enough wind for steerage way, and it took most of the day before the atoll dropped out of sight astern.

Closer to the equator we had expected the south equatorial current to give us twenty to thirty-five miles of westing per day. Instead we found that *Whisper* was getting set *east* about twenty miles a day. But it didn't matter. We were in no hurry. We had plenty of food, good books to read, and always a few odd jobs to do—fix a cockpit locker hinge, reeve a new topping lift, or sew a pair of torn trousers.

We still had the forward deck leak to think about. We were definitely close to solving the problem, which was in the hull-deck joint. At Funafuti we had removed three more feet of forward toerail on each side, cleaned the areas underneath, puttied the seams, and laid four-inch strips of special fiberglass cloth over the joint in epoxy resin. Each time we hacked off a piece of the toerail and covered more of the hull-deck joint, we found less water below. The outside appearance of the hull suffered and we lost the security of a toehold when changing sails on the foredeck, but gradually we seemed to be winning the battle.

One night at dusk the sea around *Whisper* exploded with life when a hundred porpoises suddenly surfaced around the ship. They splashed water up and down the decks as they circled around and around, diving, rolling, twisting, and frolicking, their sleek steel-gray bodies half out of the water. The cat, Kong, sat on the edge of the deck and watched wild-eyed, perhaps savoring a bite of fresh fish but afraid of the powerful, seven-foot sea creatures. Sometimes several of the porpoises would pause for a moment and emit a great *paaaahhhh* as they breathed, a sound that terrified Kong and sent him racing below. His curiosity was too great, however, and a moment later he would be back looking intently over the side.

December 7. Becalmed again and we sit quietly on a silent ocean at dawn. . . . It is an amazing experience to be becalmed and one that every sailor should know. . . . The wind gets less and less, the slatting of the sails and gear increases, the ripples on the water disappear, and you realize you are not moving. Down come the sails, one by one, and the ship sits stripped of her canvas. The sea is smooth and quiet. The only movements are from the long swells

On December 12 we crossed a moon sight with a morning sun line which gave us a noon position of 1° 58′ S. and 176° 10′ E., thirty-five miles east of Onotoa atoll in the southern Gilberts. At 1800 Margaret sighted the island, but it was too late in the day to go closer, so we hove to for the night. We expected to be pushed away from the atoll by the east-setting current, and sure enough at dawn there was no trace of land. It took us until 1030, the tenth day from Funafuti, before we tacked a half mile off the eastern shore.

"The lagoon looks marvelous," Margaret shouted down from the ratlines. "Like Rangiroa in the Tuamotus only more sand and larger beaches. I can see lots of tall palms. Oh for a nice cool drinking nut!"

There was a recommended anchorage, according to the sparse comments in the *U.S. Pilot*, but it seemed wide open to wind and swells from the west. I hoped we could enter the lagoon. We would have to sail to the opposite, northwest corner of the atoll where we could perhaps get local help to guide us. The distance was only eleven miles in a straight line, but it took us to the middle of the afternoon before we tacked north of the island and headed west. The breakers boomed along the fringing reef; however we held our own and with the sails strapped in tightly and water flying everywhere we passed through the disturbed seas that fronted the top of the island. The weather was worsening, with many squalls and some low clouds.

Our 1910 sketch chart showed a stone beacon on a motu called Temuah which we rounded in a hurry with eased sheets. I doused the genoa while Margaret steered toward the anchorage shown on the chart. Suddenly we were in an area of coral sand and coral heads with depths of three to four fathoms. I let the anchor go, but the chain was fouled in the locker from all the motion during the long passage from Samoa. The barrier reef was only fifty feet away.

"Gybe at once and run back out," I shouted at Margaret, who threw the tiller over hard and eased us back into deep water. We got the chain in order and went back and anchored in three fathoms. The wind was fifteen knots from the north-northwest with about two squalls every hour. There was not much wind with the rain, but each squall seemed a river from the sky.

I saw at once that the anchorage was wide open to the west and very rolly in any case. Already we were pulling hard on the chain, which creaked a bit, so I rigged a thirty-foot anchor spring of half-inch nylon line—a sort of giant rubber band to take the minor shocks of the ship jerking against the anchor. Suddenly all was quiet except for the fall of the topping lift, which *rat-tat-tatted* on the mast as we rolled. To keep the line quiet I led it aft and tied it off, a step I was to regret.

Margaret got ready to go ashore, about three quarters of a mile across the lagoon, while I blew up the inflatable dinghy. It was now 1700, with maybe an hour or a little longer before dark. A small rain shower whipped across us and was gone, but I could see an enormous squall coming. In a moment heavy rain bucketed down and the sky became sea, indistinguishable except for the cooler fresh water. The rain erased the reef and the island completely, and I could scarcely see the bow of the ship. Half an hour later the rain still plummeted down; now it was too late to go ashore. A good thing Margaret hadn't been caught when halfway to shore or she couldn't have seen to row without a compass. We would wait till dawn.

The prospects for dinner were good. A silvery-blue four-foot wahoo had taken our trailing feather lure while we had tacked along the island and we had a splendid fish. I cleaned the beautiful creature as the rain tapered off.

"How many steaks do you want?" I called down to Margaret from the cockpit. "How thick? The fish looks great."

"Oh, cut eight steaks about three quarters of an inch thick," she said, holding up a thumb and forefinger an inch and a half apart. "I'm starved and I bet you are too. I'll have the frying pan hot in a minute and we can eat shortly."

My hacksaw made quick work of the request, but there was enough fish for fifty steaks. It was a pity we hadn't someone to give the rest. Without refrigeration there was no choice in the tropics. Meat or fish was eaten at once or tossed over the side.

I went below and dried out a bit. *Whisper* was straining hard at her anchor. I decided to take off the genoa and put on the working jib in case we had to leave. However, once I got on deck I realized that conditions were changing rapidly and I hurried to change the headsail. The wind had veered to the west and we were on a lee shore, a sailor's nightmare. The wind was not too strong, about twelve to fifteen knots, but large swells began to roll into the anchorage. While I knelt on the foredeck and changed the jib, two waves broke across the front of the ship, the second about two feet over my head. As I tied on the jib sheets there was a small bang. The nylon anchor spring line had chafed through and broken. I rushed below.

"There's some nasty stuff rolling in here now," I said to Margaret. "We've got to clear out at once!" The ship rose on another breaking crest and the chain and windlass groaned terribly.

"Do have some of this nice fish," said Margaret. "We'll eat a little and go." I wolfed a little of the wahoo, but I was too nervous to eat.

Ten minutes later the chain was screeching against the windlass gypsy whenever the ship rose on a heavy swell, which surged in about every two minutes. On deck the ship was rolling and pitching so that I had to crawl along the deck to reach the mast. In the dark and confusion I tried to hoist the mainsail without bringing the fall of the topping lift forward from the cockpit. The sail jammed, of course, with the topping lift fouled around the main halyard. Down mainsail.

Clear topping lift. Hoist away. But the sail refused to go up more than a dozen feet.

With the ship plunging and yawing, the top of *Whisper*'s mast was scraping wild arcs in the sky. On one lurch the burgee halyard had whipped around the main halyard and jammed it. By now the motion of the yacht was simply ghastly. As we rolled back and forth, the deck on first one side and then the other slammed into the sea. I knelt at the mast, clawed down the mainsail, got a grip on the burgee halyard, and cut it away. Then I hoisted the sail again.

This time the halyard whipped around the starboard spreader. I pulled the sail down for the third time. Margaret crawled forward and managed to keep tension on the halyard while I cleared it and reeled up the slack on the winch. This time the mainsail climbed the mast smoothly and quickly. At this point it would have been dandy to have fired up the auxiliary engine for a little quick help out of the untenable anchorage. But the fuel system of the engine was still full of sludge. We would have to sail the anchor out.

Margaret ran back to the tiller while I prepared to hoist the jib. All this time waves had been surging into the anchorage, lifting the yacht, and churning past with a hollow sound as they broke behind us and walloped against the barrier reef in back of the ship. The waves were on the point of breaking, but so far only two had actually crested and sent white water across the decks. Nevertheless, the strain on the chain and windlass was enormous, and I expected both to be snatched into the sea.

Suddenly a colossal wall of water was in front of the ship. Though daylight was gone I could see the milky white of the foaming crest as it thundered across the face of the breaking wave. It looked huge and heavy. I was horrified.

"Hang on!" I shouted.

The wave broke clear across as it got to *Whisper* and with a roar lifted the ship up to an angle of perhaps 75 degrees as the water thundered down the decks. I lay flat with my head down, seized a mooring cleat with each hand, and held on with all my strength as the water rushed over me. The windlass in front of me gave a lurch and shriek as suddenly all the remaining chain was ripped out of the gypsy and stripped into the sea. There was a bang and a great jerk from aloft. The ship wallowed in broken water as the wave passed. I spit out a mouthful of warm salt water.

"The chain must be broken," I said aloud. "We must be on the reef." I had visions of fragments of *Whisper* strewn along the reef and mixed up with pieces of bones—*my bones!* "No!" I said. "We are still rolling and must be afloat." I looked up and wondered what had broken aloft. The snap at the end of the 75 degree climb and then again when the ship had plunged were frightful. Something must have broken. The rigging? The mast itself? It was too dark to see anything except that the mainsail was flapping. Rain rattled down from the inky sky. My eyes burned from the salt water.

I clawed at the windlass and found the chain limp. We were in a momentary calm after the great wave had passed. I groped at the chain and found a piece of metal that had been torn from the gypsy. With energy produced by desperation I hauled in the chain at a fearful pace—until my arms throbbed and my breath came in gasps. Finally I came to the shackle that had held the nylon anchor spring. My pliers had been swept away, so I raced back to the cockpit, got a hacksaw, and hurried forward to cut the iron shackle. Again I stripped in chain as fast as I could pull. To my amazement the chain got tight. The anchor still held. Or I hoped it held. The shock of the breaking wave had broken the hold of the windlass on the chain and it had merely run out.

"Haul in the mainsheet! Put the tiller to starboard!" I yelled at Margaret. "Stand by for the jib. Back the jib to starboard and as the ship's head swings to port, haul the jib to leeward."

As I winched up the jib halyard, *Whisper* payed off on the starboard tack and began to move. I cranked the anchor windlass until the slack chain became taut and pulled the head of the ship around to the port tack.

"I'll change the jib sheets," Margaret shouted above the noise of another breaking wave.

We were on the port tack now and moving smartly and the force of the wave—though knee deep down the deck—angled off *Whisper* somewhat. We kept short tacking as I worked in the chain. God, how black it was! I was afraid the anchor would foul a coral head and I might need the hacksaw—if I could find it on the waterswept deck—to cut the cable. But the chain kept coming. I glanced to starboard and saw that we were moving past the little motu at the end of Onotoa. The anchor was free! I winched it on board, gave Margaret a compass course to steer, and collapsed in the cockpit. Once out at sea we hove to on the offshore tack to recover from the evening.

Half an hour later a gale roared in from the west. Our late anchorage must have been a maelstrom of white water and breaking waves, a death trap for ships and sailors. We had saved the ship and probably our lives by clearing out in time. I thought back to the days when we had practiced sailing out an anchor in Drake's Bay north of San Francisco. There we had propped open Eric Hiscock's *Cruising Under Sail* on the coachroof and followed his directions like a cook baking a cake. Eric's instructions and our practice had saved us.

The next day I discovered that the shank of the forty-five-pound CQR anchor—a two-inch I-beam of drop-forged iron—was bent, and a tough, six-ton-test iron shackle at the end of the anchor chain was stretched to almost twice its original dimension, with its pin bent one quarter of an inch. Beryl Smeeton had given me that shackle and I thought of her with a good deal of affection at that moment. During the pitching caused by the great wave, both the top and bottom aerial insulators on the port backstay had shattered, and the outhaul fitting at the end of the main boom had been partially torn off. It was a wonder we still had a mast!

How comforting it was to be on the deep sea again! The motion of *Whisper*, the motion that we knew so well, seemed steady, reassuring, and almost homelike.

Had I learned anything? I hope to tell you. Forget doubtful anchorages when the weather is uncertain. Stay at sea if you would live.

12 /

The Porpoise Is Dead, the Whale Is Sunk

TWENTY-FIVE MILES NORTH OF THE EQUATOR WE SIGHTED Abemama in the central Gilberts, and a few hours later we anchored off the village of Binoinano deep inside the quiet lagoon. Because of the calms and headwinds and the anchoring misadventure off Onotoa, the 640 miles from Funafuti had taken us two weeks. We had sailed 1,171 miles.

Now the trip and the bad weather were behind us. We sat above the calm sapphire of the lagoon and doddled with coffee after a good meal. Outside the pass we had caught another big wahoo, and in the late afternoon Margaret and I and the cat munched contentedly on fish steaks while *Whisper* lolled easily at anchor.

I heard the snort of an outboard motor and looked up to see a small boat approaching. In a few minutes the local constable, the island executive officer, and several assistants, all Gilbertese, climbed on board. They welcomed us cordially but were curious to know our business and who we were.

We had crossed the border into Micronesia. The skin of our visitors shone with a deep copper. The Gilbertese were short and lean—there was no Tahitian fat here—and the men moved with a natural vigor and confidence. They had handsome, good-looking faces set off by prominent cheekbones, short straight noses, well-formed shiny teeth, and merry brown eyes. Their black hair was short-cut, straight, and glossy. Altogether the fellows looked quite alike, and I thought of a team of good-humored, small-sized athletes. I liked them at once.

"We ask you to come ashore to sign the visitor's book," said Ioane Kaitabo, the executive officer, in excellent English.

We all climbed into the launch and motored toward the land some three quarters of a mile away. The lagoon soon shoaled to a foot or so and the boatman and his helper jumped over the side to push and pull the launch over the white sand in the shallow places. I had a chance to look around.

Abemama, which means Land of Moonlight, was typical of the sixteen atolls of the Gilberts. The island was shaped roughly like a horseshoe pointing west, with its outside dimensions about nine by thirteen and a half miles. The iron rim of the horseshoe supported a thin wall of green with golden beaches on each side. At most the land measured a half mile wide and ten feet high, with a sandy marginal soil that supported coconut and pandanus palms and an inferior taro called babai. Geologically the atoll was very old, and inside the lagoon much of the coral had disintegrated into dazzling sand, often swirled into motus, shoals, and sandbanks by the force of currents.

It was dark when we touched the shore, but the sand on the village beach flared up from the harsh light of kerosene pressure lamps held by several men. We were suddenly aware of a crowd of perhaps seventy-five to a hundred people watching us. Ioane led the way to the small headquarters office of Abemama—the crowd followed—where he produced and dusted off the visitor's register, a large bound book. I opened it and saw that it had been started in 1946. In more than twenty years only a handful of outsiders had come to the island. I signed my name at the top of page three.

"Are we the first yacht, Ioane?" I asked.

"I think so," he said. "I have never seen one before."

We were taken to Ioane's comfortable native Gilbertese home across the way. The crowd was still with us and we all filed inside the high-ceilinged main room, which was lighted by gently hissing kerosene pressure lamps. Two rickety chairs, hastily fetched from God knows where, appeared, and we were bid to take them. Everyone else sat crosslegged on mats. We were given two freshly husked drinking nuts, and when we finished Ioane began to speak.

"Ships come to Abemama very seldom and the people are excited and interested in you. With your permission we would like to ask you a few questions. I can translate—"

"Where did you come from?" asked a man in back.

"America, the United States," I answered. "My home is in San Francisco." The names got no response at all. "On the other side of the Pacific," I said, trying again and motioning toward the east, "is a big land where I live. We came by way of Tahiti, Samoa, and Funafuti."

Now I mentioned names that got nods and recognition. I would have to answer in terms that these atoll people understood.

"How many days from your land?" asked an old woman who squatted in front of us in a thick grass skirt.

"Nine months, but we stopped at many islands for rest and food."

As Ioane translated into rapid-fire Gilbertese, the frowns of the people dissolved in understanding.

"Why did you come to such an isolated place as Abemama? No one ever comes here."

"To meet you, to see how you live, and to become your friends."

"But what of storms?" asked a voice in back. "How were the waves beyond the horizon? What of the gale-force winds from the north that we call Nei Bairara, the Long-Armed Woman?"

"We had a few storms," I said. "Mostly though we have sailed in the trade winds. Our ship is decked over and when the sea becomes angry we put up small sails and wait until the ocean becomes our friend again."

More and more villagers, especially women, kept crowding into the room. A few people rolled shreds of tobacco inside pandanus leaves to make particularly foul-smelling cigarettes that were passed from person to person, each of whom took a puff or two.

"Do you have plenty of coconuts and fish in your land?"

"My country is too cold for coconuts. However, our land is good for growing cold-weather fruits and vegetables—things we call apples and corn and beans and potatoes. We eat some fish but we raise animals for meat. Your staple is the coconut; our mainstay is bread made from wheat flour."

"How much did the ship cost?"

How could I reply sensibly to a man who in one day would gather and split 300 coconuts whose dried meat might fetch three dollars? "I got the ship by trading the proceeds of all my work for five years," I said, holding up five fingers. "The ship is my most valued possession."

"How was the fishing on your trip? What kinds?"

"The best fish was wahoo, a strong fighter," I said. "But too large. We ate so much that we grew great stomachs. The cat on the ship got a belly so big that he cried for two days. He almost died of pleasure."

While Ioane translated I made motions of a big stomach on me, on Margaret, and on an imaginary cat. Everyone hooted, and when I imitated an overstuffed cat the room rocked with laughter.

The questions went on and on. We were tired but our audience was delighted with the show and we saw eager brown eyes on every side. Someone handed us cups of coconut toddy, a sweet, slightly thick, amber-colored drink.

"You have come a long way," said a man whose hair was thin. "You are only two, one a woman. Were you afraid when you were out there far from land? You found your direction by the white man's method but what did you feel in your heart? Tell us now."

"Old friend, you must know the sea, for you speak wisely. The Pacific is big and powerful and when her temper is high her rage knows no limit. We were late in the year to come here and we almost lost the ship and ourselves at Onotoa because I was foolish. Now we are safe at Abemama. But of the sea . . . I have often been frightened but I don't know fear. If your ship is good, luck is with you, and the sea is on your side, you have a chance. When the Pacific smiles you must hurry. When she screams you must wait. Above all you must acknowledge that the sea is the master in your heaven. You are merely a dot of nothing, an insignificance."

Margaret and I stood up. Suddenly everyone began to applaud. Without realizing it we had put on a performance, an entertainment in remote Abemama. As we left Ioane's house on our way back to the ship the people smiled and nodded to the actors.

The next day we went ashore in the dinghy. It was a long row, the current against us ran swiftly, and my arms soon felt as if they would fall off. Finally the water shoaled enough so that I could wade and pull the dinghy along. Loss of an oar in such a place would have been serious and I was glad we had a small anchor with us.

In the bright morning the atoll was a world of dappled sunlight and shadow, of brown palm trunks reaching toward a green heaven, of long beaches of white diamonds. A crowd of golden-skinned youngsters escorted us to the village along wide pathways of coral gravel and sand that were outlined with small rocks and bordered with fluted hibiscus and milk-white crinum lilies. We began to see the quiet browns of peaked roofs and the tawny sides of native cottages.

A few children scampered in front of the houses and shrieked as

they ran past. We heard the chatter of women as they walked along the roadway and we saw several young men with handsome bronzed bodies pushing bicycles on which were balanced enormous bags of copra. I caught a sniff of delicate frangipani, and the stronger smell of something cooking drifted up to us. My heart soared for a moment as a magic curtain flapped open and I looked at the simple beauty and essence of the South Pacific.

Each home stood by itself on a raised foundation of lime made from burned coral. The corner posts, rafters, joists, and thatch for the roof had been cut from pandanus palms. Coconut-leaf mid-ribs lashed side by side were placed upright to make walls, and thin slats of bent coconut wood covered with lattices woven from white pandanus roots formed the window frames and doors. More coconut mid-ribs became flooring and the whole house was tied together with intricate cross-lashings of coconut-fiber string.

But this bald description suggests in no way the pleasant geometry of the Gilbertese houses in among the palms and the magical neatness and order of the village. The houses were light, airy, and perfectly suited to both the eye and the atoll environment. Even the arrangement of the footpaths was harmonious, and I noticed that they were swept clean of leaves and debris. We saw no rusty iron, no junky old boards, and no litter.

Ioane met us and introduced us to the assistant medical officer, Tomasi Puapua, an Ellice Islander from Vaitupu. There were no cars on the island, but both men had small Honda motorcycles. Margaret climbed behind Tomasi, I got back of Ioane, and we zoomed off to look at the island, most of which had a roadway. However, the land was not continuous, and every mile or so we came to a crude causeway that had been constructed to bridge the swift channels of water that raced between the lagoon and the sea and isolated one part of the atoll from another. We dismounted and trod gingerly across these rickety bridges, which were nothing more than haphazard collections of odd branches from trees pegged together with a few nails—teetery matchsticks that threatened to collapse with a hard step and to plunge us into the swirling waters below.

We drove through small villages, passed fields of wide-leaved babai, saw the skeletons of World War II airplanes, waved to women washing, and interrupted men making copra. Someone asked us for matches. We all searched our pockets.

"No matter," said the man. "I can use uri wood." He called to his son to bring him two pieces of the dry wood. Then he pressed the end of the first piece against the side of the second, and stroked the first rapidly back and forth. In fifteen seconds smoke began to rise; in thirty seconds the smoke thickened and we saw a spark. The man pushed his pandanus cigarette into the young fire and lighted up. Then he turned to us, held up the cigarette victoriously, and smiled a happy toothless grin.

We smiled back and drove on.

At Manoku we stopped at the Catholic station, where we were surprised to meet a French priest, Father Dureihmer, who was astonished to see two white people.

"But there's been no ship," he stammered. "Wh . . . where did you come from?"

We told about our trip and Father Dureihmer stood spellbound. He was a small, energetic, bespectacled man in middle age who had been in the Gilberts most of his working life. In his little school he was training sixteen native priests who would study for three years.

Father Dureihmer invited us all to lunch, but he didn't eat much, for he was starved for conversation rather than food. We discussed De Gaulle, the Common Market, island medicine, World War II, men in space, American politics. . . . "Ah, it's good to talk," he said, relishing the words. "I'm in another world out here.

"I regret that I can only offer you this inferior Australian wine with lunch," he said. "It's vile-tasting but all I have. Can you imagine a Frenchman offering guests such bilge? Or drinking it himself?"

We left after promising to call at the station again. Ioane and Tomasi took us back to the main village and our dinghy.

The next morning we went ashore again, but Ioane was busy with tax court. He came out to see us for a minute.

"We collect one dollar for each parcel of land regardless of size," he said. "Some people pay and some people argue but we still collect, although the rate and scheme are ridiculous."

We had lunch at the hospital with Tomasi. The hospital was a self-care institution in which each patient's family moved in with the sick person to feed and take care of him under the supervision of the doctor. Instead of a central building the hospital complex was a tiny dispensary plus a scattering of several dozen small native houses, one for each patient and his family. Several lepers were in isolation in back.

"On an island such as Abemama the only trained medical people are myself and my nurse," said Tomasi while we ate. "A self-care hospital is the only way to achieve reasonable care for the seriously ill."

I was very impressed by Tomasi. His title was assistant medical officer, but he was the doctor for three islands and he was astonishingly capable. He had been picked as an adolescent and sent to Suva, where he received rigorous schooling and practice for six years. The emphasis was not on *theory* of medicine, although there was some, but on *practice*. Each assistant medical officer, or AMO as he was called, performed dozens of complex operations under the tutelage of the staff of the Fiji School of Medicine.

"We can take care of ninety-five percent of all medical problems on our islands," said Tomasi. "For difficult cases we can radio for assistance to the general hospital in Tarawa. Much of our work is routine childbirth, fractures, or perhaps removing a fishhook from a man's nose. We spend a lot of time discussing diet and passing out vitamin pills, for malnutrition is a problem on atolls. However, when someone comes in with appendicitis we must operate at once or the patient will be dead."

Tomasi was proud of his tiny dispensary and his stocks of medicines and equipment. The United Nations, through UNICEF, had given him a motorcycle, a launch, and an outboard motor to conserve his energies for medicine instead of walking and paddling. An autoclave, scales, a number of expensive medical books, and various medical items also bore the stamp of UNICEF. I made a mental promise to support the organization forevermore.

Before we left Abemama we were invited to Baretoa to see Gilbertese dancing, which we had previewed on Funafuti. We heard the stentorian chanting of the men as they sat around a raised platform and pounded the rhythm with the flats of their hands. We listened to the earnest voices of the women and we watched the brightly dressed dancers who moved with the stiff and inflexible steps that seemed so unreal yet were so typical of these atolls.

That night Ioane and Tomasi came to dinner on the ship and they enjoyed the meal immensely. Both were exceptional men who had the twin blessings of intellect and education. The two men chafed in the backwater of Abemama, but they were wise enough to realize that their place was with their people—to heal them, to guide them, to lead them. When Ioane and Tomasi left *Whisper* late that night to cross the star-swept lagoon my heart felt the wrench of the peripatetic traveler: to make a good friend and then to leave him.

The following morning we were to start early. We had promised to take the royal mail to Tarawa, and a prisoner brought out the mail bags in a canoe and took the signed receipt back. I rowed ashore with a bottle of good French wine I had bought in Apia. I saw Father Dureihmer pushing his bicycle along.

"Father," I said, "we're leaving this morning and I want to say goodbye." As we shook hands I said that I had enjoyed the lunch the other day but that the Australian wine was simply terrible.

His face fell.

"It pains me to think that a Frenchman will have to celebrate Christmas by himself and have only that bilge to drink."

His face fell further.

"But cheer up, Father!" I said. "I've brought you a present of a good bottle of Saint-Julien Médoc that we had on the ship. We want you to have something nice for the holiday." When I whipped the bottle out of its paper sack Father Dureihmer's eyes grew big and responsive.

"You shouldn't have . . ." he began.

"Nonsense," I said as I climbed in the dinghy and began to row away. "It's my pleasure. We hope that you'll remember us with a kind thought."

"A kind thought?" he shouted across the water. "A kind thought indeed! I'm going to pray for you forever!"

Tarawa was an easy overnight sail, and shortly after lunch on December 22 we crossed the pass into its giant lagoon. Gilbertese fishermen after tuna had sighted us and a parade of their swift sailing canoes flashed by on both sides. We were aware of a large population (8,000) at once, for we saw rows of native houses along the shore and crowded ferryboats heading across the lagoon.

But we were prepared in no way for the reception we got when we pulled down the sails and glided against the seawall in the tiny man-made harbor at Betio. Above us stood 200 or 300 Gilbertese men shouting and pointing and laughing and gesturing. The sun blazed down on their handsome brown bodies, brilliant with the cheerful whites and reds and blues of trade-store prints. News of *Whisper* had been radioed from Funafuti and Abemama, but the men couldn't believe that our little ship had crossed the Pacific. Waves of delight rippled across the yelling mob when someone saw an anchor or the compass or a navigation light and pointed it out to his friends. I was overwhelmed at all the fuss; the noise and laughter seemed a little too much.

A bird circling high in the sky might have seen that the reef of Tarawa (pronounced Tare-a-wah, with no accents) looked like a vast triangle bent from a piece of rusty iron rod. The three-sided, milky-blue lagoon measured nineteen miles from north to south, and the main islets of Betio and Bairiki lay on the southern base of the triangle which ran sixteen miles in an east-west direction. Americans first heard of Tarawa during World War II when a stoutly entrenched Japanese force made the beaches of Betio run crimson with the blood of men from the U.S. Marines and Navy. Seventeen percent of a 18,313-man attacking force ended up as casualties to secure an atoll that no one had heard of before or remembered since.[23]

When we went ashore to deliver the mail we heard English spoken with accents of New Zealand, Australia, and Great Britain and saw tall men in white shirts, white shorts, white stockings, and brown laced shoes, for this was the main island of the colony and 200 Europeans lived on the atoll. Not only was Tarawa the center of government administration, but the island was also the principal shipping center for the twenty-five atolls of the Gilbert and Ellice group, headquarters for the trading company, and home of the colony hospital, secondary schools, missionary offices, copra warehouses, machine shops, and a surprisingly busy boatyard. There was a feeling of prosperity and industry in the air.[24]

We began to make friends and in a day had half a dozen dinner invitations. We got acquainted with the head of the trading company, Keith Ussher, a curly-headed New Zealander who moved fast, was capable, aggressive, and generous, but a man who never stopped talking. He and his gentle wife, Evie, were building a small yacht alongside their house and they were good to us during our visit. We were offered the facilities of the boatyard, so we unstepped *Whisper*'s mast, which needed repairs and varnishing, made arrangements to paint the bottom of the ship, and I began to overhaul the fuel system of the engine, which we hoped to get back into operation.

The mast was propped up on sawhorses at the boatyard, and as Margaret and I sanded and varnished each morning we got acquainted with the Gilbertese workmen who often stood and watched every move we made. With supervision the Gilbertese were excellent workmen. For instance, the claim at Betio was that the stevedore gangs, using barges, could unload 400 tons of general cargo per day as against 300 tons per day in a modern quayside port. The men were an enthusiastic lot, perhaps a bit irresponsible and clownish by Western standards, but they had rules of their own, main ones being the concepts of courage and shame.

A Gilbertese man constantly exhibited his courage by his performance in daily tasks. If his courage failed, he was shamed, which was tantamount to death or severe social ostracism. The standards were black and white; there was no middle ground.

The men often took their small, undecked sailing canoes into the ocean where the seas were big and currents strong. A man might sail his canoe for years and have no trouble. But if he capsized or his mast broke or the sail ripped, the owner would have to get back to the atoll by himself. His countrymen might watch—and be beside themselves with laughter—but they would offer no assistance. The victim would accept no help anyway, for if he did he would be totally ashamed and probably kill himself.

When a veteran office worker at Betio was reported missing after going fishing, the Europeans were about to send a launch outside to search for the man.

"No sense going," said one of the local men. "You won't find Kimaere alive, for I saw him drown."

We heard about a Gilbertese who had been out on the reef at low tide. The fishing had been so good that he forgot to watch the time and suddenly found himself cut off by the flooding tide. He couldn't get back to land, for the undertow sucked him seaward as fast as he swam shoreward. He was in a desperate position and covered with blood from cuts when he was slammed against the coral as he went back and forth. A group of islanders on shore guffawed at the fisherman's plight.

A European called to the men, "Why in God's name don't you help the poor fellow? Take him a canoe or throw him a line."

"Oh, sir, we couldn't do that. If the man saw us coming to help him he would drown himself."

Fortunately the man kept his wits and managed to work ashore.

A well-known fisherman from Abaiang was plucked out of the ocean by a colony ship that happened to pass when his canoe was seen upside down and his mast and paddle gone. The man lost all interest in the sea, and after cowering in the hospital for a week he announced that he was going to Tarawa and learn to be an electrician!

Gilbertese children usually obey their parents without exception. However, when a father told an errant daughter who was involved in a complex romantic situation that he was taking her back to their home island, the girl refused to go. Shamed, disgraced, and utterly ruined, the father stuck a knife in his belly.

In other words, a man must be a winner; he must not lose. The victor is courageous—according to the Gilbertese use of the word—but shame destroys him before the eyes of his fellows. I suppose this was the reason the natives were so enthusiastic when we arrived on *Whisper*. We were heroes as long as we stayed ahead of the game. I would hate to be shipwrecked in the Gilberts!

But this was only a single color from the rich rainbow of Gilbertese culture, a people we wanted to know better.

To understand those who are different from you, a person needs patience, knowledge, and respect, three traits possessed in large measure by the late Sir Arthur Grimble. He was a long-time administrator, yarn-spinner, and a prince when it came to a sympathetic ear for the Gilbertese, who less than a century ago were tough warriors who decimated their enemies with swords of fire-hardened palm wood rimmed with sharks' teeth.

Grimble wrote of the poetry, songs, legends, sorcery, magic, and wisdom of these complex people who on their last voyage might be swept into the zone of wildfire (where a man had two shadows) before he sailed over the lip of the world.[25]

The Gilbertese logic was sometimes scathing: "God and Jesus do not belong only to the Protestants and Roman Catholics," said an old man of eighty who was thoroughly fed up with the missionaries, their biased teaching, and constant infighting. "God and Jesus belong to the pagans also. They are not surrounded by a fence up there in Heaven, and we do not have to run into a mission fence to find them here on earth. They are everywhere . . . we can take them for our own friends if we want them."[26]

The Gilbertese could celebrate the end of a long dispute between two villages with a rollicking poem:

Behold! the back-and-forth, the dartings, the stabbings of my
    words are done!
For the talk is ended, the judgement judged
And there he goes now sailing over the horizon.
The porpoise is dead, the whale is sunk,
The thundercloud is fled from the sky,
The storm is over: a small, cool wind blows between the villages.
A cool wind-o-o-o! O-o-a![27]

On Boxing Day, the day after Christmas, Margaret and I went to a grand party on the *Teraka*, the colony training ship that was anchored in the lagoon. Most of the Europeans were on board and we were served by ninety enthusiastic cadets who were learning to become stewards, engineers, and seamen. The training scheme was clever and I was filled with admiration for the British.

Commercial shipping lines in the Pacific and Far East are in constant need of good seamen. The Gilbertese made excellent crewmen, but there had been no way of training the men and the shipping companies didn't take native apprentices. Someone in the colony suggested buying an old steel coasting vessel from Germany that was for sale at a reasonable price. Qualified training officers were expensive to hire and there were no funds in the slim colony budget, but the scheme looked so promising that the United Nations offered to pay the salary of the captain. Several major shipping companies from Germany and Great Britain furnished the other principal officers, since their lines hoped to hire the trained cadets. It was a wonderful idea and the thinking behind it could well be copied by others.

Margaret and I completed the mast work, and one afternoon we asked for the crane and six men. Sixty (!) showed up, all shouting and joking, and amidst pandemonium we stepped the mast, under the supervision of Sam Murdock, the capable foreman at the boatyard. A few days later we put *Whisper* on the hard white sand and at low tide painted most of the bottom and scrubbed what we couldn't reach to paint. The engine now worked, and one by one we crossed jobs off the list. Some of the deck leak was still with us, so we removed the rest of the toerail between the mast and the stem and laid fiberglass over the hull-deck joint. Finally it was dry below.

One day I happened to glance up and I saw something that appeared like an enormous kite up so high that it was among the low trade wind clouds. It *was* a kite and we noticed others. We discovered that kite flying had been a favorite Gilbertese pastime for as long as memory. The kites were huge—often twelve to fifteen feet long—and we measured one that was twenty-five feet overall. The construction was of thin sticks lashed together and covered with light cloth or plastic. The ball of string was often the size of a volley ball. We couldn't get over the size of the kites!

Large whaleboats were used throughout the colony to haul copra from shore to ship. Such service was severe, for the boats often had to go through the surf and sometimes capsized, and there were always eight or ten bashed-up whaleboats awaiting repair at the boatyard. Often the boats would sink, and as they went down the copra bugs and cockroaches would scramble higher and higher. Whenever a whaleboat foundered near us the horrible insects would begin to swim toward *Whisper*. I had always thought that cockroaches would drown, but I can assure you that the two- and three-inch brutes can swim well. We seized oars and fought them off, repelling the odious invaders with vicious smashing blows against the hull and water.

We sailed across the Tarawa lagoon in the astonishing Gilbertese outrigger canoes, perhaps the fastest in the world and one of the miracles of the islands. So-called modern concepts such as asymmetrical hulls, low wetted area, light weight, and large sail area were old stuff to the Gilbertese. Our lagoon canoe was thirty-five feet long and entirely built of small boards lashed edge to edge with coconut string. There was no metal in the entire canoe. To change direction you didn't tack or wear the ship but you physically shifted the entire triangular sail from one end to the other and carried the steering oar to the opposite end while always keeping the outrigger to windward. This was not as awkward as it sounds, for the reaching winds were steady and the courses often ran for miles.

When the mainsheet was pulled in we flashed across the turquoise lagoon at eighteen knots. Two men danced in and out on the balancing outrigger, one man steered, and the captain handled the mainsheet and ran things. The idea was to attain a balance between the wind and the sail so that the outrigger would be just clear of the water. With no drag from the float and the enormous sail full of wind, our knife-edge canoe hurled across the lagoon fast enough to bring tears to my eyes. When a puff of wind came, the acceleration was unbelievable. What excitement!

The other miracle of the Gilbertese was the maneaba. This was

the great meetinghouse of each village, and somewhere among each collection of native houses you would see a lofty peak and a huge mat of thatch pushing almost as high as the palms. The maneaba was not only an attraction for the eye; it was the social hub, the assembly hall, the dance emporium, and the news center of the village. Each clan in a village specialized in one part of the construction. According to Sir Arthur Grimble:

One manufactured thatch pieces for the roof, another lashed them into place; there was a clan to gather the timbers, a clan to dress them, a clan to lay them in place; and so on for the capping of the ridge pole, the trimming of the eaves, the setting up of the corner-stones, the shingling of the floor, the plaiting of the coconut-leaf screens to cover the shingle and hang below the eaves. The ridge soared sixty feet high, overtopping the coconut palms; the deep eaves fell to less than a man's height from the ground. Within, a man could step fifty full paces clear from end to end, and thirty from side to side. The boles of palm trees made columned aisles down the middle and sides and the place held the cool gloom of a cathedral that whispered with the voices of sea and wind caught up as in a vast sounding box.[28]

On New Year's Day we heard shouting and clapping from the great maneaba at Betio, and we walked up to watch half a dozen groups take turns singing and dancing. The performance had some of the aura of a revival meeting, with a thousand or more people involved, and the leaders, who stood in back of the puppetlike, brightly dressed dancers out in front, whipped up the shouting and singing to a frenzy. Another day we saw youngsters from the island of Tabiteuea practice crab and ghost dances. A leaf skirt around the wriggling hips of a three-year-old was quite a sight.

On the day before we left we gave a small party for the friends we had made on Tarawa. Forty-five people signed our guest book. The next morning we discovered that *Whisper* was hard aground.

"No problem," said Sam Murdock. "I'll call out the fire brigade."

Fifty men appeared, waded into the water, and put their shoulders against *Whisper*'s hull. "Hip hip hip *haaaaaaw*," shouted the leader, and the ship began to move. The men got laughing so hard they had to stop, but at the signal of their leader they soon boosted the yacht into deeper water.

As we sailed away from Tarawa I thought of the richness of the Gilbert and Ellice islands and the wise and unmeddling government. A child's good night poem kept singing in my brain:

> Mr. Star, thou, the little one,
> Wink once, wink twice.
> Thee I have chosen: thou art sleepy!
> Thou sleepest, Mr. Star, thou, the little one,
> In a little cloud.
> O-o-o-a-a-a! Sleep![29]

A Large Outrigger
Has Been Sighted

AT FIVE O'CLOCK IN THE AFTERNOON ON JANUARY 16, we had logged 332 miles on a course west and a little north from Tarawa. It was the third day out and we ran easily before light easterly winds and a favorable current, halfway to Kusaie, the easternmost of the Caroline Islands.

With 8,662 miles behind us since San Francisco we knew our sailing routine well. When a fair wind blew we put the mainsail out flat before the wind, with one line to hold the boom firmly forward and a second line on a tackle to pull the boom and sail down so the belly of the sail wouldn't chafe on the rigging. Opposite to the mainsail and a little forward, the genoa was held out with a long white pole whose inner end was clipped to the mast and whose outer end was controlled by three lines. The thrust of the wind pushed evenly on the balanced sails—one out to port and one out to starboard—and we sped along hour after hour while the wind vane easily steered the ship.

I looked up at the neat triangles of sails enclosed by the strong rigging and varnished spars and marveled that man could harness the wind in such splendid fashion. Like the steam locomotive, the windmill, and the stagecoach, sailing was hopelessly outdated, a kind of archaeological oddity; yet it was a wonderful, free kind of life where money and possessions counted for little. You lived at a level where a simple act like identifying a curious bird became profound and surrounded with wonder. You would see a coconut be-whiskered with barnacles and grass and speculate where its parent tree grew. A fish would jump out of the water and you had time to think about the complex world of sea creatures below you. At night there were the stars! I never saw the world above until I went to sea.

January 19. The stars are so brilliant and beautiful that it is worth taking extra naps during the day so that you can sit up at night to watch them. (Those of the equator and northern hemisphere are much more splendid than the paltry few of the south.) Orion's complex is the best with its leading lights of Sirius, Betelgeuse, and and Procyon. Early in the morning (here at 5° N.) the Big Dipper comes up and with it (on the sweep of the arm) Arcturus and Spica. Capella is then a glowing guidepost of blue in the western sky. Surely the splendor of these night skies is the best thing I have ever seen. And it's all free.

Margaret and I played games with the stars. On a good viewing night we would try to impress each other by rattling off a dozen stars—and then point out a new one.

"Look! There's Schedar," Margaret would say, gloating with su-periority after some secret homework with the star charts.

"Oh? Where's that?"

"*Everybody* knows Schedar. It's at the bottom and right of the W of Cassiopeia. See, over there . . ."

As we neared Kusaie (Koos-eye) we had lots of squalls. Most lasted only fifteen or twenty minutes but they persisted, and when we were below we always listened for the sudden calm and severe silence that presaged these minor wind and rain storms. Then one of us would go topsides and douse a sail until the disturbance passed. We were slowly working north but still in the unsettled southern fringes of the north-east trades, a wind pattern that got increasingly vague as we sailed toward the Far East.

At 0715 on the sixth day from Tarawa, Margaret looked up from feeding the cat to see the high silhouette of Kusaie scratched across the horizon. We were in the American Trust Territory, on the outermost fringes of the Carolines, a scattering of 963 small islands that was sprinkled from Kusaie (163° E.) all the way west to the Palau Islands (130° E.), a distance of 2,000 miles. In addition the Trust Territory also includes the Marshalls and all of the Marianas Islands except Guam. In total the territory takes in three million square miles of the Pacific and encompasses 2,137 mostly tiny islands whose land area adds up to 687 square miles on which live some 94,000 people who speak nine different languages.[30]

The islands belonged first to Spain, then to Germany, and finally to Japan. After World War II the area became a United Nations strategic trusteeship with the United States as the administering authority. Or to put it more simply, the United States promised to look after the islands in exchange for rights to build military bases. But the islands are far-flung, conditions abysmal, transport nonexistent, and the United States—with little colonial experience—has had only slight concern over its distant possession. Few Americans have ever heard of the Trust Territory and care less.[31]

We knew all these things and wondered what we would find. On our chart we saw that Kusaie was roughly a circle about nine miles in diameter, and looking ahead we watched verdant, green-clad mountains slowly take form and substance.

By late afternoon we were off Lele on the eastern shore, and I was surprised to see two boats come out to escort us into the harbor. As we glided through the pass we saw perhaps 100 people lined up along the village shore on the north watching us. We glanced at the people, but our attention was drawn to the village. And what a village!

It was worse than Pago Pago in American Samoa. I saw an eye-smashing horror of huts, warehouses, boat shelters, and houses, mostly roofed with torn scraps of rusty iron sheeting. Everything was built up from beat-up scrap boards and junk lumber roughly nailed or propped into place without any sort of plan or guideline. Some of the decrepit, unpainted structures were built around old concrete foundations and walls of Japanese style from an earlier era. Several shiny motorcycles bounced along the dusty waterfront, which was bordered with thickets of weeds. Piles of broken wooden boxes and debris littered the foreshore. I thought back to the neat villages of the Gilbert Islands and groaned.

"I don't understand Americans," said Margaret. "It's truly incredible how junky the waterfronts of these U.S. islands are. It almost seems there has been a carefully worked-out plan to make the villages as ugly as possible.

"We've visited French and British islands and I've seen photographs of these places during the German and Japanese times," she said. "Each administration except the American manages to have neat villages, reasonable roads, and some order. The money is here for new motorcycles and outboard engines. Plenty of energy is present, for I can hear hammers pounding away. Can't the American authorities furnish a little enlightened control? Must the slums of America be exported?"

Shortly after we anchored, five officials came out to see us. We met Leo Delarosa, the acting district administrator, who jumped on board and showed us a message from one of the elders of Lele.

A LARGE OUTRIGGER HAS BEEN SIGHTED. TWO SAILS AND COMING VERY FAST. ALL THE PEOPLE OF THE VILLAGE ARE WATCHING. YOU HAD BET-TER COME.

Leo asked whether we had "authorized permission" to visit the Carolines.

"Authority? Permission?" I said, dumbfounded. "I am an American citizen. This is a U.S.-documented vessel. President Kennedy said over and over that it was official policy to encourage visits and tourism."

"I will radio the U.S. Navy strategic command on Saipan to see about authority for you to visit here," said Leo, surprised at my outspokenness.

You have to get away from America to realize that no officialdom on earth is worse or more cumbersome than that of the United States. Any action on an administrative level is years behind policy statements. Second-echelon officials hide behind phrases such as "Headquarters says ..." or "According to present regulations ..."

The next morning we went ashore to look at Kusaie, which has the reputation of being the garden isle of the western Pacific. The soil was extremely fertile, the growth lush and heavy, and we were soon eating delicious oranges, brimming with juice. We met two men almost at once—Paul Ehrlich of the Peace Corps and Frank Grossmann, an American teacher from Idaho, who took us on a tour of Lele. We visited some old stone ruins that were said to date from 1500 and were supposedly once the residence of the kings of Kusaie. A series of stone walls built up from columns of black basalt laid horizontally on top of one another rose from the floor of the forest. Each stone column was five- or six-sided, ten or twelve inches in diameter, eight or ten feet long, and resembled the trunk of a small tree. The stone walls looked like the sides of a log cabin, except that the walls were longer and higher and overgrown with giant banyan trees and heavy vines and creepers. The ruins covered perhaps a half square mile, at least the parts we saw, but were hard to envisage as a dwelling place because of the jungle growth and the roofless, tumbled-down condition.

Leo drove up in his Datsun truck and took us for a bouncing ride along a road that finally petered out five or six miles north. Along the perimeter of the high tropical island we saw a thick confusion of brown palm trunks soaring to a green overhead, and we looked at the big-leafed breadfruit trees, a few hardwoods, and the cream and crimson of flowering hibiscus. We listened to the twittering of small birds—something we hadn't heard for a long time—and walked along the edge of mangrove swamps, which, according to Leo, were found only in a condition of both fresh and salt water. We inspected nipa palms—short, nutless trees—whose tough leaves were used for roof thatch. The road was truly terrible and got no maintenance at all.

Back in Lele, Leo's wife had us all to a big lunch, which included mangrove crabs, giant fellows with enormous pinchers whose red legs had big chunks of rich and succulent meat.

We found Frank Grossmann great fun. Though not quite up to the appearance of a Hollywood leading man, Frank was a number-one character actor who was well traveled, urbane, and kept us forever chuckling.

"I was on one of the islands during an outbreak of disease," said Frank later in the day, "and I was instructed to brief the local chief about an emergency air drop of vaccine.

"O.K., Chief," said Frank, with many motions of his hands. "Listen carefully. Tomorrow—next sun—a great silver bird will come over the island past the tall mountain—over there. The medicine will—

" 'You mean the DC-6?' said the chief. 'Let's see. Medicine is Code Yellow. I will alert my men to watch for the airdrop of the paratyphoid bacillus in the primary target area. . . .'

"But seriously," said Frank, "you must forgive me for my small jokes. It's the only way to keep your sanity in this place."

We visited the small hospital in Lele, the sole medical facility for Kusaie, and were shocked at the peeling paint, the sagging doors, the rusted screens, and the insects buzzing around inside the decrepit building which had plenty of patients but hardly any medical equipment. I opened my mouth to speak but Frank held up his hand.

"I know what you're thinking," he said. "And I agree. It's a grim community joke that when an operation is over, not only are the doctor's tools counted, but so are the bits of plaster that fell from the ceiling.

"Every Congressional committee that comes here is horror-struck just as you are," said Frank. "The Trust Territory hired a special team to make an expensive study which pointed out that the whole village of

Lele was situated in the wrong area and should be relocated across the bay on higher ground where the drainage is better. Then when the new village is built a proper hospital can be constructed. It's a grand scheme but only a ridiculous notion, for the five million dollars it will cost is never going to come from the paltry budget."

"Such grandiose schemes are hopeless," said Margaret. "Americans mean well but are too idealistic. It's not necessary to rebuild the entire world like a suburb of Philadelphia. People resent too much intrusion anyway. Do you think the natives of Lele are going to want to leave their ancestral home?

"What is needed is not five million dollars in the vague future," said Margaret, "but five thousand dollars this month to paint and patch the existing hospital. In fact I could make a good start with five hundred dollars and a couple of local workmen."

Later Frank showed us the school where he taught that had been constructed after long planning and fought-over funds. The new building had tiny windows because the stateside architect had specified artificial illumination. Unfortunately there was no electricity. The small windows allowed no ventilation.

"Everybody knows that windows should be floor to ceiling when you're on the equator," said Frank. "Too bad the architect never got out of Washington, D.C. In addition the rest rooms and the general plumbing are unusable because there is no way to get water down the mountain. It's regrettable the architect didn't put a water-catchment system on the roof, which is the usual, simplest, and cheapest arrangement in the tropics."

Back in Lele we saw some excellent local handicrafts made from native fibers. I bought a hat and Margaret got several shopping baskets. Strips of material dyed purple had been cleverly worked into the weaving. "Probably root dyes discovered by the people of Kusaie in ancient times," I said.

"Nothing like that at all," answered Leo Delarosa, who happened to be walking past. "The purple coloring is from A.B. Dick mimeograph ink!"

We stopped at Kusaie only a few days. It was a pretty island whose lofty greenness reminded us of the Marquesas. When we went hiking with Frank Grossmann he took us through great gardens of jungle where we saw guavas, mangoes, papayas, and giant stalks of bananas. (Little did we know it would be the last good fruit until we got to Japan.) It was hard to realize that in 1874, Kusaie was the place where

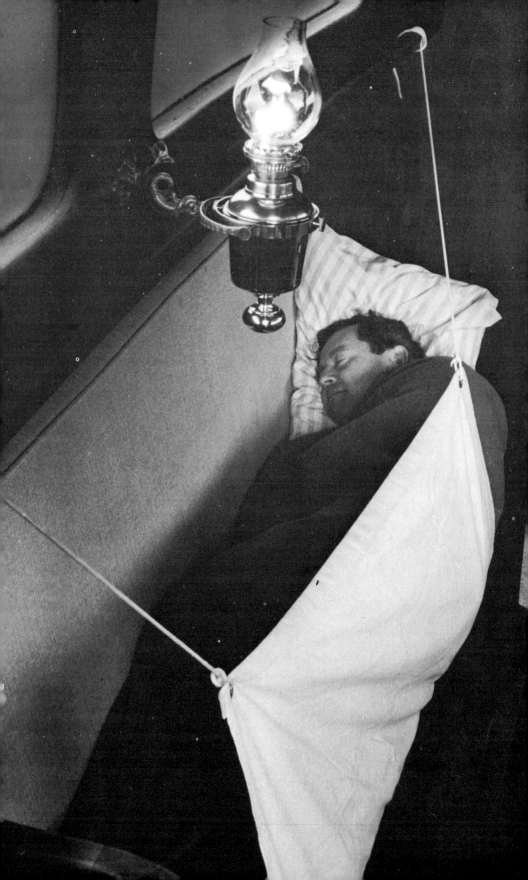

Captain Bully Hayes had reached the zenith of his career as a forger, ship stealer, swindler, confidence man, child raper, kidnapper, blackbirder, murderer, thief, and general nuisance to the human race.[32] Kusaie too, on the other end of the human scale, is where present-day native Protestant pastors, trained by zealots from Boston, still exhort their people to "confess" in public.

From the top of the hill above Lele, Frank pointed out the traces of Japanese days—the alcohol plant, the fish factory, the shipping docks, and the dim outlines of fields where rice and sugar cane once flourished. We had seen Japanese features in some of the Kusaie people, had heard Japanese spoken, and had bought Japanese foodstuffs in the trading stores.

"I sometimes think these places might be better off under the Japanese," mused Frank. "Of course the Japanese colonized the Carolines for their own benefit. We Americans have a lot of plans . . . if we only had better people out here."

The trip from Kusaie to Ponape was an easy 320 miles with northeast winds of fifteen to twenty knots behind us. On the second day we passed Pingelap atoll just as the swift night of the equator fell on us. We were exactly on course, but it was good to have the low island behind us before dark. When the daylight was gone I stood on deck and hunted in vain for the atoll which was astern and to starboard only a mile or two. In the moonless, overcast night I could see nothing, though I have good eyes and looked carefully. No wonder atolls are dangerous at night!

When the wind was fair we were often able to open all the hatches and ports, which allowed lots of fresh air below. Kong, our cat, liked to jump from the floor of the toilet compartment up through the open ports to the deck. He would wait until the middle of a roll and then jump. Sometimes he did this a dozen times in an afternoon and then would scamper up and down the decks looking for flying fish.

One morning about 0700 I was dozing on the port settee and I vaguely heard the cat jump on deck. A little later when I got up to check our course and to look around, I suddenly had the feeling that Kong was gone. I called Margaret and we raced to search the ship. We were running hard at six knots with a small jib flying and when Margaret and I stood on deck and looked back at the heavy swells that reached endlessly toward the rising sun we knew it was hopeless to go back. I had no idea when Kong had gone over the side. His little head would have been impossible to find in the seas that were running. I think he would have gone right down.

We were sick about losing Kong, absolutely disconsolate. People get attached to pets more than they realize and even as I write these lines twenty months later I feel regret and sadness.

January 24. 0900. Of all the islands we have approached, the landfall here has been the most frustrating. Yesterday we ran our distance and were confident of our course but saw nothing except misty clouds to the west. Finally after a lot of hard looking I made out part of a mountain. We piled on all sail and hastened to the west for hours until we could distinguish a bit of the north and south extremities of Ponape. We carried on until dark, feeling that the island was on rollers and that as we approached Ponape it was automatically pulled away from us another ten miles. We finally gave up and hove to at sunset.

This morning at first light, we again made all sail westward. But the men had pulled the island away from us on the rollers again. No sign of land. Finally we saw a bit of mountain through the mist. (Our eyes ache from all the searching.) We carried on but it took us two hours before the bearings on the north and south points were the same as yesterday afternoon. Now an hour later we can begin to see the separate peaks, knobs, and ridges through the heavy veil of mist. No doubt there is a stream of hard-running current from the west. We expect the island to be pulled back on rollers any minute as we hurry toward the phantom.

We knew the main settlement of Ponape was at Kolonia on the north coast. However, we wished to visit the ruins of Nan Matal, so we sailed into the big bay of Matalanim on the east coast, glided around the protecting hook of south-facing Pantieinu Point, and anchored in four and a half fathoms. The waters of the bay were opaque with particles of soil carried down by the Retao River above us, and the dark water reflected a tumbling waterfall, mountains mantled in heavy green, and afternoon cumulus clouds billowing above the highlands. Three rickety native houses on stilts stood near us on shore, and two miles to the south the buildings of Father Costigan's big Catholic school loomed up from clearings in the velvety growth. *Whisper* swung with a cat's paw of wind and I looked at a thick mangrove swamp 150 yards away. Bird calls fluted across the quiet water.

The next day several outrigger canoes came alongside. We saw at once that the people were darker than those we had met before, and their standards of dress were poor. The long, lean canoes were hollowed from logs that sat low in the water and needed constant bailing. The owners paddled, set rude sails before the wind, or used outboard motors. Any women on board invariably carried big black umbrellas.

We soon found that the ambition of every young Ponapean man was to install a large Johnson or Evinrude motor in his outrigger canoe and to flash around the waterways at high speed with a great rooster-tail of water splashing up behind. The larger the motor, the more ecstatic was the smile of the owner. Last year ten horsepower. This year twenty-five. Next year fifty!

We rowed across Matalanim Bay to Nan Matal, the site of an ancient stone city that is spread across perhaps 100 low islets near the southern entrance of the bay. Long known as the forgotten Venice of the Pacific, Nan Matal has the appearance of a series of feudal fortifications. The stout, dark-colored walls are built up from stone logs of columnar basalt ten or twelve inches in diameter and eight to ten feet long, stacked in log cabin fashion like the ruins we had seen on Kusaie.

We rowed along the mangrove-choked canals and tied the dinghy up at the front of a giant ruin whose black walls jutted thirty feet above us. We walked up broad steps through a large entrance and, once inside, we found the stone ruins cool and strangely quiet. Some of the low chambers had roof beams of stone logs. We speculated on the people who might have constructed this ancient city with its straight canals and precise walls which presumably once supported colossal peaked roofs of wood and thatch or else harbored hundreds of small individual dwellings. Except for the water, Nan Matal reminded us of the Inca city of Machu Picchu high in the mountains of Peru. Certainly these departed races had a good knowledge of civil engineering and stone work. U.S. scientists have recently dated charcoal fragments that were 700 years old, showing that native fires burned in Nan Matal in the thirteenth century, but how the ancients transported stones that weigh many tons remains a mystery, a puzzle for future archaeologists.[33]

Before we left we met an old man with wide vertical bands of blue tattooing on his legs who was collecting breadfruit and carrying them to his canoe. We returned to *Whisper* by way of another canal route—passing tumbled-down ruins everywhere—and glided down waterways with heavy steaming jungle on each side. It was good to break into the open and to feel the cool northeast trade wind again.

The next day we sailed along the east coast and around the north barrier reef to Kolonia, the principal settlement of Ponape and the head of the eastern district of the Caroline Islands. In my mind's eye I had hoped for a neat little town nestled beneath the dark-green mountains that rose behind the Tawenjokola River, but we saw the usual junky American waterfront, an ugly amalgam of rust, dust, and debris. Wags have sometimes called the Trust Territory the Rust Territory, which is not far from the mark. So much World War II debris still litters Micronesia that scrap metal is the territory's second most valuable export a quarter of a century after the war.

When I landed I was handed a copy of the harbor regulations, but I soon discovered that the river near the settlement hadn't been dredged since Japanese days and was silted with mud so that we went aground at low tide. I leafed through the regulations and found that I would have to pay harbor dues of $5 a day even though I anchored out and had access to no facilities. Once ashore, however, I explained that I was a small pleasure vessel and after some trouble managed to get the harbor dues waived.

In Western Samoa and Kusaie we had met members of the U.S. Peace Corps and now we got acquainted with many more. For the most part these were young people who had come to a foreign place for several years to work with the local residents on a grassroots level. They instructed island women about balanced diets and nutrition, helped with better village sanitation, taught elementary school, worked on roads and water reservoirs, and cheerfully labored in a dozen disciplines. There were a few misfits and some wheel-spinning because of inexperience, but the men and women of the Peace Corps had the twin advantages of youth and energy, and best of all they lived at the level of the local people. The Peace Corps volunteers generally stayed in native villages, often wore local dress, and tried hard to speak the language of the land. Their goals seemed realistic and practical.

But it was quite a transition for Martha Bridges, aged twenty-two, from Grand Island, Nebraska, who suddenly found herself distributing anti-filariasis pills in a remote village in the Kiti district of Ponape instead of attending classes at the University of Chicago.

"I liked the Micronesians very much," said Martha when I spoke to her in Kolonia, "and as I learned to speak Ponapean better they accepted me more and more. I had a little house of my own and my life was secure and interesting except for one thing: I could get no privacy. Every hour of the day and night the villagers were with me or looking at me. In the evening I would be in my house reading or cooking or combing my hair and there would always be a few locals peering in the window. I liked the people but their constant presence began to bug me."

Martha knew the Micronesians were intensely superstitious, so one night at dusk she wrapped herself in a white sheet and lighted a tall candle, which she placed on a saucer in the middle of her one-room hut. Then she knelt in front of the candle and began to wave her arms and wail a high-pitched chant.

"*Whish!* The Peeping Toms were gone," said Martha, "and have never come back—even at noon!"

We met Jim Zeiger, the plant pathologist at the agriculture station. Jim gave us a grand tour of the impressive plantings and trees—begun by the Japanese—and we saw such exotics as the mangosteen, star apple, cherimoya, Malabar chestnut, ixora, soursop, tiarre gardenia, and Surinam cherry. Jim showed us pepper vines which grew on neat rows of fern posts and explained about the processing and marketing of this new Micronesian crop. Jim's most important project was research on breadfruit disease.

"The breadfruit is a major staple of tens of thousands in the South Pacific," he said, pointing to brownish spots on infected fruit. "We are working to inject a plot of sterile breadfruit seedlings with different viruses to learn about the course of the blight and possible ways we can attack its cause."

A number of American teachers came to see us on *Whisper* and we got to know many men and women—often married—who had come from the United States to teach school for two years. Invariably some-one would appear who was keen on sailing or travel and who would ask a hundred questions about our trip and the yacht. Without doubt the social acceptance we got in many places depended largely on the fact that Margaret and I were doing something that represented a dream to many people. The romantic delight of sailing at leisure from one island to another is enormously appealing, and during our Pacific trip hun-dreds of people told us that they too had similar plans—uh—someday.

A parallel consideration of such a trip pivoted upon the needle point of fear. Many people told us they would like to make a similar journey but they were obviously afraid of the sea. When I tried to explain how small-ship sailors worked to minimize the hazards of the sea by careful planning, I got only stares, hesitations, and vague answers.

Or to say it another way: Most people like the known, the positive, and the certain. Our friends on land distrusted what we said about the dangers of the sea. When I said that storms were infrequent and we tried to be where the gales weren't, my listeners didn't believe me. When I suggested a coastwise trip for a starter, I saw heads slowly shake. Their minds were made up in advance. Twice I invited keen schoolteachers to come with us to Guam to try out an ocean trip; neither the man nor the woman accepted. Yet the fascination with our trip continued.

We had some splendid evenings with the American teachers who worked in Kolonia, but we began to discover that the different groups from the United States squabbled fiercely among themselves. The educators—themselves split in factions—hated the plant people, who reciprocated with gusto. The head of the cooperatives was quitting, he said, because his plans were constantly frustrated by headquarters and those who controlled his finances. Public Works wanted more money and less work, and the transport people claimed their shipping schedules were reduced to shambles by the demands of the Peace Corps. Even after twenty-five years, a dozen studies, and untold expenditures, a proper airfield hadn't been constructed on Ponape (the Japanese had two fighter strips during World War II), and the only official transport was via tiny amphibian planes that used the lagoon. A good administrator could have dealt with these problems, but unfortunately the number-one man on the island had a drinking problem and was often absent from his office.

The situation was humorous in a way and Ponape would have been a good place for a novelist. But it was a pity, an absolute shame, that so much energy was wasted in petty bickering—foolishness that dissipated the time of expensive people whose talents should have been used for the good of the Micronesians. "Misfits are the plague of the administration," wrote Willard Price after a long visit.[34]

This is a book about a sailing adventure, not a political work, but if I can be allowed one comment it is this: The U.S. will never have any success running the lives of foreign people until it establishes a *career* colonial service based on the British model. The service should be staffed with outstanding, carefully chosen people—*employed for their entire working lives*—who wish to deal fairly and firmly with foreigners under U.S. control.

The question at the moment is not intent, for our intentions are pure. The question is not money, for we spend far more than anyone else. The question is not motivation, for we want to do well. The question is *experience*. We are bungling amateurs.

"Few of the Trust Territory positions are even under our civil service," writes James Ramsey Ullman. "There is, on the one hand, neither the machinery for preparing a man for a career in the islands, nor, on the other, the rewards to make it attractive once he has undertaken it."[35]

The use of the words "wards" and "colonial service" may sound presumptuous today, but the need for these concepts exists. The Pacific people I saw weren't a bit concerned over the blue-sky slogans of nationalism, colonialism, and self-determination. These people were worried about getting something to eat.

You can't rule stone-age people with computers and pie-in-the-sky planning studies. The Micronesians need leadership. They have to be told what to do. Money is important but *leadership* is the critical thing. The Gilbert Islands were run for only a fraction of the money spent in the Carolines. Yet we saw busy, happy people who lived in neat villages in the Gilberts. In the Eastern Carolines we saw confusion, indolence, and apathy in an environment of abysmal living conditions. The young people don't need to study the humanities and social studies (whatever that means) but to learn to read, to write, and to perform simple arithmetic. What Kusaie and Ponape lacked was craftsmen of all kinds—carpenters, welders, cement workers, seamen, offshore fishermen, plumbers—men with practical skills. This shortcoming was quite unrecognized by U.S. officialdom, and met so far as I saw by only a single Catholic priest, Father Hugh Costigan, a twenty-year Ponapean veteran, who ran a useful industrial trade school designed to help the actual *needs* of his island.[36]

As we got ready to leave Ponape we thought of Adriano Selhar, who had come aboard *Whisper* in Matalanim Bay and had told us about the astonishing yam culture on the island.

"Growing yams is very important on Ponape," said Adriano. "They are raised for food but more important they are cultivated for prestige."

We found out that over one hundred varieties of yams are grown, some long and skinny, and others short and round. The individual tubers grow up to six feet long, six to eight inches in diameter, and weigh 200 to 250 pounds. Sometimes six men are required to carry a single yam! The Ponapeans often grow the yams deep in the forest in hidden places where each farmer works with secret techniques, special fertilizers, skills handed down from father to son, and varieties of yams that date from pre-Spanish days.[37]

"The cult of the yam is complicated," said Adriano, smiling broadly. "If you grow a yam bigger than anyone else and give it to the chief at the annual festival, you become famous and the chief awards you a special title. To present the biggest yam is a wonderful honor, which not only reflects a man's ability, generosity, and initiative, but shows his love and respect for his elders. I would give anything to be able to grow a two hundred-pound yam. Just think of it!

"Who knows?" said Adriano, pausing in glorious thought, "maybe I will be lucky with the plants I have in the forest."

14 / ∿∿∿∿∿∿∿
∿∿∿∿∿∿∿∿
∿∿∿∿∿

Where Are You, Magellan?

As we slipped northward through a pass in Nankapen-param Reef, a full-throated northeast wind ballooned out *Whisper*'s sails. The overcast dawn of February 6 was an hour old, but in the dim light the dark mountains of Ponape were already fading behind us in the mist. 、

The great game in small-ship cruising is to arrange your passages so that you go from one place to another without intermediate islands in the way. Or if that is impossible, to plan things so you will see the inter-vening obstacles during daylight hours. In more civilized parts of the world, powerful flashing beacons and various signals help the mariner. But in the trackless voids of the nether regions you are on your own. God forbid any surprise atolls in the middle of a moonless night!

The complex of the Caroline Islands bulked to our west. We aimed to leave these reefs and atolls to the south by holding a course of 296° T., which gave us a straight run for Guam, 900 miles away. We were in the northeast trades and had plenty of fair wind across our starboard quarter. The wind was squally, however, and for the first few days we seemed to be forever pulling the sails down and running them back up.

On the second day we logged 156 miles noon to noon, our best ever for twenty-four hours, but the motion was too wild as we whished ahead on big rollers, so we carried on with less sail. Even so our average remained 137 miles per day, good daily runs for a sailing ship twenty-five feet on the waterline, especially when we generally flew a double-reefed mainsail and a storm jib. The wind varied from twelve to thirty knots.

With *Whisper* guided unfailingly by the self-steering vane we had to be careful not to fall overboard. A sailing yacht is designed to come into the wind and stop if no one is at the helm. If you were steering by hand and fell over the side you could probably swim to the stopped ship. But with the vane in control of the helm, the yacht would merrily continue on course while you—alas—watched forlornly from the water. For this reason we had double lifelines around the ship, and when the sea was rough we wore safety harnesses so that we could clip ourselves dog-leash fashion to the ship somewhere. Alone up on the foredeck at night with the other person asleep you had to be especially careful—one hand always firmly on the ship or your legs jammed against something.

Margaret and I wore police whistles around our necks so that we could summon each other in case one of us fell over the side, got fouled in a line, or otherwise desperately needed help. Fortunately we never used the whistles.

We spent a lot of time studying the next charts and reading the *Pilot* books for the islands ahead. Of course if you took the *Pilot* books seriously you would never leave your home harbor. No writing on earth is more filled with gloom and black warnings than the sailing directions of the various governments. We read of "uncharted rocks, numerous and fang-like," "hostile tidal streams that seethed with sudden overfalls," "poisonous shell fish," "severe magnetic anomalies," and about "vicious undersea volcanic activity."

Margaret and I often held contests to see who could come up with the most melancholy passages and we would soon be hooting with laughter.

"Listen to this one," I said. " 'The anchorage is obstructed with a loaded ammunition ship below the surface.' And here's happy news: 'The life-saving station has been shut down.' "

"Try these," said Margaret. " 'Unlighted concrete fish traps obstruct the channel.' Or 'Mariners are warned that oyster farmers have sometimes fired on small ships thought to be poaching.' "

Guam is the southernmost of the sixteen Marianas Islands which extend northward for 420 miles and include such well-known places as

Tinian and Saipan. Our plan was to work north along the chain and to cross 280 miles to the next group north, which was the Nanpo Shoto, some two dozen small volcanic islets which extended north another 640 miles to the Japanese coast. I spent days studying the charts, reading the *U.S.* and *British Pilots*, and examining weather maps.

As I read the *Pilots* I followed the descriptions with the appropriate charts. This was slow work with Japanese place names because the names were sometimes different. Was the mountain called Hagashi Yama the same as Mihara Yama? Was I right in assuming the Kyodoga Hana was a spelling variant of Koiwadoga Hana? Was the village of Yaene the same as Kanado? Was the 215-foot cape named Funatsuke Bana that I saw on the chart the same 215-foot place that the *Pilot* called Funetsukega Hana?

I began to have serious doubts about my scheme to work northward along the two island groups. The strong Kuroshio current—the Japanese current—set toward the northeast at thirty to forty miles per day, and the prevailing winds above 25° N. blew from the north and northwest. I feared that we might find ourselves beating against the wind on the port tack trying to make westing as we headed north while being set eastward by the Kuroshio current. The prospect was dismal. After much deliberation I decided to strike out boldly for southern Japan directly from Guam. According to my studies, a gale or two was likely, but we would have plenty of room in the Philippine Sea, with Okinawa and Chichishima as refuge places on the extreme limits of our route.

"The distance between Guam and the southern tip of Kyushu is 1,310 miles," I said to Margaret. "We should stay in the northeast trades for 64 percent of this distance or some 840 miles. That leaves 470 miles —call it 500—of more uncertain winds. Typhoons are unlikely in February. We can cope with gales, though not pleasantly. With luck we can make the 1,310 miles in ten days."

I had made my decision. So much for the homework.

We were somewhere over Nero Deep, a submarine trench whose bottom lay 31,680 feet beneath us, an inverted Everest of the Pacific. The weather continued to be overcast and the moonless nights were black. The illusion of speed was remarkable with the ship running hard. When the wind blew strongly and the seas stayed moderate, we seemed to hurl along in the darkness. At such a time it always appeared to me that we were running downhill—maybe into the other world of the Gilbert Islanders. It is strange how the notion persists. But the feeling of sailing down and down recurs and I have experienced it many times at night.

An hour before dawn on the seventh day I saw a brightly lighted Japanese fishing vessel lying quietly on the sea. That morning was gray, but at 1135 we saw the sun for a moment and a questionable position line put us twenty-seven miles from Guam. I was worried about passing the island and having to beat back, but two hours later we sighted Guam some twelve miles to starboard. How beautiful it was! We immediately put *Whisper* hard on the wind and began to beat toward the island, which, with its cloud cap, looked like a fairy-tale illustration.

February 12. 1340. I am quite pleased to see how well we are going to windward with the storm jib and three rolls in the main. The wind force is 24 knots with fairly large but quite regular seas. There is water over the foredeck but only occasional spray in the cockpit. This landfall has been something like Rarotonga. Twice now I have not allowed enough leeway for the trade wind drift.

Guam is a big American military base and the approach by sea is controlled by the U.S. Navy. We were required to radio twenty-four hours or more ahead for permission to enter Apra harbor, a gigantic military installation on the west coast. Since we had no transmitter, I had asked the radio people on Ponape to contact Guam, which they did. However, when we arrived at Apra at night, no one had heard of us. We were not allowed to enter the commercial harbor but were sent to a remote quarantine anchorage on Cabras Island, a place known locally as Outer Siberia. We were soon cleared, but we discovered that we were miles from stores, shops, supplies, main roads, and transport. I wanted to apply in person for permission to tie up at the docks in the inner harbor, but the gate at the main Navy area meant a ten-mile walk.

We were told to sail to the small-boat harbor at Agana, the main city of Guam. After bashing to windward for most of a day we followed the leading marks through the tiny windswept pass and bang! We were on the coral! We managed to get turned around and off, and fled out to sea, feeling particularly bitter at a Navy that would send a small ship to a harbor that required local knowledge. Wet, tired, and discouraged, we returned to Apra. Again I tried to go to the commercial docks—where a Navy band was serenading a cruise liner—but we were sent to Outer Siberia. What was particularly frustrating was that I couldn't even get to anyone to plead my case. We had no choice but to stay among the area of broken-down docks, moored barges, and new construction.

We saw a parade of big U.S. Navy ships, nuclear submarines,

immense drydocks, and tall, giraffelike cranes, presided over by swarms of dungaree-clad sailors and civilians in hard hats. Overhead a steady procession of B-52 bombers departed and returned from missions in Vietnam. The bombers were painted a dull black and, with their long droopy wings, looked immensely forbidding. Not far from us an ammunition ship was unloading bombs, and trucks stacked with the ghastly missiles rumbled past *Whisper*.

Now on the third day at Guam we were particularly anxious to get ashore and to Agana, where we hoped to find several months of mail. Margaret managed to ride into the city with a friendly construction worker and brought back packages, film, books, charts, a few urgent parts for the ship, and letters from our friends.

We looked on our chart and saw that Guam was about twenty-nine miles long and four to eight miles wide, with a spine of 1,000-foot mountains paralleling its major dimension. Once heavily wooded, the vegetation is now sparse and the general color of the island is light brown. Our attention was drawn to the automobiles, which were everywhere. The island's 230-mile road system was choked with 28,000 motorized vehicles. The biggest problem was to get across the main street in Agana at quitting time when the Navy workers headed for home. After a year in the South Pacific the traffic seemed unbelievable.

"I discovered that the two-car family is out of style," said Margaret. "Modern families have three!"

Technically Guam is a U.S. territory run by an appointed governor and a legislature of twenty-one members, but in practice the island is operated by the military establishment (for example, since most telephone calls are military-oriented, the Navy furnishes free phone service for everyone). The local people number 55,000, with another 38,500 connected with the armed forces.

Guam might easily be called an aircraft carrier with trees, although its used-car lots looked suspiciously like those of Los Angeles and New York.

We found that food prices were higher than the sky. Food cost more on Guam than in San Francisco, and a 25 percent cost-of-living bonus was added to wages. What we could not understand was why certain Japanese and American foodstuffs cost more in Guam than in the Caroline Islands, where the transport charges were infinitely greater. Margaret was amazed that bananas cost fifty cents a pound in the markets.

"The bananas are *grown* here," she said with incredulity. "In California I buy bananas from Costa Rica that cost only ten cents a pound."

With *Whisper* tied up in Outer Siberia it was a miracle that we made any friends, but several schoolteachers happened to drive past and kindly invited us to their homes for meals. One day when we were out walking, a man named Marshall Bridge picked us up in a very battered car. "I thought you were in the Peace Corps with your camera bags," said Marshall. "No matter. I recruit people for the educational program out here and if either of you can teach and are fluent with Japanese and can pass a security check I can offer you a job with a vast salary."

A little later we met Bill Moody, a foreman at one of the Navy shops, who helped us with a repair of *Whisper's* tiller fittings. Two people loaned us automobiles, which made shopping easier and gave us a chance to look at the island.

We sailed to the southwestern coast of Guam to visit Umatac Bay. This was something we had dreamed of when we had first outlined the Pacific trip, for it was in Umatac Bay in 1521 that Magellan had anchored his three ships after his long Pacific crossing.

At dawn [writes a historian] *they coasted along until the watchers crowding the rail sighted a break in the cliffs and saw a little bay between the shoulders of the highlands. They could make out a number of canoes drawn up on its sandy beach while back from the shore a row of thatched houses on stilts was visible.*[38]

Now 447 years later we sailed *Whisper* along the same coast. The wind whipped down from Jumullong Manglo mountain as we skirted the fringing reef. We tacked in toward the little bay and thought of Magellan and his men, sick, scurvy-ridden, and dying, after crossing the strange Pacific from South America. We wondered at their emotions.

The bay was small, only 350 yards wide, and I was surprised that Magellan's weakened men could have worked their unhandy ships inside. Like Magellan we saw the village, now with a church, built along each side of a narrow road. And we saw the Chamorros—the natives of Guam—who were generally small people, a mixture of Micronesian, Filipino, and Spanish stock. We heard the staccato Chamorro language, a Micronesian tongue with Spanish and Tagalog words.

That night we thought how fortunate we were in our little ship. Four centuries ago Magellan had no food, no charts, little medicine, and his navigation was pitiful. On *Whisper* we had a variety of excellent health-giving foods, first-class charts, ample medicine, and we could navigate with ease. The design of our little ship was good and she was made of materials beyond Magellan's dreams. Yet he was the first Western man to cross the world's largest ocean and to demonstrate its existence to an unbelieving world.

That night we drank a toast to Magellan.

We left for Japan on February 24 and learned right away that the Philippine Sea in winter has a mind of its own. An hour out we put one reef in the main, followed a little later by a second reef. Before midnight we pulled down the number two working jib and replaced it with the storm jib. We were headed a little west of north, bashing into big seas churned up by twenty-five to thirty knots of wind from the northeast. Our lives had suddenly become wet and noisy. Japan seemed a long way off.

Margaret was ill and out of it all in her bunk and I didn't feel too well myself. About every third wave thumped on board and bombarded the coachroof and cockpit with sea water that sluiced everywhere. The sea conditions were different from those we had experienced before, and water ran all over the ship, especially around the main hatch, which leaked alarmingly. We had long known a few drips, but now we had first a trickle, and then a stream which soon flooded out the quarter berth, the chart table, and sloshed over the tools stowed beneath. I tried to lash a piece of canvas around the hatch, but without proper fastenings the canvas came adrift.

When we sailed against the wind we pounded into the waves, and big ones would almost stop the ship. *Whisper*, angled closely into the seas, climbed the swells as they passed and crunched into the troughs that followed. You felt the ship rise on a wave, hesitate, and then fall with a great thud into the pit between the last wave and the next. Below in your bunk hanging on, you wondered how the ship could take such knocks. Certainly her stout hull would break in two.

In heavy windward going, the self-steering vane was not too good because the head seas shoved the bow sideways. Adjusted to go more against the seas, the vane steered well until we got into a calmer patch when the vane headed *Whisper* into the wind and tacked the ship. With no one to release the jib sheet, the ship wound up hove to, riding easily on the seas but going nowhere.

"This will never do," I said. "We've got a long way to go." At midnight I began to steer by hand and we got along much better. I was able to stay on course until a big sea approached, when I headed off a little to take the wave on its side. This way we kept the ship moving and lessened the terrible banging.

We were still in the tropics and the sea water was warm. During the night I wore oilskins without boots. After a while there was as much water inside the oilskins as outside, but I was warm and comfortable and cheerfully steered hour after hour. In the dark you could see the big seas coming by the flash of their crests. The water churned and tumbled as it approached and I sometimes thought there were a thousand crested dragons charging the ship, their spines erect and mighty as they converged on our little world. The dragons hissed as they approached and sighed as they swept past, leaving a tingling smell of iodine that freshened the cool air of the black night.

In the first eighteen hours from Guam we logged eighty-two miles. At noon on the second day the gray sky darkened in the north and the wind increased to a steady thirty-seven knots, almost on our nose. We hove to on the starboard tack and I retired to my bunk with a handful of crackers and a book. Margaret was listening to the short-wave broadcasts on the radio.

"It's marvelous to tune in to the political broadcasts of each nation," she said. "The reports of Radio Moscow, Radio Peiping, Radio Australia, and the Voice of America are so different that you think each announcer must be reporting separate events. What pretenders people are! How they bend the truth to fit their own purposes!"

Margaret had her sea legs at last, and we soon had a hot meal, which we ate from bowls while we wedged ourselves against the cabin bulkheads. At first light on the third morning I looked out on a lead-colored sea striped with foam-crested rollers that marched in unflinching rows from the north-northeast. The wind was a little less, and the Ventimeter read twenty-four to thirty-two knots. I was fed up with being hove to because we weren't getting anywhere, so I began to steer again. Close-reaching on the starboard tack, we made good time, but water flew everywhere. Before noon a sea bounded up over the coach-roof, filled the port Dorade ventilator, and poured in below. About half the time there was a foot of water in the cockpit. However, *Whisper* scooted along, and by 2300 the log read ninety-seven miles, an average of six knots, a figure I doubted. A little before midnight the wind became very gusty. We hove to on the port tack.

At 0700 on the fourth day Margaret cautiously slid the hatch back, looked outside, and measured the wind. "Oh joy," she said. "There's an easterly wind of only twenty-four knots."

We got under way at once. During the morning the cloud cover dispersed a little and celestial observations put us 235 miles northwest of Guam. The weather stubbornly stayed foul and in the afternoon the wind backed to the northeast and increased to thirty-five knots with gusts that put the sides of our lee coachroof in the water. We hove to again and I pulled down the third reef in the mainsail. Later I doused the storm jib.

February 28. 1230. We have been steering since dawn and have made 33 miles northward but during the last two hours the seas have gotten bigger. One broke on board and washed Margaret to the opposite side of the cockpit. While I was steering I got caught by a large wave which swept me and a sail bag on to the lee deck, filled the cockpit, and snapped the boat hook in two. Margaret and I have both been wearing safety harnesses plus an additional bight of line tied around us and made fast to a cleat. After a second wave put me across the lee deck I hove the yacht to.

The sky has a low roof of slate-colored clouds with patches of sun here and there which make me think the gale will soon be over. However, the waves are a bit frightening now, and the largest I have seen. In the last 24 hours we logged 31 miles.

When the third wave broke on board Margaret saw the kettle fly upward from the sink and cross to the outboard part of the chart table without spilling a drop. A remarkable act of levitation!

The next day the gale went on. The seas were easier—perhaps more regular—and we banged along and did 135 miles. The yacht was a shambles inside. We had rolled heavily from a big wave and everything flew off the shelves above the chart table. A pair of pliers smashed the stove pressure gauge to bits and spread glass all over the galley floor. While I was asleep the books catapulted off the shelves above the port settee, flew across the cabin, and landed on top of me.

"Help! I'm drowning in books," I shouted, suddenly awake, with dozens of books piled on top of my head.

February 29. 1900. Incredible how you see glimpses of life beneath the surface. Yesterday at the height of the big waves I spotted a whale 25–30 feet long. A little later when the sea was quite wild I saw something off to starboard which after a few minutes proved to be a dozen porpoises leaping and frolicking. How rich with life the sea must be beneath the surface.

2100. Wind up to 40 knots from the east. I tried steering for an hour and filled the cockpit again. Hove to on the starboard tack now. With the current, fore-reaching, and leeway, we are probably making 2 or 2½ knots straight for Japan.

Whisper was so hard pressed that on the next morning—the seventh day of gales—we put up the number three storm jib (fifty square feet) and continued to thump along. At midnight warm rain began to fall. A frontal system was passing over and the wind was definitely less. I was grimy, salt-covered, and weary beyond belief. I sat in the cockpit with the warm rain running over me and watched a ship ten miles off to port.

"Hooray!" I said. "There are other people in the world after all."

The next day we reveled in fine weather and sun. The wind and seas both decreased, and we ran up bigger sails and cautiously opened the hatches and ports. The lifelines were festooned with clothes drying out, and while I picked up below and replaced a few lengths of running rigging, Margaret cooked several hearty meals. Our spirits, now immensely restored, climbed higher when our noon position showed that we had only 680 miles to go.

I had begun to think that in the Philippine Sea the prevailing winter winds always blew from the northeast at forty knots. For a week the sailing had been rigorous, with the ship shut up like an agitated oyster and the sails of laughable size—so full of wind I expected them to blow into a million threads.

At times one perhaps has doubts about sailing in a small ship, but the storm always passes and with it the uncertainty. Like the smile of a pretty girl after an argument, the blue sky, the warm sun, and the easy seas soon restore one's faith in the enterprise.

By March 3 we were at 22° N., and a shirt and a pair of trousers felt good. At night we spread blankets on the bunks, and sea boots began to appear from their long storage. We even fired up the cabin heating stove to dry out the ship below. No one complained about the heat.

I started the engine to charge the batteries. The little Diesel was running nicely when suddenly there was a horrendous bang, followed by a crash, and then silence. I opened the engine-room compartment and was surprised to find the engine gone. The flimsy, built-up wooden mounts had fallen to pieces and the unsupported engine had dropped into the bilge. Once again we were a true sailing ship.

We began to see an occasional smudge of smoke on the horizon, and we kept careful watch for ships, particularly at night. One morning I sailed near an old moss-covered floating tree that was almost twice as long as the yacht. From time to time we had dolphins around us, and once we ran alongside a big turtle. Under the clear skies the sea was no longer blue but dark-colored, for we had worked into the mainstream of the Kuroshio current—the black tide—that swept northeastward from the Philippines to Japan and beyond.

At noon on March 8—1,221 miles from Guam—we were smoothly broad-reaching in front of a twenty-knot southwest wind when I noticed a swell from the northwest. Rain splattered on deck and the wind began to veer and blow harder. I knew something big was coming. Our little vessel was strong, but she was only a tiny ship and we had to drive her sparingly. We yanked down the mainsail, set the storm trysail, and put up the number three storm jib, our two smallest and stoutest sails.

Two hours later we were hove to in a gale with a steady forty-six knots of wind from the northwest. The swells from two directions tumbled against one another, and the sea was as nervous as a caldron of boiling water. *Whisper* lurched into a complex of roads and pathways that capered and bucked like scenery waving in an earthquake. The lanes and ditches not only formed and disappeared in a twinkling, but of a sudden rose and heaved down as the ship tried to go ahead. When she hobbled east she was knocked south, and when she was shoved north she was jerked west. Cross seas banged and slapped on all sides.

I stood in the hatchway and looked out on a leaden scene of bitter gray sparked now and then with a stray shaft of sunlight. The wind had real weight in it and I could scarcely turn to windward because needles of spray hurled against my face and blew my eyes full of water.

The ship rose on a swell, and all at once I looked out on several miles of snorting ocean. Here and there wave tops exploded into block-long cascades of foam, etched white against the dark sea. In the distance immense combers broke and toppled, and when the light was right you could see green water furiously tumbling down.

Then the ship slid into a trough and our world shrunk to a single wave mountaining up behind us. As the sea climbed higher and higher I wondered whether the ship would lift as the swell swept forward. Somehow the ship always rose, and as the water roared ahead, the wave whished under the hull with a bubbling sound.

Storms in the ocean sometimes give the crew a good drubbing. But though you get weary, your senses become immensely heightened. You grow alert to every movement, every shudder, and every vibration of the sea. You hear better, see farther, and somehow touch toward the nerve of the shrieking wind and ocean. You take great breaths of super-clean air, and your nose and tongue pick up the sharpness of the iodine and the faint aroma of sea creatures. You learn the sense of the sea itself.

I stood in the hatchway for hours watching it all, sometimes shouting for pure joy as the big waves scoured past. "You haven't got me yet," I yelled like a blubbering fool, with my words twisted by the wind. "You may be big, but I've still got my wits and my ship."

The grandest experience of my life was to look upon the sea in storm and later at the sea in calm. It's a thing everyone should experience. Reading about it won't do, and photographs are a poor substitute. You need to gaze upon the brooding soul of the tempest itself, and on another day to ponder an ocean of utter tranquility.

During heavy weather we always saw storm petrels, small soft-gray birds that fluttered a few inches above the wave tops seeking bits of food on the surface. The storm petrels often flitted behind the yacht to look over the water churned up by the passage of the ship. The birds would dance above the wave tops a few feet from you and almost touch the water with their tiny webbed feet. In the lee of the waves the wind must have been less, for the gales didn't seem to bother the birds. I often wondered why they weren't swallowed up by the toppling crests, but the petrels somehow rose just enough to stay above the water. No matter how close they were the birds never took any notice of us. Their job was to get food, it appeared, and the task seemed to take their entire attention.

I grew very attached to these slender-winged little fellows—called Mother Carey's chickens by sailors—who came next to us again and again and never showed the slightest fright. Sometimes when I was on the foredeck changing sails and rising up and down on the plunging deck I would look out and see these dainty little birds fluttering—there is no other word—a few feet away, only inches above the water.

By noon on the fifteenth day the gale was gone and we were under way again. The next day we saw a ship, a glass float, and a waterlogged Japanese basket. The following night Margaret called me at 2200 and nodded toward a Japanese coasting vessel about a quarter of a mile astern.

"This fellow has circled us twice," she said. "I haven't made any

motions nor changed course. Evidently the honorable captain has never seen anything like us."

At 0345 on the seventeenth day Margaret picked up a lighthouse signal on Tanegashima, a small island south of Kyushu. We skirted its east coast and in thick weather headed across the Osumi Kaikyo, the broad strait leading to Kyushu.

I was asleep on my berth when I heard a familiar voice. "Oh do come up," called Margaret. "I see Japan."

The visibility was poor—driving rain, low clouds, and light squalls —but we caught glimpses of a high, rock-bound coast. The scenery was wild. Steep mountains disappeared into clouds, and along a black and white and gray coast gigantic rocks were dashed and buffeted by the wind and sea. Hiroshige would have liked our landfall.

We kept plenty of sail up for power since there were strong tidal streams and our engine was only ballast. When we rounded the entrance to Kagoshima Bay we got becalmed behind a current-swept rocky headland and had a few worrying moments when I wished for a big sculling oar. But we finally got wind and began to work up to the city of Kagoshima, the port of entry at the head of Kagoshima Bay, forty miles to the north.

In the middle of the next afternoon, with the magnificent volcano on Sakurashima erupting mightily to starboard and a ferryboat hooting for right of way off to port, we glided into Kagoshima. While the port officials blinked at us with astonishment we clumsily climbed on the docks with our lines and bowed deeply. We had reached the Far East.

15

A Sail in Japan

FIVE MINUTES AFTER WE HAD TIED UP *Whisper* IN KAGO-shima a crowd of a hundred Japanese looked down on us from the big commercial pier. A sailing yacht like ours was unknown, and under the shadow of hulking freighters and enormous, double-decked ferry-boats the people gazed with fascination and curiosity at *Whisper*'s tiny hull, her diminutive mast and sails, our little anchors, and the toy self-steering vane. The children pointed at our U.S. flag, the Japanese cour-tesy flag, and at the yellow quarantine flag that flapped idly.

We weren't quite sure what was going to happen, so we busied ourselves with furling the sails and tidying up the lines.

"Good afternoon, Captain."

I looked up to see three uniformed Japanese officials lowering them-selves on deck. They were nattily dressed in dark blue, with crisp white shirts, carefully pressed trousers, and elegant officers' hats. Two carried briefcases.

I ushered them below and had just begun to get out the ship's papers and the clearance from Guam when I felt more people step on deck.

"Immigration, please."

Four more men filed below, and as I looked still others appeared on deck. Some of the men were young and smooth-faced with plain uni-forms, while several of the gray-haired officials had lots of gold braid on the visors of their hats.

"Customs inspection, hello." More Japanese officials stumbled on

JAPAN

ALEUTIANS

HOKKAIDO IS.

Kushiro

HONSHU IS.

Yokohama
Aburatsubo
Mt. Fuji
Miki Ura
Kobe

SHIKOKU IS.
Inland Sea
KYUSHU IS.
Hososhima
Uchinoura

KOREA

Kagoshima Bay

TANEGA SHIMA IS.

board. Someone asked for passports, but there were so many men in the saloon that I couldn't get forward. Margaret had half a dozen in the cockpit, more were along the side decks, and I heard heavy footsteps on the foredeck.

"Health and agriculture officers, please." A new face smiled in the hatchway.

It was all too funny and I began to chuckle. I guffawed. I giggled. I laughed. I roared. I wept. It was hilarious. I made motions of a little ship, pointed at all the people, and began to count on my fingers. Everybody began to laugh with me and the ship trembled with the gusto of a good joke. The contagion spread to the crowd on the dock, and the laughter rose like a great wave of happiness.

What had happened was that the word had spread that a strange little sailing ship, a yacht with a woman on board, had suddenly come in from across the sea. All the officials wanted to have a look. It was a vast entertainment, an amusement on a dull winter workday. Everybody who could came—apprentices, clerks, inspectors, supervisors—and we were suddenly overrun. Twenty-eight uniformed officers had climbed on board and each claimed to have serious business.

We soon satisfied the agriculture and health men, and the immigration authorities stamped our passports. The customs people, however, concerned with smuggling, searched the ship from the chain locker to the after lazarette. But instead of opium they found rusty cans, in place of gold bars they uncovered wet blankets, and the guns they sought turned out to be dirty laundry.

We wanted a change of scene, so we tied the ship securely, snapped the padlock on the hatch, and left the yacht to the crowd that still watched.

Kagoshima was a bustling seaport of 300,000, and, like so many Japanese cities we were to see, it had a quality of rawness, a feeling of not being quite finished. Many of the streets were torn up and dusty, building projects stabbed the sky with steel and concrete, and the sidewalks were invariably incomplete. The first thing we wanted was a hot meal. We had brought a few yen from Guam and were eager to do business, but first we had to find a restaurant.

We were far from the tourist routes and, once away from the port officials, heard only Japanese. We couldn't read a single letter, much less a word or sentence. We couldn't decipher a street sign, a bus designation, and we could only gaze upon a sign which said 危険建物破壊中 (Danger! Building Demolition!) with idle curiosity.

However, a friend we had made in Guam, Ria Bridge, had loaned us a special English-Japanese dictionary prepared by Oreste Vaccari which had the Japanese words in both Japanese characters and spelled phonetically in Roman letters. This meant we could look up the word for restaurant (*ryoriya*), for example, which we could read and pronounce. If that didn't work, we could show someone on the street the word written in Japanese characters (料理屋). Without the little dictionary our life would have been hard indeed.

Westerners were unusual in the streets of Kagoshima, and people stopped to stare at us. Once downtown, and very hungry by now, we entered a little eating place which had *noren*, half-curtains with large Japanese characters written on them, hanging across the entrance. As soon as we entered, the waitresses began to giggle. One timidly approached and bowed.

"*Hai* [yes]?" she said.

I pointed to the dish being eaten by the person next to us and gestured that we wanted the same. The waitress made the motions of small, medium, and large. I chose medium. She withdrew, immensely relieved, and soon brought bowls of Chinese *soba*, delicious thick noodles in a steaming broth. We each paid 70 yen (19 cents).

As we walked around the city we were delighted with the Japanese food markets, which had dozens of varieties of oranges, all arranged in geometrically precise rows. The early strawberries were individually wrapped, and each early melon lay resplendent in a separate gift box with a window. Enormous bottles of dark-brown *shoyu* sauce alternated with giant bottles of *sake* of half a hundred varieties. We saw stacks of scrubbed carrots, fat cucumbers, giant white radishes called *daikon*, and cabbages with heavy green leaves.

The fish counters gleamed with a circus of colors and shapes—the pink flesh of salmon, the silvery-blue sides of salted mackerel, and big solid chunks of dark-red tuna. The fish sellers stacked up heavy slabs of dried bonito and arranged trays of crayfish whose feelers waved above the edges. Some fish were long and eel-like, others round and thick, and still others flat and spined. There were neat mounds of tiny shrimp, pungent shreds of squid, and purplish sections of octopus.

It was good to have wholesome fresh food again, and we soon had a variety on board, which kept quite well since we were almost 2,000 miles north of the equator. We found the winter nights cold in Japan and we usually fired up the cabin heater.

The harbor authorities moved us next to the ships of the Maritime Safety Agency, the Kaijohowancho, the Japanese equivalent of the U.S. Coast Guard, whose sailors and officers tied us alongside one of their patrol vessels and helped us with the crowds. We were glad to see people and to talk with them, but the men and women and the uniformed students never stopped coming. Night and day we heard them loudly reading our name and home port, *Wheez-pear*, Sahn Frahn-sees-ko. Fortunately for us the Maritime Safety Agency acted as a buffer and a question-answering service about the strange black sailboat. One man who was particularly helpful was a slight-figured chap named Kenrow Iwamoto, a junior officer.

Wherever we went in Japan we tied up to these friendly ships which flew a dark-blue flag with a single eight-pointed gray star on a gold shield. The crews helped us with repairs and shopping and we became good friends with many of the men, who loved to practice their rudimentary English. Most of the Japanese sailors seemed extremely cautious and at the slightest sign of wind or rain came rushing over with the latest weather maps, urged us to double our lines, and pleaded with us not to go sailing—even when the wind was fair and moderate. Their idea of a good day to go to the next port was a flat calm. How they thought we had ever gotten across the Pacific by sailing on windless days I will never know.

As a visiting captain I was invited to many *sake* parties, which were held at the drop of a noodle. The duty hours of the Maritime Safety Agency men often dragged and a few cups of *sake* helped brighten the gray hours. Then a few more cups and soon a full-blown celebration was under way.

Sometimes at 0200 the main hatch of *Whisper* would suddenly bang open and a seaman would shout: "Very important, Captain, this ship go my ship."

I would sleepily step on deck and climb to the next ship to find half the crew drunk and singing and pounding their fists on the table in the cabin. The captain was generally way ahead in the drinking and in the consumption of little cans of smoked oysters, some of which had dribbled across his uniform. I was hailed as a hero and heard a lot of bubbling Japanese amidst red eyes and empty *sake* jugs. A new bottle would be opened, heated, and I would be given a stiff glass together with handshakes and vows of United States–Japanese friendship forever.

Since I was four hours late for the party and couldn't understand a word, I was a little out of it and could only smile and feign unmitigated happiness until I could slip away and go back to bed.

The next afternoon the honorable captain, now alert and in a fresh uniform (you should have seen him last night), would nod curtly at me. I wondered whether he remembered the night before and all those pledges of international good will.

We found the docks filled with life and vitality. Most of the ships were Japanese, but we saw freighters from the Philippines and Australia, and trading ships from Taiwan and Indonesia. We watched green-helmeted crane operators hoist bright-red farm machinery into cargo holds. Stevedores lugged sacks of fertilizer and pushed carts piled high with crates of brooms and straw baskets overflowing with cabbages wrapped in plastic. Men with bulging shoulders wrestled steel rods into long piles on the dock while frantic train brakemen waved striped signal flags, which brought strings of dwarf railroad cars that were pushed by nervous, soot-belching locomotives. Funny little three-wheeled trucks backed into impossible corners to pick up giant bottles carefully cushioned with straw and tied with straw rope. Sometimes the dock workers paused to drink from miniature plastic teapots or to slurp down a fast bowl of noodles. Then back to work quickly, for other ships waited and hooted with impatience.

When we first got to Kagoshima we had a visitor, Sukefumi ("Fumi") Kabayama, a university student whose home was in a nearby village. Fumi was very keen on sailing and a member of the Nippon Ocean Racing Club, a national sailing organization, and he wrote a number of letters of introduction to various members along our route. Fumi was on vacation from his Kyoto school and came to *Whisper* each day to help us on the yacht. He was a good worker and, unlike most of the dreamer types, didn't have to be watched and constantly supervised. Fumi had a twenty-five-foot sloop which he kept on a lake near his school.

We became quite fond of Fumi, who not only worked hard but insisted on bringing us presents. He appeared at 0900 each morning after a one-hour bus ride from his village, smiling brightly and carrying a blue sailbag with his work clothes.

"I am like Santa Claus," he would say, sitting down and opening his blue bag. He would extract a bag of oranges, a cake, or a box of sweets.

Fumi had studied English for many years, but his conversation was terrible. However, we spoke with him every day and after a week we began to notice remarkable improvements in his English.

Kagoshima was a key transport center for the many small islands south, and ferryboats arrived and departed at every hour. No people are more sentimental than the Japanese, and fierce tears appeared at farewells. The departing passengers bought rolls of colored paper tape and held one end while their relatives on shore grasped the other. As the ship left—the loudspeakers blaring "Auld Lang Syne"—the people on each end of the paper tapes held tightly as the streamers unrolled and stretched farther and farther. Amidst more tears and frantic waving, the colored tapes finally broke as the ship got up speed. Then the music changed to a spirited march, and the people on shore dried their tears and went home.

I had been working on the engine of the yacht and had managed to get the mounts partially rebuilt. A local machinist made several critical parts, and with his help and some hoisting with the main halyard we got the engine up in place and working, though the repair was incomplete.

After a day of struggling with the ailing engine, and well infected with spots of grease and splotches of fiberglass resin, I was only too ready for the curing grace of the *o-furo*, the Japanese hot bath. Margaret and I took our towels and clean clothes and walked to a nondescript building with a tall iron smokestack. Men (男) entered on one side and women (女) on the other.

I paid 25 yen (7 cents) and stepped into a small room where I undressed and put my clothes in a straw basket. With my towel and soap in hand, I slid back the glass door to the main bathing room and heard gasps of astonishent as a dozen or so Japanese men turned to see a *gaijin*, a foreigner, enter their hot bath. However, I had learned to merely nod hello, and I picked up a plastic bowl, sat down on the tiled floor in front of hot- and cold-water taps, and began to wash myself.

The drill in a Japanese *o-furo* is to wash and rinse completely before you lower yourself into the steaming main bath, which is *very* hot. (You must show no emotion as you descend.) As you soak in the hot water for perhaps five or ten minutes you find that the heat relaxes all your tense muscles. Though a bit enervating, the Japanese bath is totally refreshing and sensible and something the Western world should adopt.

"I paid twenty-five yen plus an extra five yen because I washed my hair," Margaret told me later. "The women and children couldn't believe what they were seeing. The children, especially, had never seen blue eyes, and they put their little faces so close to mine that our noses almost touched.

"And such washing," said Margaret. "The women scrubbed every square inch of themselves so hard I thought their skin would come off. We all helped one another with our long hair and then had a good soak.

"I always wondered how the women survived the winter weather wearing only light kimonos," said Margaret. "You should see the layers and layers of woolens they put on underneath."

Stories and photographs about us and *Whisper* appeared in the newspapers and on television, and we continued to have many visitors, several of whom invited us to their homes for dinner. One night we took the streetcar to the house of Manabu ("Mab") Fukudome, another college student. We left our shoes at his door and put on slippers before we stepped onto the woven tatami mats with which all Japanese homes are floored.

Mab's widowed mother and sister welcomed us with bows and smiles, thick cushions to sit on, beer to sip, and little Japanese cakes to eat. The family was worried that we might have missed some vitamins on our trip, so we had an enormous salad of delicious mixed vegetables. Japanese women concern themselves particularly with the appearance of food, and the ingredients of the salad were chosen both for taste and arranged for prettiness.

We then moved to a room next to the kitchen and sat crosslegged around a small table with a thick blanket tacked around the edges and an electric heater underneath. The rooms were chilly, and we all put our feet and legs beneath the table and drew the blanket around for warmth. Mrs. Fukudome began to cook sukiyaki in an electric frying pan on the table. The two women had dishes of beef sliced thin as onion skin and plates of carefully washed cabbage, carrots, mushrooms, bamboo shoots, bean cake, and various ingredients. When the food was cooked we helped ourselves with chopsticks, dipping each mouthful into a beaten egg before we ate it.

We hadn't sat crosslegged since Samoa, and my legs began to tingle with stiffness. However, I feared to straighten them out because I didn't want to upset the little table and to electrocute myself on the rickety electric-plug arrangement which had wires radiating octopus-like to the frying pan, electric rice cooker, room lights, phonograph, heater, and television set, all of which were going.

American Westerns were big on Japanese television, and the sound dubbing was astonishing. I heard gun-toting desperados from West Texas suddenly spout a mouthful of rapid-fire Japanese. Mab asked me whether I had a gun and my cowboy suit on the yacht.

"I have my horse too," I said, and we all roared with laughter. I motioned toward the TV cowboys and thumbed through my diction-ary. "*Otogi-banashi mattaku desu* [fairy tale absolutely]," I said, which put our hosts into such hysterics that they almost upset the table.

The evening was good fun for everyone. We got along surprisingly well with Mab's modest English, our scraps of Japanese, and lots of gestures. The next day the family visited us on *Whisper*.

On our last night in Kagoshima our friend from the Maritime Safety Agency, Kenrow Iwamoto, whom we had seen every day for several weeks, gave us a sukiyaki party aboard *Whisper*. Kenrow and Fumi, our voluntary crewman, got our permission, rushed off to shop, and returned a few minutes later with a big box of vegetables and groceries. We fired up a one-burner Tilley cooking stove in the main cabin, and Kenrow and Fumi took turns putting in the thinly sliced beef and the precisely cut vegetables. The meal was wonderful—hot, tasty, fine-smelling, and novel to eat—a supper to linger over while we chatted and told jokes.

"This is the second sukiyaki feast in two days," I groaned. "I will get big like a sumo wrestler," I said, indicating a big belly. "*O-sumo.*"

Kenrow had brought us a going-away present of green tea. "I will be very lonely when you go," he said wistfully. "It is good to have you in Kagoshima."

I was quite touched by his statement. Earlier in the week I had been ill. Kenrow had looked in and had been genuinely distressed to see me flaked out in a forward berth. "Do you need a doctor?" he had asked. "I can call one right away."

He went over our itinerary and approved or disapproved our various stops. "Be careful of the headland of Sata Misaki," he counseled. "Hard currents there. Go far outside before you turn."

Kenrow was twenty-six and had been with the Maritime Safety Agency for eight years. He had two children, and his wife was a tea-ceremony instructor and a pupil of flower arranging. He was thrilled by our trip and liked to come aboard *Whisper* (with his two dictionaries) for a hot rum punch and a chance to practice his English.

Kenrow was a junior officer. His rank badge had two stars and two horizontal bars and he was qualified to command ships up to 1,500 tons. "But I want to get better certificates and to go to the Maritime Safety Agency University," he said.

I will long remember his slight figure in his trim blue uniform. I hope I can see him another time.

Again and again as we made friends with the ordinary people of Japan we were convinced that ghastly wars would be impossible if countries exchanged more visits on a person-to-person level.

We sailed from Kagoshima on a sunny April morning with Fumi on board for a few days. As we left, Sakurashima erupted mightily and spewed bits of rock that floated and covered the water with a froth of pumice that extended for miles and looked alarmingly like land. We touched briefly at Yamagawa and Odomari in the Kagoshima area and headed north along the east coast of Kyushu. We had the choice of continuing north via the Inland Sea or of going on the Pacific side of Shikoku and Honshu. We elected the Inland Sea because we had heard vaguely of its scenic attractions.

Sailing in Japan was a new experience. Close in, the hills and mountains were distinctive, but once a few miles offshore the land disappeared in a gray haze that seemed part fog, part industrial pollution, and part the nature of the country itself. We had to steer careful compass courses and to note our distance run. We were better off at night, for the Japanese had excellent aids to navigation, and the light signals were frequent and powerful.

Of course when we were close to shore during daylight we kept track of our position by reference to land features, using Japanese charts and the usual books of sailing directions. But the pilotage was a muddle in gray.

Our *Pilot* books identified places by solitary mountains. I saw mountains everywhere. The *Pilot* books described prominent points of land. I saw dozens of spurs of high land. The books spoke of small islands and conspicuous trees. We saw scores of islets and I often wondered whether the energetic Japanese woodsmen had spared that conspicuous tree so often mentioned but so seldom seen. Indeed with enough patience you could fit a given landscape—especially when it was half submerged in gray—into almost any description.

What we did find were small and large coasting vessels whose captains skirted in closely to shore with knowledge learned from lifetimes of working along the Japanese islands. Whenever we saw ships appear out of the murk we knew we were near the shore and on the shortest course between the two nearest towns. As we worked north we saw more and more Japanese fishermen in the big offshore tuna fishery in the warm Kuroshio current. The fishermen had ships of every sort, usually high-prowed wooden vessels twenty to forty-five feet long with thumping Diesel engines and decks cluttered with nets, poles, floats, gaffs, barrels, rows of night lights, laundry, fish boxes, and sometimes a small riding sail at the stern.

All fishing stopped when we came near. The crew would line the decks, pointing and smiling at us, and eagerly discuss the ship and flags and sails. "Yacht-o, yacht-o," the men would exclaim.

The Japanese seamen were always helpful. When I was unsure of a headland I only had to point and to shout "Hetsuka Ura?" for example, and I would get eager nods or aggressive head-shaking. When I gestured toward several villages and called out the names, the Japanese sailors would smile and nod. If I indicated a detour around a danger with my hand they assented eagerly. If I questioned the depth of the water in a nearby harbor I got immediate motions to indicate how many men high the water was deep. If I shook my fist at an approaching squall the fellows on the other ship knew exactly what I meant. In short we were all from the sea, and though from different cultures, we understood and helped each other, for one never knew who would need help tomorrow.

Fumi knew the Kitamura family in Uchinoura and had written them, so we sailed into Ariake Wan and slipped behind the quiet breakwater next to a few fishing boats. Uchinoura was an old-style Japanese village surrounded on the land side by rows of orange trees whose dark foliage climbed the surrounding hills. Time had darkened the wooden sides of the small houses, and the gray tile roofs curved gracefully above the narrow lanes. We put out a bower anchor from the ship and tied up stern first to the concrete quay, a method we were to become expert at before we left Japan.

The whole Kitamura family—father, mother, daughter, four sons, and grandmother—was along the shore when we docked and we were whisked away for a bath and meal. It was comfortable in the Kitamura house and we felt well settled and at ease at once.

In Japan the rooms are sized according to the number of soft straw mats, tatami (each measures about three by six feet), that make up the floor, a single mat being the smallest area in which one person can sit, work, rest, and sleep. You have six mat rooms, eight mat rooms, and so on. The entire house is conceived in multiples of this fundamental modular unit, and every dimension—the width of the sliding doors, the height of the room, the size of the veranda—is worked out in terms of the basic tatami.[39]

We sat in the parlor of the Kitamura house, a ten-tatami room walled in by sliding panels (*fusuma*) and translucent screens (*shoji*) that opened to the formal garden a few feet away. One wall had a small Shinto shrine with a purple cover raised above it. A photograph of grandfather, the late patriarch, hung above the shrine. An old Japanese scroll (of sailing ships, to honor us) decorated another wall. An *okoto*, a thirteen-string harp, lay at the foot of the scroll, and we admired a Japanese doll in a glass case. The ceiling was high and the upper parts of the walls were finished in hand-sawed cedar embellished with long wood carvings. The main furniture was a low table with surrounding cushions on which we knelt and later were told to sit.

We ate meals of many courses, each exquisitely prepared and served on dozens of small dishes that were carried from the kitchen by mother and sister. There was no clutter of wires and no sound of television. Only the peacefulness of the traditional room and garden and the quietness of the sea and countryside.

The next morning we ate in the same room, but the environment of breakfast was quite different. The shoji screens had been opened, and with the garden beyond, the feeling was that the room was part of the garden. The flowering cherry and plum seemed to flow right inside the house. The ordered rocks and sea shells and green shrubs all worked together with the cedar walls and roof tiles. The feeling was a satisfied one of neatness, order, and tranquility. Just over the garden wall we saw the varnished mast of *Whisper* with the Japanese courtesy flag leisurely flapping in the morning sun.

The people of Uchinoura all wore kimonos and bowed deeply, their knees and hands and foreheads touching the floor when they greeted you or departed. We were startled at such bowing, but the people—of all ages—kowtowed from habit without a thought. We were the first foreigners that the Kitamura family had ever entertained and the first that the grandmother had ever seen. We stayed for several days and visited the nearby family farm, where on ten acres of rich Kyushu land some 1,500 orange trees each bore about 200 kilos of sweet-tasting fruit every year. True to the Japanese custom of gift-giving, Margaret was given a beautiful kimono. Grandmother presented us with a set of "married couples tea cups" of special pottery. The next night we countered (after much hunting in the yacht) with a fancy Swiss handkerchief for the grandmother, a piece of costume jewelry for the sister, and a Samoan fan for the mother.

We of course invited the Kitamura family to *Whisper* for a meal,

but the tide was low and the women had trouble getting down to the ship with their long kimonos until we found a ladder.

"I feel as if I am deep in the heart of old Japan," I told Mr. Kitamura through Fumi, who translated. "The values in your life are much the same as mine. You respect beauty and tranquility as I do."

Mr. Kitamura nodded gravely and looked thoughtful behind his thick glasses. I thought I saw the beginning of a tear. All of a sudden there was a deafening explosion. I jumped up.

"O.K.! O.K.!" said Mr. Kitamura. "Only Japanese rocket firing at nearby rocket base of Tokyo University."

Obviously the twentieth century had come to Uchinoura. I wondered if the rocket man bowed before he pushed the button.

Fumi left us and returned to college. We sailed north into the Bungo Suido, the strait between Kyushu and Shikoku, and stopped at several places before we entered the Inland Sea. This great finger of the Pacific, encumbered with islands and peninsulas, is about thirty miles wide and 230 miles long in an east-northeasterly direction. We had had many warnings about strong currents, but with the appropriate tidal tables we had no difficulty. What we did find was heavy shipping traffic and that new terror of terrors, the hydrofoil, a ship that looks like a giant mosquito and skims on top of the water at forty knots with a siren and a red light to clear the way.

The buoyage and navigational light system was excellent. However, instead of clear skies and fresh winds combined with exciting scenery we often found a murky atmosphere and calms, and generally we didn't see the picturesque volcanic islands with their splendidly formed pines until we were close to land. At Saganoseki we left behind a colossal smokestack hundreds of feet high that spewed reddish dust from blast furnaces into a somber sky.

Margaret and I stood watch and watch as we sailed from buoy to buoy and island to island, steering careful compass courses. We heard the sound of big and little ships and felt the vibrations of their engines. Sometimes we saw ghostly silhouettes appear and disappear, but generally the sounds receded without us seeing anything. We came upon frail little fishing boats, floats that marked submerged fishing gear, plastic debris, and derelict fifty-five-gallon oil drums that were easy to confuse with buoys.

When the tidal stream ran against us we anchored. At Obatake Seto the current roared by at eleven knots in the 850-foot channel, and when we started out with a fair stream we rushed by a signal tower with the ship making fifteen knots over the ground. We covered five miles in twenty minutes, the fastest *Whisper* has ever traveled. I was at the helm and Margaret was in front of me. I asked her to move. There was a misunderstanding because of the noise of the water, and during a brief argument the chart flew over the side and somehow got into a counter-eddy of the violent current.

"Look!" shouted Margaret above the roar. We watched unbelieving as the chart was swept out of sight in a twinkling.

April 15. 1100. Much heavy industry along the Honshu coast off to port. Sounds of riveting from new oil storage tanks carry across the water. Jet fighters overhead (one formation of three close-flying, dark-colored, bat-wing planes). Many ships loading at a refinery. The whole area smells as if it's ready to blow up. Small wooden ships jammed with barrels, big and little oilers, and super tankers. A moment ago I looked at the super tanker Gloric *from Monrovia through the glasses and I suddenly realized that the pier I thought she was against was the forestructure of the* Gloric *herself!*

We anchored near several ferries at the shrine of Miyajima on the island of Itsukushima. We took the dinghy ashore to see this famous attraction, which was thronged by hundreds of Japanese, who are certainly the world's most energetic tourists, carrying their maps and cameras and lunch baskets. Some of the Japanese wore kimonos, some sported Western clothes, and a few young people had on jeans and leather jackets. However, we all stopped to exchange our shoes for the straw sandals of pilgrims before we stepped onto the wide camphorwood walks of the Shinto shrine which led to various places of worship, rows of stone lanterns, ancient buildings with religious relics, two remarkable pagodas, and to a near view of the *torii* gate itself.

The great red *torii* of Miyajima, perhaps the most impressive of the 100,000 *torii* in Japan, is built of six enormous camphorwood trunks and is so located on the edge of the sea that the tide alternately covers and uncovers its impressive base.

"The universal presence of the *torii* in Japan is, I think, comparable to the sound of church bells in the West," writes Japanese scholar Fosco Maraini. "The popular belief is that to pass under a *torii* is a first stage in purification."[40]

April 18. Hiroshima. On Tuesday we had dinner at the apartment-office of Dr. Keiichi Tanaka, a sailing enthusiast and a busy throat specialist. The dinner was pleasant and the talk was all about yachts

*and cruising. Dr. Tanaka, however, made it sound as if he was about
to go off on a big sailing trip which I think is doubtful because
of his enormous one-man practice and his level of living.*

*Dr. Tanaka hired Watanabe, one of Japan's leading naval
architects, to design a new 33-foot sloop for him. Tanaka employed
Okazaki, a small shipyard on Shodoshima, to build the yacht. But
in order to afford all this, something not common in Japan, Tanaka
works very hard and has a practice so big that he cannot find
time to enjoy his ship and certainly not to go away on a long or
even a short cruise.*

*His life is a paradox, as are the lives of many Americans, sort
of quivering ulcers, who in order to afford something they want
very much, must work so long and hard that they have neither the
time nor the energy left to enjoy their hard-won gains. Perhaps
their salvation would be to reduce the height of their goals a
trifle. . . . Maybe a 30-foot yacht instead of 33 feet. And must it be
double-planked with expensive teak on the outside? Better a modest
trip to paradise than no trip at all.*

In Hiroshima we tied up to a Maritime Safety Agency ship. One
morning Margaret was on the dock washing clothes in a bucket with a
hose and a box of detergent when a sailor happened by. He watched

Margaret closely for a moment and hurried away to return a little later with a friend. The two sailors stood next to Margaret and vigorously discussed her box of detergent. Finally the second man spoke.

"Wrong box," he said. "Only for vegetables. Please wait."

The two men disappeared and soon came back with a box of detergent with different Japanese writing on it which they gave to Margaret. "Please use now," said the second sailor. "Other for vegetables only. No power for clothes."

We discovered later that the Japanese have at least three detergents. One for vegetables, one for dishes, and one for clothes, all used in cold water.

We continued east through the Inland Sea and found more heavy shipping traffic. We saw old rust-streaked sailing hulls that had been repowered with lumbering engines, high-sided trading vessels, sleek low-slung steel oilers, big fishing boats on their way to the Pacific, cargo vessels from Europe, and small undecked dories without paint that were patiently sculled by a fisherman's wife while he fiddled with his lines and hooks.

Often the motor vessels would come near to have a look at us. A ship stacked with lumber and bamboo would slip alongside, the door of the pilot house would slide open, the helmsman would step on deck, and we would exchange waves and smiles. But we had to be careful when ships approached because sometimes they ran on automatic pilot with no helmsman visible. Three times during our stay in Japan, vessels came close to us on collision courses and I saw no one in the pilot house.

The little islands were exquisite—steep and rocky with delicately branched pines and always with a tiny Shinto shrine, a few statues to Buddha, and perhaps a small *torii* arch. We marveled at the patience and resourcefulness of the hard-working Japanese farmers who grew such splendid crops in the rocky soil. If the weather or the season was too cold for strawberries, for example, a little bamboo frame and plastic cover was fitted over each plant, which was tended with what seemed almost like adoration.

The islands were timeless and blemished only by the national curse of Japan: plastic. On every beach and road, in every river and harbor, in every estuary and pond—everywhere—we saw plastic junk. Plastic toys, plastic buckets, plastic bags, plastic everything littered the shores and roads and lanes in wearying windrows which will never disappear.

Whisper's hull was foul with marine growth, for we had not taken the ship out of the water since California. Dr. Tanaka had suggested that we go to the shipyard where his new yacht was under construction. The yard was on the island of Shodoshima, in the eastern part of the Inland Sea, and on a rainy April afternoon we sailed in silently to the little settlement of Kotozuka on the north coast. Mist-shrouded green hills rose up in back of a sandy beach on which were scattered the ramshackle buildings of the boatyard and the few houses of the hamlet.

The shipyard was a small place that specialized in yachts and sailing dinghies and was run by a smiling Mr. Okazaki and his four sons. The yard employed forty men, mostly locals who had been trained as apprentices and who worked cheaply and well. We hauled *Whisper* out on a rickety marine railway that seemed certain to collapse. Indeed the power windlass used to pull the ship from the water looked as if it had been designed and built by Archimedes. The Japanese knew their job, however, and we were soon high on the beach. While the carpenters did a few jobs inside I repaired the rudder, which we had damaged on the coral at Guam, and I replaced all the shut-off valves below the waterline.

"Good morning" in Japanese is *ohayo gozaimasu*, but in these remote Shikoku islands the dialect eliminated the first word and used only the final sibilant of the second. "Good morning" sounded like a plain "ssssss." We presumed the morning smile and hiss was a pleasantry, so we smiled and hissed back.

The Japanese carpenters used tools I had never seen before. Most of their work was by hand and their saws cut when you pulled (instead of when you pushed as in America or England). Each man had five or six small pull saws made of thin, high quality steel that cut quickly and precisely. Every carpenter had a dozen planes and chisels and seemed a fanatic at sharpening them, for we often saw a man bent over a set of abrasive stones flushed with water while a steel blade was rapidly scraped back and forth.

To make a long line for a saw cut or other measurement a worker employed a kind of ink pot with a roller and a string, something like a miniature spinning wheel. In use the carpenter stretched the string between two points raised slightly above a plank. He plucked the ink-stained string and presto! A sharp black line—perfectly straight—appeared on the plank between the points.

Women do hard physical work in Japan. Often you would see them slaving on road construction gangs or cutting trees in a forest. In the shipyard two little women with their hair wrapped in white towels

worked as janitors. For some reason they were terrified of me, and whenever I appeared they would seize a basket of shavings and rush down to the beach to burn them.

Every day we looked at Dr. Tanaka's new wooden ship. Plastic and steel and aluminum may be good for yachts but for romance and feeling nothing equals wood. I don't know whether it is the fragrance of the flying wood chips or the delight of watching the skilled joiners and shipwrights expertly fit the planks together. Maybe we all know wood better (everyone has whittled) and feel an acquaintance with teak and oak and fir and spruce.

The island newspaper reporter did a story on us, and every day the newspaper was delivered to the ship with great seriousness, as if the paper were a document of huge importance. No one seemed to realize that we couldn't read a word.

One morning the number-one Okazaki son, Yoshihira, rushed down from the office. "Shipping Bureau telephone. You must go mainland Shikoku quick. Big trouble if no go."

I sighed and began to change my clothes. We had been plagued by the Shipping Bureau all through Kyushu. The problem was that certain large specified ports in Japan are open to foreign shipping. All other ports are closed and can be entered only with special permission, which is tedious to get.

By their nature yachts prefer the smaller and more isolated ports rather than Tokyo, Nagoya, Sasebo, and so forth. Japanese vessels are not subject to this rule, of course, and practically no Japanese has ever heard of the Shipping Bureau. The first problem was to find the agency (whose existence was usually denied). The second was to explain what I wished to do, which usually took several hours of earnest talking (through a translator) to unbelieving civil servants. In the end I found the best answer was to say that I had put in at so and so for emergency repairs, a white lie perhaps but a reasonable defense against regulations drafted in 1912, long before tourism.

We liked the Okazaki shipyard whose men did excellent work and even cast and machined their own metal fittings. The language was a problem, however, and sometimes Yoshihira and I had to work hard with our dictionaries, which fortunately for scholars have lots of terms that deal with love and poetry but have few words for practical sailors. We hoped to end the floods of water into the accommodation of the yacht with a box to contain the main sliding hatch, which had leaked so badly. In addition an expert carpenter fitted splash boards from the new hatch box to the sides of the cabin to direct water that fell on the coachroof to the decks instead of at the hatch and cockpit.

With two coats of anti-fouling paint on *Whisper* and number-two Okazaki son on the windlass, the ship was lowered into the water. We paid our bill, exchanged bows with the whole staff, and headed east toward Kobe. At Nishinomiya we met Professor Kensaku Nomoto, an expert single-handed sailor who kindly marked our charts for the rest of Japan.

We had been in the Far East for two and a half months and the summer typhoon season was approaching. It was time to get north. At the end of May we sailed toward the Tomogasima Suido, the channel between the Inland Sea and the Pacific.

We were with a vast flotilla of big ships going in and out from Kobe and Osaka. Swarms of fishing boats crisscrossed around us, independently pursuing their business of straining the sea with nets or trying to outsmart the fish with baited hooks.

May 28. 1300. 60 ships in sight. Mostly coasters and fishing vessels. One giant passenger ship, a tug pulling six barges, a large ferry, small cargo ships, and various tankers. I can feel the vibrations of fishing boat engines as I write. Incredible amounts of smoke and fumes stream skyward from the Wakayama steel mill and refinery complex to the east.

A little later Margaret called me on deck. "Look ahead," she said. "I see what looks like a breakwater with city buildings at the far end. I've plotted bearings of it but the chart shows open water."

We watched with interest. Half an hour later the breakwater and buildings turned into a vast white super tanker being maneuvered by tugs.

By nightfall we were in the Pacific and surrounded by red and green and white ship lights on all sides. We marveled that there were no collisions, but each helmsman watched carefully and sorted out the lights as they approached. Many of the Japanese fishing boats used bright floodlights to attract their prey. A row of the little ships blazed like a downtown street at carnival time. As we passed the individual boats we saw that each captain carried a green light over a white light to indicate that his trawl was down. The wind had been fitful, so we started our little Diesel to help us through the traffic. However, the vibration of the engine was severe and we shut it off. The engine mounts needed to be rebuilt entirely.

By dawn we were around the southernmost point of Honshu. The

shipping traffic from the Inland Sea had fanned out and we were almost alone. We headed northeast along the east coast of the great Kii
peninsula and by early afternoon glided into the steep and wooded
shores of Kata Wan, where we followed a fish boat flying an enormous
flag into a protected anchorage. We tied up stern to at the village of
Miki.

The people of this remote village had never seen anything like us or
our ship, and they were as delighted as children with a new toy. We
tied the ship near the familiar iron chimney of the *o-furo*, but Miki
was small and had the hot bath only three days a week. It wasn't
long before we were invited to someone's home, where we scrubbed
and soaked and then shared a meal of raw fish, octopus, tomatoes, and
beer.

Soon after we sailed in, four beamy net-tending boats appeared.
Each of the unpainted tenders was about forty feet long, weighed
many tons, and was entirely handled by two men with sculling oars. All
the crewmen wore large round straw hats with white towels wrapped
around the brims. *Whisper* was in the docking space of the net tenders,
but with a little pushing and shoving there was room enough for all.

The men put up awnings over the four boats and kindled a wood
fire on the deck of one. They soon had tea and rice and raw fish before
them. It was a wonderful scene. The chattering men in their straw hats.
The cooking under the awning. Hawks circling overhead watching for
bits of food. Ribald comments from one ship to another. The putt-putt
of a passing boat. The sounds of children raking leaves and scraps of
paper from the quay. The old man on shore recollecting his fishing
days. . . .

I adjusted several tires for bumpers between the ships by slipping a
clove hitch on one of the lines holding a tire. One man didn't know that
knot. He distrusted it and insisted on adding two half hitches to each
of my clove hitches. This amused his fellow fishermen as much as
Margaret and I, and we all smiled. Then someone gave us fish for our
dinner and another man passed a hose with fresh water to us.

Of the seventeen ports we visited in Japan we liked the village of
Miki and its neighbor Kuki more than any others. Everything was new
and novel and exciting.

We watched the busy fish market and learned that when a fish boat
came in with a big flag flying it meant a huge catch. We looked over
the shoulders of Japanese shipwrights while they hammered away on
new wooden fishing ships. We took long walks in the lovely country-

side. One morning the returning crew of a night fishing boat hailed us on board and we shared their breakfast of beer, raw squid, and *sake*, a powerful diet at 0700.

Even mailing letters was fun. Japanese stamps are beautiful and I hoped to put a variety of stamps of small denominations on each letter to my friends in America. But how to explain this? In Miki I opened the stamp tray of the postmistress and helped myself to stamps (while the whole staff watched with big eyes). When I had my letters checkered with a variety of bright colors I totaled up and pushed my yen across the counter. Suddenly one of the clerks understood that someone in America collected stamps. Smiles all around and chuckles of delight.

The day before we left, a Maritime Safety Agency Patrol launch came to check the strange foreign ship. Communication was difficult, but I dutifully filled out the papers which had questions in English and Japanese. The captain of the launch asked me to fill out a second set and then a third. I felt a bit harassed and I suppose my impatience showed.

Satisfied at last, the captain took the papers, bowed, and rushed to his launch. The crewmen started the engines, threw off the lines, and the ship started away. Suddenly it came back and the lines were tied up again. I watched as the captain jumped ashore and headed in my direction.

"Oh no," I thought. "Not more forms!" But the captain merely handed me a slip of paper on which he had laboriously printed in unfamiliar block letters: BON VOYAGE.

The trip to central Honshu took three days. Tokyo Bay was unsuitable for yachts, so we sailed to Aburatsubo in Sagami Wan, the next bay west. Aburatsubo was one of the main yachting centers in Japan and over 100 sailboats lay on moorings. Most were twenty-five feet in length because of the 40 percent tax on larger yachts. We tied alongside our friends Jens and Keiko Jensen, who lived on their thirty-two-foot gaff ketch *Tortuga*.

To get *Whisper* ready for the North Pacific I had three big jobs and many small ones. I took six of my eight sails to a Yokohama sailmaker to have a third row of stitching zigzagged along every seam. I had been using a jury-rigged port backstay since the anchoring misadventure in the Gilbert Islands, so I ordered a new backstay plus two new upper shrouds and one lower shroud, all of which had broken strands of wire. Jens Jensen and I removed *Whisper*'s engine with the main halyard and got a local shipwright to strengthen the mounts by adding immense specially welded angle irons which were through-bolted to the hull.

While I was busy with the ship, Margaret and Keiko Jensen bought many cases of stores and patiently tracked down the charts and *Pilot* books for the North Pacific.

These jobs often took us to Tokyo and Yokohama where we learned that patience and time are the requisites for Japanese shopping. Taxi-cabs are cheap in Japan, but the problem is the address, since houses and businesses are numbered according to when they were built. To go to a company you have a Japanese friend telephone ahead for instructions. Your friend then writes out the directions in Japanese, which you hand to the cab driver.

"O.K., O.K.," the cab driver would smile, his gold teeth glinting. He would pin the directions to the windshield with rubber suction cups, which left him only a narrow slit for forward vision. The driver would then pull on his white gloves, gun the engine, and we would lurch away ready for combat with traffic.

Japanese drivers pass on hills, around curves, and think nothing of swerving around big trucks and buses. Once a Japanese driver pulls out he never retreats. "Full speed now!" is his cry as he floors the accelerator. The only saving grace is that everyone drives alike and expects cars from all directions. When I would think a head-on collision was imminent, everyone would honk and squeeze aside just enough so that all would get through. "O.K., O.K. Plenty room," my driver would say, turning from his narrow slit to face me while he practiced his ten words of English.

A critical part of the directions was the telephone number of your target so that when your driver got lost he could telephone for additional help. ("Follow the double streetcar tracks until you come to the blue noodle factory. . . .")

The other terror of shopping is that the Japanese hate to say no ("Yes, I would not like another cup of coffee"). Often after you had arrived at a business house which had assured you by telephone that it had the tubing or wire or chart or whatever, you would be told (after a cup of tea and much time-wasting talk) that last year the Primus franchise was sold to a company on the other side of Tokyo. Or "Yes, we will have the parts in a few days as soon as the next shipment arrives from Sweden."

But the Japanese were kind and meant well. Sometimes a clerk would accompany me for hours while we went from store to store. When we finally got the part, the clerks would laugh with pleasure, a delight so genuine that you had to smile with them.

The day before we left for Hokkaido another cruising yacht came to Aburatsubo and we met Paul Hurst and his Filipino crewman Abraham Magpator. Paul had sailed from the Philippines in his sleek white-hulled Alden ketch *Staghound*.

When we headed north to Hokkaido we sailed offshore far enough to get outside of coastal shipping. The first night, however, we had plenty of company.

June 29. 2150. Seventy-seven fishing boats in sight, each with five powerful floodlights directed at the water. When we pass one of the ships we can feel the Diesel chugging away, hear the screeching

Japanese radio, and see the busy hands of the fishermen as they pluck the silvery fish from the lines as they are hauled in.

The passage north was slow. The 671 miles to Kushiro took eight days, generally with gray weather and fitful winds. At the start we were helped by the north-flowing Kuroshio current, whose temperature we measured every day and found to be 73 or 74 degrees. But by the time we had reached 41° N. we had left the warm current behind and were in the cold Oyashio current. The water temperature fell to 55 degrees, and under foggy skies and unused to the cold, I found myself wearing long underwear, two pairs of woolen socks, a heavy shirt and trousers, sweater, neck scarf, oilskins, sea boots, a winter coat, and two pairs of gloves. In July!

Along the southeast coast of Hokkaido we saw that the fishing boats were big and strong. The bulwarks, ground tackle, engines, and gear in general indicated severe conditions, and the way the men worked showed they were tough and rugged in these northern waters. None of the tissue-paper boats and frail crews of the Inland Sea in these waters.

We found Kushiro a raw, unfinished sort of place, a center for fishing, shipping, and paper- and plywood-making. Gray and colorless, the foggy bit of Hokkaido that we saw must be a frigid terror in winter. In every office and home was a giant stove. The windows were double, and when the stove fuel was wood I saw cord after cord of it piled high against the side of a house. The sidewalks of Kushiro always seemed to be under construction on both sides of the street at once, and with the taxicabs and trucks roaring along the narrow streets, walking was an exercise in survival. But the people were cheerful and friendly and the women seemed better dressed than anywhere else in Japan.

The Japanese fishermen are masters of the sea. In American Samoa we had watched their ships come in from the Pacific almost sinking under the weight of gleaming tuna, shiny blue wahoo, and whopping big-eye and yellowfin. In the Japanese ports we had looked at ships laden with bottom fish of every kind and with almost every edible crustacean known to man. The Japanese netted billions of tiny fish that were chopped into meal or made into paste.

A Japanese fishing vessel bound for the South Pacific had tied alongside us in Guam because of engine trouble. What was the first thing the men did? They all started fishing. "To see what fish are in this distant ocean." In a little village in Kyushu I had watched a shrimp specialist spend two hours baiting 100 tiny hand-made traps and then lower them to the bottom of the harbor in a *selected* place in a *selected* pattern at a *selected* time. Now in Kushiro a fisherman gave me four *ka-re*, delicious flatfish caught in gill nets set at forty meters. "Higher depth no good," said the fisherman. "Lower no good. Must be forty meters exact."

Fishing is a national passion in Japan. The people excel because they practice. They specialize. A father teaches his son and the skills go down the line of generations. "When I seek the tuna I become a tuna and I think like a tuna," an old man told me. The Japanese are not too hidebound to change, however, and they are often the first to adopt new machinery or an advanced technique.

A popular game in Hokkaido is indoor fishing. You buy a ticket and enter a room mostly taken up with a tank about thirty feet long, twelve feet wide, and four feet deep. The tank is filled with water dyed an opaque blue to keep the fishermen from too much success. You fish for goldfish (which you can keep) with a sliver of bamboo for a rod, a thread for a line, and a hook you can hardly see.

The tough fishermen of Hokkaido loved this game and on their days off would spend hours hunched over the opaque water starting at a red-and-white bobber the size of a pea while their buddies shouted encouragement and made jokes. Yet when the bobber went down, the fish came out. I like to think I am clever, but when I tried it I caught nothing.

On the day of our departure we secured our clearance for the Aleutian Islands and walked to the regional weather building. No one spoke any English and we were sent from office to office. Finally we got to a large room with dozens of small desks around the walls. At each desk sat a clerk with weather maps and one or two telephones. As the reports came in the charts were marked and sent to the chief fore-caster, who sat surrounded by telephones at a huge desk in the center of the room. The desk was cluttered with weather charts, reports, clip boards jammed with statistics, and an ashtray full of cigarette butts.

The forecaster was a small, nervous, tired-looking fellow with deep lines in his face. Barometric pressure seemed to ooze from his skin. He had obviously worked up through the ranks and was responsible for storm warnings for thousands, perhaps millions, of people. He was treated with vast respect and obeisance by his underlings, who ap-proached him in a semi-bow as one might a king.

I explained that I was about to sail to the Aleutian Islands in a ship eleven meters long and—

He held up his hand. "You have come at the right time," he answered in excellent English. "My new forecast is ready now." He explained how weather information came to his office from ships all across the North Pacific.

Suddenly the telephone rang. The forecaster listened. Another phone rang. The inscrutable face of our friend collapsed into a horror of uncertainty. He slumped forward with his face in his hands.

"No use," he said. "All changed now. But for you going northeast, O.K. Winds ten knots from the west."

As we bowed, more telephones rang. We fled before we heard something bad. We hurried to the ship, cast off the lines, and left Japan.

16 / ~~~~~~~~~~ ~~~~~~~~~~~ ~~~~~~

Are the Aleutians Cold?

WITH A SPRIG OF PINK CHERRY BLOSSOM LASHED TO THE headstay and a friendly hoot from an escorting Japanese customs launch, we left Kushiro and headed east across the North Pacific. The date was July 11. We wondered what was ahead.

The start was our poorest ever. We sailed out into four days of calms and fog off the southeast coast of Hokkaido. On the first day we did four miles—our all-time low. The following three days we had runs of fifty-six, twenty-five, and forty-seven miles, not much better. We heard the dim hum of fishing boats from time to time, but in the cottony mist around us their sound seemed to carry for miles and we didn't worry until the thump of their engines was quite loud.

Our last contact with Japan was one morning when six mackerel ships discovered us waiting for wind on the fog-shrouded sea and motored near us. I motioned that we would like a few fish. One ship maneuvered alongside on the calm water and a crewman passed us a tub with seven salted mackerel. We threw packs of American cigarettes across and soon the whole crew—in long underwear shirts and with towels tied around their foreheads—had lighted up and was smiling. We had a good look at one another, exchanged bows, and the ships moved off to continue fishing.

It was a small incident but one of the things that makes travel so worthwhile.

When we were becalmed it was important to pull in the rotator and its fifty-foot line which drove our distance-recording Walker's Log. Otherwise the rotator would sink and pull the line down, which would foul the rudder or the propeller. I had issued stern orders to *always* pull in the log line when becalmed or hove to. But when we lost our wind gradually, it was easy to forget. On my watch the log line got wrapped around the propeller. I took down the jib to stop the ship, stripped off my clothes, put on a face mask, jumped into the sea, and freed the line. I was only in the water half a minute or so, but the Oyashio was cold and I was soon gasping. Afterward I dried off and put on my warm clothes but I shivered for a long time and was a little sick.

A dark-brown seal appeared on the still water and followed the ship. He went faster than we sailed and was soon swimming in circles around *Whisper*, mocking our progress. Margaret translated a French magazine article and I spent an afternoon with a novel by Joyce Carey.

We saw a number of headfish, sometimes called ocean sunfish, gigantic relatives of puffers or porcupine fish, that swam just below the surface with a ragged black dorsal fin that knifed through the water like the fin of a shark. Only the fin flopped lazily from side to side. The headfish were strange creatures, perhaps from the age of dinosaurs, and seemed only the remnant head of a larger fish. Yet the heads—up to ten feet long—had fins and eyes and mouths and gills and swam around us curiously. We read in our fish book that their leathery skin was two inches thick and they weighed up to 2,000 pounds. The book added that headfish were not good to eat, but the fish were safe from me in any case, for the last thing I wanted aboard was a one-ton sea monster! The headfish showed no fear of us. We watched the great gray creatures with awe and wondered what else we would see if the ocean remained calm.

During the third night we got a light northeast wind, which increased with rain during the morning of July 14. By noon we had enough breeze to change to the number two working jib and to tie one reef in the main. The wind backed to the north, and at last we began to make good our course toward the northeast. We had been worried about being too close to the Japanese coast in case of an onshore gale, but with a run of 131 miles on July 15 we had a good offing. Laysun albatrosses, parasitic jaegers, and both Leach's petrels and fork-tailed petrels flew around the ship.

We had thought of visiting the Russian islands. However, we had neglected to ask permission at the Russian embassy in Tokyo. In addition, the Japanese Maritime Safety Agency officers in Kushiro strongly

advised us not to go to the Kuriles or to the Kamchatka peninsula. In spite of the warnings and lack of visas we were tempted when we saw several of the Kuriles dimly off to port. Our main reason for not stopping was the lack of time. The summer sailing season in the North Pacific was short and we had far to go.

On July 16 we passed a small Russian trawler and on the radio we heard Russian stations from Petropavlovsk and the Siberian mainland. The music was heavy and syncopated (often with soapy tenors) and the announcers were always women.

When we had planned our Pacific voyage we had three basic weather problems. The first was to avoid the South Pacific hurricane season. The second was to get away from Japan before the typhoons started in the late summer. The third was to miss extensive gales in the North Pacific.

We had gotten past the first two problems and now we faced the third—to cross the North Pacific at the most favorable time.

The monthly *Pilot* charts indicated the average gale frequency for each five degree square of latitude and longitude, and we had spent a long time studying the little blue squares and their inset numbers. In

January—according to the charts—we would find gales up to 14 percent of the time. In February one square read 17 percent. April looked better, with only one reading of 10. June was mostly 1 and 2 with a maximum of 3. In the westernmost Aleutians the gale frequency rose to 5 percent in July and 7 percent in August, while most of the northern Pacific had 0, 1, 2, or 3. In September three squares had 8, and the percentages of gales increased sharply during the rest of the year.

Clearly we would have the most storm-free passage in midsummer. An easy July–August passage was tempered, however, by heavy summer fog, which ran from 30 to 40 percent south and west of the Aleutians to 10 percent in the Gulf of Alaska. In the vicinity of the Aleutians the sea temperature was about 45 degrees, and whenever a warm wind blew from the south, fog formed at once. Ice was not a problem.

We had already run into plenty of fog. It blocked the horizon and reduced visibility to a few hundred feet. Yet though it was thick it was not high, and often we could see blue sky if we looked overhead. Sometimes the fog rose as a body and we could see the horizon but no sky.

For celestial observations we needed both the sun (or another heavenly body) and the horizon at the same moment. The fog was a constant problem, however, except during the nights, which were sometimes clear. But when the sun rose it heated the air, which formed convection fog on the cold water. All in all we found that star sights at dawn were often our best chance for celestial observations.

We had unlimited sea room now and were north of the steamer lanes. The ocean was surprisingly calm, the barometer remained high (as much as 1022 millibars), and we made good daily runs. The winds were generally light, with a southerly component, and we carried a lot of sail area. We wore plenty of warm clothes and at night we often used the cabin heating stove. We were pleased with our progress although I wondered about a fog-bound landfall. We still had our wits about us, though, and lots of confidence.

Even if we arrived in thick fog there would be plenty of signs of land. We knew that the bird population was enormous in the Aleutians and that many birds flew out to sea to fish in the morning and returned to their nests in the afternoon. We would see kelp and seaweed on the ocean and could listen for the booming of waves on the rocks and the swish of the sea on the beaches. Large populations of seals and sea lions and sea otters lived in the Aleutians, and we would see them and hear their snorting and barking. The *Pilot* books spoke of strong tidal streams between the Pacific and Bering Sea, but we had read of various fog-bound ships that had been safely swept from one ocean to another by the currents, which sometimes ran swiftest in the deepest channels between the islands. We had no reason to doubt our excellent compass and we could sense a shoaling bottom by the difference in the feel of the swells. We had a good depth sounder to tell us the fine measurements when close to land, and we would certainly sail slowly if we approached in fog. The Aleutian land masses would tend to upset the sea winds and at some stage we ought to have a fog-clearing wind. And if we watched for the sun and horizon carefully there would be a few chances to fix our position.

In any case we had asked for adventure. Our undertaking was bold and exciting and I was anxious to press on.

As far as we knew we were the fifth yacht to sail from Japan to the American continent via the Aleutian islands. Five British naval officers pioneered the route in 1933 in *Tai-Mo-Shan*, a fifty-four-foot ketch that displaced twenty-four tons. The second was *Tzu Hang*, a forty-six-foot ketch (twenty-two Thames tons) owned by Miles and Beryl Smeeton, who with two others for crew sailed via the Aleutians in 1965. *Stormvogel* (seventy-three feet and forty-two tons) with six aboard made the trip in 1966. The American yacht *Awahnee* (fifty-three feet and twenty-four tons), owned by Bob and Nancy Griffith, together with three crewmen, crossed in 1967. *Whisper* was number five. She measured thirty-five feet and weighed six tons. But though she was the smallest, we like to think that she was the proudest.

On July 21 I got a good round of observations. "We're three hundred and eighty miles from Attu, the westernmost of the Aleutians," I said. "But Petropavlovsk on the Kamchatka peninsula is only three hundred and twenty miles away."

"I knew it! I knew it! *Whisper* wants to go to the Russian ports," cried Margaret, who secretly wanted to go too. "All these southerly winds and north-setting currents are trying to tell us something."

The next day remarkable clouds formed overhead. From the northeast to the southwest great horizontal bars of dark gray reached across the sky in colossal wavelike rollers as far as we could see. It was almost as if a gray-haired sea were upside down. The water temperature was 49 degrees now, and the weather had turned crisp. We were almost to 50° N. latitude and in the eastern sky the summer night began to turn pink and pale blue at 0200.

On July 23 the light southerly winds increased to gale force. We changed to a small jib and triple-reefed the mainsail. The sails were still too large, and solid water exploded on board, so we handed the main altogether. The seas got up, of course, but they had started over a calm ocean and were even and regular. The wind vane steered the ship perfectly and we stayed right on course with the jib pulling us at hull speed.

I stood in the companionway for hours with the hood of my winter coat around my head while I watched the gray seas push up from astern and rush forward, hissing as they passed the ship. *Whisper* rolled from side to side as she hurried along, while the vane, the ever-steady steering device, kept our heading true. I say "device" but surely the steering vane has a heart and soul, for how else could she hold the ship so firmly in her cord-bound grasp, safely steering the yacht in gale and calm, by moonlight and sunlight, day after day, mile after mile?

Three black-footed albatrosses flew round and round the ship, sometimes dropping behind the swell of a wave. Yet they never wet a wing. "Surely they are God's answer to perpetual motion," I said, as the thin seven-foot wings dipped and wheeled with scarcely a flap. We had last seen the dark profile of the squat brown bodies and the dusky, saberlike wings off the California coast. The birds seemed like old acquaintances.

By 0300 the next day the gale was over, more sails began to go up, and we slatted and rolled on a windless North Pacific. One might expect a gradually diminishing wind after a gale, but it seems that when a big wind is over, the curtain bangs down and there is little or nothing until the next scene opens some hours later.

July 24. 0700. Wind light. Hoisted genoa. Log line around rudder again. Spent two hours getting it free. Lashed small spinnaker pole and boathook together. No luck. Cursed log line finally freed by dropping a dinghy anchor over the side to pull the line down from the rudder. Stone-age sailing.

Yesterday the fog cleared a bit. I was asleep when Margaret saw a ray of sun. "Sun! Sun!" she shouted. I rushed on deck with a sextant and took a series of observations. After dinner I shot star sights of Deneb, Altair, Arcturus, and Polaris which gave us a good fix. Fierce headache from the eyestrain connected with the star sights and their arithmetic.

On the fifteenth day from Japan I climbed on deck at 0415, swathed in layers of clothes. The midnight fog had dispersed and the cold air was as clear as the lens of a telescope. The eastern sky glowed reddish in the dawn and I saw two islands to the northeast, more than forty miles away. We identified the long island with snowy mountains as

Attu, the westernmost of the Aleutians. It lay off to port. Agattu, dead ahead and smaller, was overlaid with a mushroom of thick fog.

If you were to put the point of a giant compass on the North Pole and swing an arc between the southernmost tip of the Alaskan mainland and the middle of the Kamchatka peninsula near the end of Russian Siberia, your curving line would follow the sweep of the Aleutian Islands. These fifty islands—depending on how many fragments you count—extend through 24½ degrees of longitude or 885 miles at 53 degrees N. latitude.

The Aleutians were discovered in 1741 by Vitus Bering, and the severe and cruel occupation by Russian freebooters that followed soon erased most of the native Aleuts together with practically all the fur seals and sea otters. The United States acquired the islands as part of the Alaska purchase in 1867. Dutch Harbor on Amaknak Island became an important transshipping center after the discovery of gold in 1898

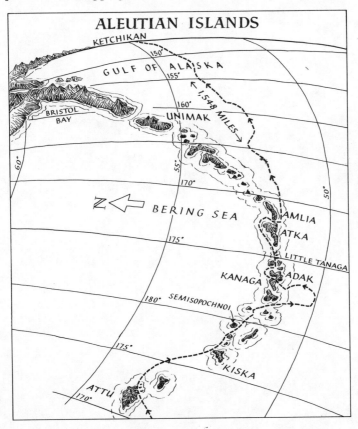

turned Nome into a boom town. In June 1942 the Japanese bombed Dutch Harbor and occupied Attu and Kiska as a diversionary action for events farther south in the Pacific. The United States launched a counterattack from bases that were established on Adak and Amchitka. In 1943, after bitter fighting, U.S. forces took Attu, and the Japanese withdrew from Kiska with the message, "It's all yours, Yank."[41]

Most of the American GIs who spent time in the Aleutians during World War II cursed the weather and isolation. A number of myths have grown from the experiences of the soldiers, and most people shudder at the mere mention of the name. The Aleutians are a land of ice and snow (false). The scenery is depressing and monotonous (false). The islands are a military outpost where poor Army recruits

resolutely march back and forth (false). Only Eskimos live there (false).

Margaret and I looked across twenty miles of sparkling Pacific to the bold skyline of Attu, topped by the flashing teeth of snowy mountains. The supporting land mass was a stony arctic blue, a heavy and powerful indigo, rather than the easy cobalt of the tropics. Even in the sun the ocean air had a chill to it and our gloves and wool caps felt good.

Birds flew everywhere now, especially large glaucous gulls with frosty white wingtips and pink feet, fork-tailed petrels, and murres. As we neared the southeast coast we saw thousands of tufted puffins. They had stocky black bodies a little over a foot long, bright orange-red bills, and tufts of white hanging down the backs of their heads as if it were time for the whole flock to go to the barbershop.

The puffins were truly the comedians of the sea. As we sailed along, the ship startled the young birds resting on the water and they attempted to take off. The puffins flopped and splashed and made a colossal commotion trying to get airborne. Some made it and then flapped madly a few inches above the water, their little wings drumming the crisp air. We stood on the foredeck and laughed as we watched. The puffins' ultimate defense was to dive just as the ship went over them. They would reappear far astern, shaking their clownlike heads as if to say, "You so and so."

Attu is thirty-five miles long and fifteen miles wide and uninhabited except for a thirty-two-man U.S. Coast Guard Loran station. The wind was light as we approached Massacre Bay, the best anchorage. Fog began to appear in the west. We took continuing bearings of principal points—all with unnerving names—and as we tacked past Murder Point under the shadow of Terrible Mountain at the western entrance, white mist swirled around us.

Margaret steered a careful compass course while I stood on the foredeck and we worked near several enormous tumbled-down World War II docks. The fog lifted a bit and we saw a U.S. flag above the main Coast Guard building. Through the glasses I watched a man disappear. In a moment the front door opened and a dozen men ran out. They jumped into a truck and speeded toward the rickety pier we were approaching. We handed the jib, dropped an anchor, veered fathoms and fathoms of chain, and as the ship swung we passed lines to the men on the pier.

"Where—where did you come from?" asked Lieutenant Martin

Hoppe, the commanding officer, as we furled the mainsail. "You suddenly appeared out of the fog. It was like a dream. We couldn't believe it. No one *ever* comes here. You are the first ship since the yearly supply vessel. Most of our food and goods come by air—uh, when the fog lifts," he said, motioning at the clammy mist.

"We left northern Japan fifteen days ago," I said. "We . . ."

"Come up to the building," chorused the men, "and tell us about it."

Our five-day stay on Attu was like a wonderful vacation. We were invited to take our meals with the men, who seemed always to be having steak. Margaret was the only woman on the island and she was treated royally. The area around the bay had been a military base for both Japanese and U.S. troops during World War II and there were hundreds of disintegrating buildings and Quonset huts and tons and tons of abandoned war goods. But over the first hill these rusting relics were largely gone. We visited inland lakes and plunging cascades and marveled at the steep, ice-carved Aleutian slopes that were so incredibly green, a solid and powerful green that seemed to represent a whole year's growth compressed into the short weeks of the northern summer. There was no tall growth, but we walked through waist-high wild flowers everywhere. Patches of fog alternated with the sun, which was warm and delightful. In the streams we caught Dolly Varden trout and along the shore of the bay we saw tens of thousands of silver salmon. Every cast brought in a big fish.

Reeves Aleutian Airlines had a monopoly on the least wanted air route in the world, and a DC-6 flew in mail, food, new men, gossip, and a stewardess (!). In theory the plane came every three or four days, but fog often canceled the flights week after week. When the plane finally arrived it was like Christmas.

There was a legend that dogs were needed on Attu (false), and whenever anyone wanted to get rid of a dog from Anchorage westward, he was put on the plane and sent to the last stop. The dogs were fed choice scraps from the kitchen and were soon sleek and fat. When we walked, the pack always came along, and a romp in the hills was good fun for all.

The morale at the Loran station was excellent. Most of the men were young recruits who treated their twelve-month tours on Attu as an adventure in the north and a lark. They were full of life and in their spare time were radio hams, beachcombers, photographers, fishermen, stamp collectors, and so forth. All were kind to us and curious about our trip, which we told about at length.

On July 31, with all thirty-two Coast Guard men waving goodbye, the dogs barking, and a gift of vegetables and frozen salmon in the galley, we headed east. Two small false killer whales crossed in front of us as we left Massacre Bay and sailed north around the island into the Bering Sea.

We wanted to visit an uninhabited island in the Aleutians but sheltered anchorages were rare. We finally decided to stop at Semisopochnoi in the Rat group, attracted by the jaw-breaking Russian name, which meant "seven extinct volcanoes." Although I was a bit wary, the three-day sail was a delight and we stayed on the northern, Bering Sea side of the Aleutians where the *U.S. Coast Pilot* said we would find better weather and less fog. We stood watch and watch, followed the compass carefully, and took celestial observations when we could. Fog was part of the scene, but it occurred in patches and often streamed above an island in high caps of white vapor. Or the fog billowed leeward in long horizontal teardrops with the bright sun behind. The differential in both temperature and wind velocity around the small islands made the fog a local condition and often it formed and disappeared before our eyes. As the sun heated a land mass it too influenced the fog.

The panorama of the islands to our south was a fluttering screen of changing weather. We used the hand-bearing compass together with vertical sextant angles to establish our position, and one by one we checked off the islands as we passed some ten to twenty miles to the north. At one time we had eleven small islands in sight. There was unlimited sea room to the north, west, and east, and if a prolonged northerly gale arose we could run between the islands to the south.

We anchored in a bay on the eastern side of Semisopochnoi, well protected on three sides but open to the east. We buoyed the anchor, tied a reef in the mainsail, and as night fell we hanked on a storm jib. The next morning the barometer was high and the weather settled, so we went ashore.

No trees grow in the Aleutians, but the beaches were piled with thousands of logs and pieces of driftwood carried by the ocean currents. We found glass floats from Japan and remnants of fish boxes with Russian markings. As we walked along the beach we heard a barking noise and turned to see a blue fox romping over the big logs. The fox looked and sounded like a small dog except for his magnificent bushy tail. He was as curious about us as we were of him, and we inspected each other for several minutes before he bounded off. Almost at once we saw a fox kit among the rocks and wood debris. Margaret picked up the little fellow and we marveled at his fluffy brown fur and endearing manner.

We kept an eye on *Whisper* and the weather and walked up on a ridge behind the beach, where we found a small, stoutly constructed building surrounded by waist-high grasses. The weather-worn structure was an Aleut fox trapper's cabin and probably dated from the late 1930s. It had been heated by a wood stove and we saw a pile of wood and a hand saw as if the trapper had just stepped outside. In back was a grave marked with a tall, weathered Russian Orthodox cross engraved with beautifully chiseled Cyrillic letters. You couldn't help but wonder who had lived in the cabin, what his story was, and who lay buried out in back.

The island measured ten miles across and we wanted to go to a small lake in the middle, but we found what looked like an easy walk to be a boggy swamp masked by tall grasses. It was both hard going and you needed hip boots. On the better drained shoreside ridges, however, we discovered the same wildflowers that we had seen on Attu—big bushes of blue lupine, clumps of golden paintbrush and purple irises, and sunny showers of yellow asters and daisies.

I found the land forms of the islands exciting. The slopes of high, snowy peaks plunged into ice-hollowed ridges of intense green. Reddish volcanic domes rose above lettuce-colored valleys. Sometimes you could look up precipitous avalanche slopes that climbed hundreds of feet above sea-dashed cliffs. With the trees entirely gone there was no softening of contours, and the general feeling was of new landscapes that had just emerged from the heart of the earth. It was only when you went over the land on foot at close hand that the birds and animals and plants and fish and streams and beaches eased the harsh impression you got from a distance. The changing light and cloud forms made the scene new every hour. Seals and sea lions and sea otters swam in the bays, and we watched colossal flights of birds so thick they were like smoke before a wind.

August 2. 1530. Away from Semisopochnoi with a light northerly wind and a warm sun. Three Japanese fishing trawlers nearby. Correct time and date unknown since we are astride the International Date Line. I am totally confused. Margaret has moved the clocks ahead two hours and decided that yesterday's date will remain today's. Just so tomorrow doesn't become yesterday!

At 2000 I was asleep and Margaret was reading. We were twenty-one miles east of Semisopochnoi, almost halfway to Gareloi Island. Suddenly I heard Margaret's voice.

"On deck! On deck!" she shouted.

I jumped up to see an enormous U.S. Coast Guard vessel almost alongside. Many of the crew lined her decks to look at the strange little sailboat in the Aleutians.

"Do you need any assistance?" boomed a voice from the bridge through a loud-hailer.

Margaret passed me the Aldis signaling lamp and I replied in Morse that we were quite O.K. As I flashed "thank you" the big white ship with its cheery red-and-blue bow stripe moved off. I later wrote to the master of the *Taney* and thanked him for his kindness and offer of help. That November we had a cordial letter of reply from Captain R. E. Young. The *Taney* was a 327-foot cutter built in 1937 and driven by steam turbines, which explained why Margaret had been caught unaware by the almost silent vessel when she slipped alongside.

It was still quite light at midnight and we had Gareloi Island in sight. The south-setting current had pushed us back into the Pacific and the northerly wind increased, so we handed the genoa and put up the small working jib. At 0200 we tied a reef in the main and paid

close attention to our course, for the Delarof Islands, a series of small islets and rocks, lay only seven miles to leeward and we were uncertain of our southern drift. By 0500 the tidal stream had begun to set toward the Bering Sea and the opposing, increasing wind kicked up severe, irregular seas over the mountainous bottom, which varied in depth from twenty-one to over 500 fathoms, according to our charts. It was light now and we took bearings of the southern points on Tanaga Island to check our position. The wind increased and the clouds lowered.

At 0900 we had three reefs in the main and the storm jib up. It was crucial to keep sailing eastward to pass the dangers to the south, but the force of the wind had the starboard deck entirely under water. The push of the seas from the north shoved us bodily to the south almost wave by wave. However, by 1030 I stopped steering because I judged that we had sufficient sea room so that the storm couldn't drive us among the rocks and shoals of the Delarof Islands. We then pulled down the storm jib and mainsail and hoisted the storm trysail. How easy it is to write what was such a struggle! Under the trysail, *Whisper* lay relatively quiet. No longer were we bashing across the seas but riding with them.

"The wind registers a steady forty-six knots on the Ventimeter," I noted, "and it takes a real hero to look to windward, because the spray feels like hot gravel."

August 3. 2215. The gale has stirred up a tempest above this shallow sea bottom and our cockleshell rolls and pitches like a tea leaf in a boiling pot. We lie huddled under a pile of blankets in the lee berth. I am astonished at the nastiness of the seas in the supposed lee of Tanaga.

During the afternoon Margaret went forward to secure a loose anchor. She came back choking from swallowing sea water and was very red in the face from wind-hurled spray. She has lots of pluck. Deck leaks fierce. Maddening to be stopped like this when our goal of Adak is so close.

The gale lasted twenty-four hours and afterward we found that under the storm trysail we had jogged along on a course of about 50 degrees to the north wind at a rate of one and a quarter knots while we made leeway of half a knot. In twenty-four hours we blew offshore some twelve miles and made roughly thirty miles of easting.

As usual, the gale ended as quickly as it began. We soon had more sail up, headed northward, and managed a sun sight through thin clouds. The barometer began to drop again as we picked up Kanaga Island. We hunted along the southeast coast for a protected bay mentioned in the *Pilot*, but the land was deeply indented and the rocks and kelp extended far offshore. I was hesitant about getting too close to shore in the rough water and foggy cliffs. We bore away for Adak Strait and by 2000 on August 4 we had two anchors down in the innermost finger of Three Arm Bay on the uninhabited west shore of Adak. For the next two days we lay in this calm anchorage while gales whistled outside and fog howled down the mountains above us. It blew so hard I thought the wind would whisk away the green of the grass. Finally on the third day we sailed around the northern part of Adak to Sweeper Cove in Kuluk Bay, where the U.S. Navy had an airstrip and 5,000 sailors and civilians.

Contrary to our experiences with the Coast Guard, we found the people at the Navy base generally colorless. Adak was as starkly beautiful as the other Aleutians, but most of the Navy people and civilians we met seldom looked farther than the rim of a glass during their off-duty hours. They seemed to regard their northern duty as a jail sentence and spent a lot of time watching abysmal reruns of old television programs. There was an incredible number of automobiles for a place with scarcely any road system.

We called on the base commander, Captain Hubert Glenzer, who in turn visited us. Glenzer was also the local game warden and keen on sea otter management and Aleutian geology. We met Jim and Muriel Welte, two civilian workers who were old hands at world travel and who spent their spare hours hiking, identifying flowers, taking photographs, and studying correspondence courses. We also met Ken Van Horen, an officer who worked as a commercial halibut fisherman on the side and loved it. But these people, we felt, were out of the ordinary. It was the old story of well-adjusted people leading useful and productive lives while the complainers were bored and frustrated. The main business of the base was supposed to be military surveillance of the northern waters, but from what we saw, it seemed mostly a memorandum-passing game between dreary bureaucrats.

We sailed for Atka by way of Little Tanaga Island. We were in the Andreanof group now, in the middle of the Aleutian chain, and fog was often around us. We found it best to sail only by daylight and to go from point to point with our compass and elapsed mileage to guide us when the swirling mists descended.

However, on many days there was no fog and the air was so clear that we felt we could see all the way to the North Pole. On such a day we sailed past Great Sitkin and marveled at its 5,740-foot peak and nearby volcano which pushed a steady stream of smoke and ash into a sky of silk-ribbon blue. We could see the sun glinting on the snout of a glacier high on the main peak and a black rim of ash around the huge caldera lower down.

On foggy days our world was different, a constricted arena only a hundred yards wide. You stood at the front of the ship and peered into a thick shroud of gray. The fog was cold and wet and I felt thankful for the layers of wool and the oilskins and the thick gloves. My nose dripped like a leaky faucet.

I couldn't afford to daydream. The land was near and my eyes were all that stood between success and disaster. The only things I saw were fog and water, both featureless and unchanging. All at once three murres flew in front of the ship, their narrow wings beating in a whir. Then the silent hand of fog again. A few broken pieces of olive-green kelp appeared in the water and looked like enormous, water-soaked

noodles. The swells were smoother now. Certainly we were across the strait that separated Tagalak Island from Atka and were in the easier water behind Cape Kigun.

"A sea otter to port," called Margaret from her position at the helm. We saw a gray-whiskered otter leisurely paddle away on his back while he watched us closely.

"Depth," I called.

"Thirty-one fathoms," shouted Margaret after glancing at the dial of the echo sounder.

The fog was thicker now. I could see only seventy-five or a hundred feet. We continued to sail fast, too fast.

"Ease all sheets," I called. "Let the sails luff."

We passed more kelp and I watched for protruding rocks. Suddenly I saw something whiter than the gray of fog. The white was water breaking at the base of a rock or a cliff.

"Change course to 060 degrees," I shouted.

"060" came the response as the ship swung to port.

Now I could see cliffs and the shore of an island, certainly north-western Atka. The fog cleared higher up and mountains rose above the

mist. I dashed aft for the hand-bearing compass, took bearings of everything in sight, and began to match the angles with the chart.

More murres flew past, along with puffins and guillemots. We saw
otters paddling around and big patches of kelp appeared to starboard.
I had calculated that we should be abeam of Bechevin Bay at 1803. But
our speed across Atka Pass may have exceeded four knots. At 1753, ten
minutes earlier, I saw the land close to starboard begin to fall away.

"Stand by to gybe," I called, hurrying aft to haul in the mainsheet.
Margaret shoved the tiller to windward and we changed course to 170
degrees. As we headed almost south we passed high cliffs that I hoped
led to Bechevin Bay. I looked for the gray bluffs of White Point mentioned in the *Pilot*—and there they were. We followed the cliffs toward
land, and the fog was suddenly less. The echo sounder read twenty-five
fathoms, twenty, fifteen, ten, eight, five, and I let go the anchor and lots
of chain. We were safe in a protected bay. Now let the fog and wind
come.

We found the isolated Aleutian anchorages wild and exciting, a
part of America that no one knows. Your footsteps pushed into untrod-
den sand and in a few minutes you might discover a Japanese broom, a
piece of Russian fish net, a coil of old rope, and the skeleton of a whale.
The shore birds and foxes and sea otters scarcely noticed you, and
where a stream entered a bay you walked over boulders and sandbars.
Often the river bottom became the way across the land. The cliffs and
hills above the beaches loomed enormous in the changing fog and the
growth was thick and almost impenetrable, a green jungle of grasses up
to your waist. It sometimes took half an hour to struggle up a small hill,
and we soon learned to wear our oilskins when we went for a walk. The
land was harsh but it had a fascination. The longer I stayed the more I
liked it.

We headed for the Aleut village at Nazan Bay on the east coast of
Atka. As we sailed past Korovin Volcano on the north point of the island, a great blast of wind—a williwaw—came hurtling down the black
mountain. A moment before we had had all sail up and barely made
two knots. Now the port deck disappeared under water.

"On deck," I shouted. Margaret hurried topsides from below. "Pull
down the genoa." I kept the ship on course while Margaret clawed
down armfuls of madly flapping Dacron. We were only a mile from
land and the water was quite smooth in spite of surface whitecaps. But
great torrents of icy wind thundered down on us. The port deck remained a boiling river.

"Never mind a small jib," I yelled, tossing the roller reefing handle at Margaret. "Reef the main."

Margaret quickly cranked the reefing gear and the mainsail got smaller and smaller. The wind shrieked louder, and with no jib and the mainsail area reduced by half we whished across the calm water mile after mile while we held our breath and marveled at the strength of the wind and the speed of the ship. Finally near Cape Shaw it began to get dark. It was too late to enter Nazan Bay, so we headed offshore until we got out of the big wind and hove to until morning.

At first light we sailed into the bay, slipped between two islets, and while rain brushed our faces and clouds swirled above the mast top, we rounded a low bluff. As I looked ahead a handful of gray houses and white and red buildings swept into view, a remarkable contrast to the firm green of the undulating hills.

We anchored in front of the village. Two Aleut teenagers in a pulling boat soon came out and told us to take the ship to the shelter of a small nearby island. We moved at once. A squally wind gusted at forty knots, so we veered all our chain for the main anchor and laid out a second anchor on a 200-foot warp.

Atka Village had eighteen families and a hundred residents. The Aleuts are short, dark, and muscular. Most have round faces, large eyes of a remarkable brown, and vague traces of Asiatic features. The men and children dressed in ordinary Western working clothes, often with boots and jackets and baseball caps from Sears, Roebuck. The women wore cotton dresses or slacks. Except for their stature the people might have been from a farming community in Iowa when viewed from a short distance. We soon learned that the Aleuts had little in common with the Eskimos who lived farther north and whose culture was materially different.

"Would you like to come in for a warm-up?"

The greeting came from Sally Snigaroff, a teenager who dashed up to us and led us up the steep hill to her home. We were welcomed into the weatherbeaten frame house by Sally's mother, Clara Snigaroff, a stern-looking, thickset woman with a pleasant smile who held a big coffee pot into which she was rapidly spooning fresh coffee.

We talked with Mrs. Snigaroff about our trip and passed on news from Adak. We met her other daughter, Frances, and a son. Both the girls and the young man were about to leave for schooling on the mainland. The girls had a battery-driven phonograph going full blast with country and western songs and couldn't wait to show us their photograph album. Their father was away working on a commercial fishing boat.

Mrs. Snigaroff didn't quite understand where we had been on *Whisper*, but when we told her we planned to sail to the mainland she got very upset.

"The mainland from *here* in that little boat!" she cried. "That ocean is terrible. I'll worry a lot until you write me that you're safe." Mrs. Snigaroff jotted down her address and made us promise to send a letter.

Most of the houses we visited had little furniture. The principal item was a large coal or oil stove, generally the center of family life. Rows and rows of woolen stockings hung on nails or from string clotheslines above the stove. In a nearby sink sat the evening meal—a couple of salmon or a piece of caribou meat. Kerosene lamps furnished light.

We looked at the new red schoolhouse, a two-room affair up through the eighth grade that was modern, large, well designed, and impressively equipped. It was to replace a decrepit old building. The villagers hoped to have the new school ready for the fall semester. The almost completed quarters for a teacher from the mainland were commodious. A new generating plant chugged nearby, and half a dozen Aleut workmen scurried around with tools and equipment.

As we walked through the windswept village we often saw a face in a window watching us, a face that flashed out of sight when it saw

that we had noticed it. We visited different families and began to realize that the Aleuts were painfully shy. They were self-conscious about being Aleuts and greatly feared shame and ridicule. It was a pity, for when the Russians first traveled to the islands more than 200 years ago the fifty-odd islands had an Aleut population of perhaps 25,000. But the unbelievable cruelty brought by the Russians, together with those familiar footprints of the devil—smallpox, tuberculosis, typhus, syphilis, and influenza—destroyed these people who had had a remarkable and highly developed primitive culture related to their seaside existence. Agattu Island, our landfall in the Aleutians, for example, had had thirty-five native Aleut villages when the Russians first came. Now there were no villages and no people at all.[42]

The faces that we saw were the remnants of the Aleuts whose strain has been weakened by successive waves of hunters, fishermen, and soldiers. According to the 1960 census only 2,099 Aleutian Islanders have 25 percent or more Aleut ancestry. Even today their health is generally poor, and, because of inbreeding, dullness is a problem. With their old skills largely gone and a strong desire to copy mainland life, the villagers probably couldn't make it without government assistance, too much of which goes for drink, canned goods, and worthless U.S. junk.[43]

However, in spite of these dismal facts we saw lots of life and plenty of children in Atka Village. The green hills were wonderful for running and the kids charged up and down the slopes laughing and tumbling, their cheeks red and their yells shrill. The men brought in enormous halibut and heavy pieces of caribou. The teenagers appeared with salmon and trout, and everywhere we saw racks for drying reddish strips of smoked salmon. The people were clever with their hands, and Nadesta Golley, a bright-eyed young woman with beautiful long hair, let me see a small basket she was weaving from fine grasses.

Her father, Sergius Golley, showed us the Russian Orthodox church with its two green balloon-shaped domes on top of a neat, white wooden structure. The inside was white too, with carefully painted blue diamonds and squares around the altar area. Sergius, who was seventy-four and one of the village leaders, read a few lines from the big Russian Bible. During services the interior was lighted by a large brass candelabra that held two dozen candles. There were no seats or pews. Everyone stood for the infrequent services when a priest came from Unalaska.

The Aleuts speak a language akin to Eskimo. The sound was unique to me and totally indescribable. The word for "hello," for example, is *du-lù-maqx*. "Thank you" is *kaxgasikuq*. "Come again" is *akaqdali-daq*.

The people were astonished at our interest and delighted to teach us a few words, though they roared at our fumbling pronunciations.

Shortly before we left Atka three teenagers came out to *Whisper* for a visit and brought us a piece of halibut. Edward Nevzoroff, Ronald Snigaroff, and Frank Snigaroff sat around eating cookies and examining a chart of their island. Frank was a smart lad and about to leave for an Indian school in Oklahoma, where he hoped to learn to be an automobile mechanic.

"Will you come back?" I asked. "Do people come back?"

"No," answered Frank. "They don't come back 'cause there's nothin' to do here. They just keep goin' . . . nothin' to do here but hunt, fish, and camp."

The Aleuts often went camping during the summer. They fished and hunted and gathered edible seaweed, shore plants, and shellfish—perhaps as they had in the old days. There was lots of driftwood for fires and in good weather the climate was mild. Margaret and I went to several of these camps, where we were given shells and a few late flowers.

"What do you see here on Atka?" I asked Clara Snigaroff at her family camp one day. "The life is hard and there's no future. You say you've forgotten much of the Aleut lore, and the old customs are dying."

"I know," she said. "But this is my land and I love it. This year the wildflowers came early and they were so lovely. We had fresh bouquets every day for a month."

Clara's eyes lighted up as she spoke, and she touched a tall stalk of grass with affection.

"The young ones go," she said, "but I want to stay. My heart would break if I left."

17 / ～～～～～
～～～～～～
～～～

Gales, Totems, and Eagles

WITH HALF A DOZEN SLEEK KILLER WHALES DIVING AND
spouting around the ship, we sailed from Atka and headed south across
Amlia Pass. The winds blew lightly from the east and we glided along
the uncharted south shore of Amlia Island, whose mountainous skyline
looked like a fairy's dream in the hazy sunlight of the golden afternoon.
I had laid out a course across the Gulf of Alaska, and as we headed
roughly eastward from the center of the Aleutians we began to leave the
islands as they curved northeastward.

The pleasant weather didn't last.

*August 20. 2110. Three hard days. Weather black and nasty and a
southwest wind up to 40 knots. Enormous seas, large enough so that
the vane is powerless and humans are powerless too. We started
out with the genoa and full mainsail. Then one reef and the #2
working jib. Next two reefs in the main together with the storm jib.
This was followed by the storm jib alone, and then bare poles. The
last, bare poles, does not work for Whisper. Too much windage
aft and the ship gets pushed around and drifts sideways with the
rudder useless. In any case we lay a-hull for seven hours today.*

*With no sails the motion was horrible. I fixed a torn batten pocket
on the mainsail and repaired a broken part on the steering vane.
Finally at 1400 today I got the trysail up after a struggle but
afterwards I was so tired I could only sit in the cockpit and steer
weakly.*

Margaret hoisted the tiny #3 storm jib which got the ship going again and later we hooked up the vane. Now we are making three or four knots with somewhat better motion since the seas are more regular. (Actually the ride is still pretty wild but compared to what it was, the ship seems positively comfortable!) Wind southwest at 32 knots. The ship is a shambles below, a jumble of oilskins, bedding, books, cooking pots, charts, and you-name-it.

When we ran into these severe seas I got violently ill, the sickest I have been on the whole trip. This coupled with two sleepless nights and the grim motion along with many sail changes took all my strength. Never have I been so feeble. Tonight I finally ate a hot meal, had a two-hour nap, and feel much better.

By midnight the following night the gale had blown out and we were becalmed on a windless, lumpy sea.

We were headed for Ketchikan in southeast Alaska by way of Dixon Entrance, the twenty-five-mile strait between Alaska and Canada that opens into an island-studded archipelago that runs northwest above Vancouver Island for 560 miles. The center of Dixon Entrance was at 54° 28′ N., so our course was 84° T., a little north of east. The distance from Amlia Pass in the Aleutians to the seaward side of Dixon Entrance on the mainland was 1,548 miles. We hoped to make the crossing in two weeks.

After a day of light westerly winds the breeze backed to the southwest and stiffened into a gale again. We stripped *Whisper* down to storm canvas and whished to the east with nasty-looking seas curling up astern. We found the gales in the Gulf of Alaska to be of short duration and rapidly moving. The pointer of the barometer marched up and down with alarming jumps as the storms tracked their way across this northern corner of the Pacific. The wind veered when the eastward-moving depressions went north of the ship and backed when they passed south of us.

The second gale lasted the eighth and ninth days of the passage and then eased off with the wind out of the west. Though both gales had been from the southwest, we found that we had been set far to the south and at one time I thought of squaring away for San Francisco. However, we continued pushing north and east. By noon on the tenth day we had made 750 miles and had about 800 to go.

One dark night we were changing a headsail with the spreader lights on when a small gray bird suddenly fluttered to the deck at our feet. I picked him up and stroked his soft, high-domed head. He seemed quite content to rest, so when we finished with the sail we carried the bird

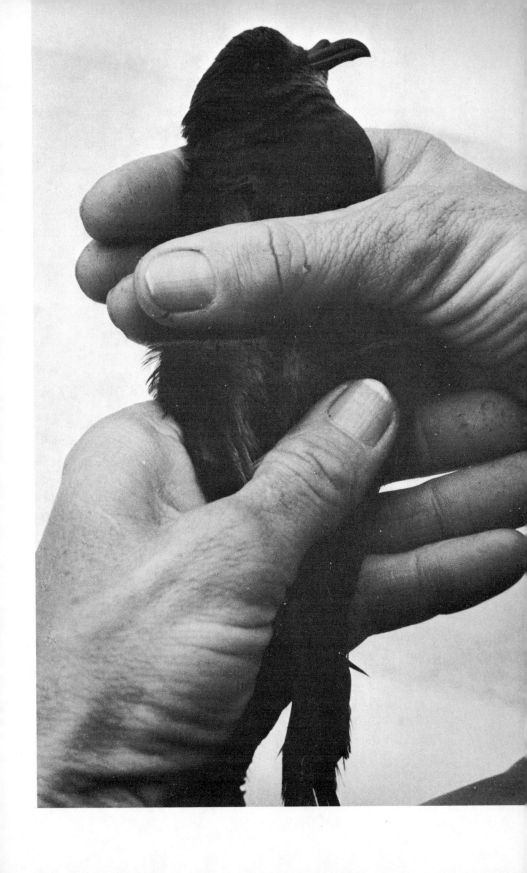

below for a good look. He was entirely dark gray except for a patch of white near the end of the top of his tail. His long, jointed legs and black webbed feet were not made for land use at all, and when he walked he had to help himself along with a wing for a crutch. His bill was slender and hooked and had nostrils on top in a tube. His eyes were two dots of bright black.

Margaret had the bird books. "How long are his wings?" she asked.

I opened one wing and measured it. "Five and a half inches," I said. "The tip is pointed and swept back," I added, feeling that at last I couldn't miss an identification.

"Is his tail notched?"

"A deep V-notch."

"A Leach's storm petrel," said Margaret. "Sailors know them as Mother Carey's chickens."

Margaret put the bird in a cardboard box, but he didn't like it and spent the night under the saloon table. The next morning we photographed him and he peeped a little while we held him. Margaret then tossed him into the air and he raced off, diving and skittering a few feet above the wave tops.

I felt I knew a storm petrel well after our interview, and I often saw several of the little soft-gray fellows flitting over the sea, especially when the weather was stormy and the seas were disturbed. I might be kneeling on the foredeck, encased in oilskins, with my safety harness clipped to a piece of rigging, and be stuffing a sail into a bag, when I would hear a quiet squeak. There in front of me would be two storm petrels dancing and diving like joyous butterflies just above the wave tops. Whenever I saw the birds I felt I was no longer alone. I had company, lively company, and we shared our ocean world together.

Margaret did wonders with meals and I never regretted the lack of refrigeration. We went the extreme from munching a few dry crackers during gales to elaborate dinners when the weather was reasonable. One memorable night Margaret handed me a warm plate with crispy pieces of golden fried chicken, sauteed Maine potatoes, and well-buttered Japanese corn—all from cans. Dessert was New Zealand peaches and cream (two more cans) plus almond cookies followed by many cups of lapsang souchong tea. But usually the meals were simpler. Our two-burner kerosene Primus stove worked well, although sometimes the motion of the ship made the stove swing so violently in its gimbals that we had to lash it down. Then we missed the stove sorely, for its top was always level and the only place where a hot cup or pot could be left unguarded for a few minutes.

August 27. 0145. The night is black and a two-foot-wide stream of phosphorescence glows behind us as we hurry along and leave a luminous path. The log line is a glowing bluish thread afire on the dark sea. The air is dry and the deck does not run with condensation which is unusual. At sunset last night the sky was layered with clouds. . . .

The barometer had begun a dance downward and the wind backed from the west to the south to the east, indicating that the center of a depression was moving south of us. In twelve hours the barometer fell from 1013 millibars to 1001, and we went through the usual sail drill and wound up hove to under the storm trysail as the wind increased to a steady forty-five knots from the northeast. By late afternoon the barometer had plunged to 993 mb., the drone in the rigging had become a remarkable hum, and the storm trysail was clearly too much for the ship, which lay with the starboard deckhouse ports entirely under water. Spray and scud grayed out the windward ports and the ship below was plunged into aquarium darkness. (I thought of Vito Dumas and the canvas he carried over his deckhouse.) The bend in the mast from the strain of the trysail was scary. How I wished for running backstays and a lower headstay to brace the mast!

If a big ship had passed us 100 feet away I think we would have been invisible, half submerged in the hiss of spray and sea.

I could have handed the trysail, but I hoped to keep a little canvas up to preserve life down below. After some thought we took down the trysail and hoisted the mainsail which flapped madly in the strong wind. I then quickly rolled the boom fourteen turns with the roller reefing gear, lashed the handle in place, and hauled in the mainsheet. With only the top twelve feet of the mainsail showing—half the trysail area—we lay reasonably well about six or seven points off the wind.

The seas that streamed toward the southwest were large and surprisingly even, for the wind seemed to have blown away much of the crests. The horizon was gone and the ocean and clouds had melted into a single element, a substance that was new to us. If you darted a glance to windward you saw only gray-white patches and streaks of dense foam in the moment before your eyes were stung with salt. As the hours went by we became aware of a tempest that was chilling in its intensity and fundamental in its violence. We learned that the heart of the storm gave the sea a rolling, thundering motion, and our tiny ship staggered as she heeled to the shocks that snapped through the water.

Just before dark Margaret pumped the bilge and captured the end of a spinnaker pole topping lift that had escaped. I prepared some tools

and pieces of stout plywood in case one of the cabin ports got broken. We had done what we could and retired to the lee berth, where we napped, read a little, and played nonsense word games. I fell asleep trying to think of a river that began with Q.

On the morning of the twelfth day of the passage I awoke to hear the wind much less, but I missed the sound of the steering vane, which made a slight clatter from time to time.

"The vane's gone," I said to Margaret when I looked out. "From now on we'll have to steer by hand." The gale had snapped the one inch stainless steel shaft and we lost the wind blade that had steered us so faithfully for 16,530 miles. I had a spare blade, but I never thought the shaft would break.

As the wind went down and the barometer climbed we got under way again, missing the help of the vane. We took turns steering, four hours on and four hours off.

The sea was vile after the great storm. Without the drive of the wind, the water tumbled and fell every which way. Cross-seas smacked against one another, and instead of a regular, oscillating, predictable motion, the feeling on board the ship was like going up in an elevator during an earthquake. A steady rising motion was interrupted by a sudden sideways push. Then the bottom dropped out and the ship plunged into a pit where the sea no longer was. The ocean was a huge rock quarry, and the ship kept falling into abandoned holes.

We had become so accustomed to the help of the steering vane that guiding the ship by hand soon became a bore. It was a cold, wet business in spite of thick clothes. Since we were still 580 miles offshore, I put blocks on the lifelines outboard of the tiller on each side and led steering lines from the tiller below deck. We then remounted the compass on the forward side of the bulkhead aft of the port settee and zing! We had a warm, inside steering position. True, our movements were backward and the helmsman sat facing aft, but you soon got used to the reversed steering.

We pushed to the northeast and gradually got closer to the Alaskan coast, changing a sail now and then and heaving to when the wind freshened from ahead. On the fourteenth day we had a fair westerly wind, so we took down the mainsail and poled out a jib on both the port and starboard sides. We led the sheets to the tiller and got the ship to steer herself for forty-one hours. The icy rain squalls stopped, the weather warmed up, and we opened the hatches for a great airing and drying out. Jaegers and black-footed albatrosses circled the ship, and with clear skies and reasonable seas we determined the ship's position each morning and afternoon. On the seventeenth day our radio picked up a fine Mozart piano concerto from CBC, Vancouver.

> *September 3. 1145. Because of a wind change, Margaret called me to gybe the running sails. We finished and while I steered for a moment she went aft to free the log line which had gotten around the self-steering gear. She then accidentally put her left hand into the mechanism of the powerful vane gear, which, routinely swinging, crushed her hand and particularly her third finger. Suddenly I saw 1½" of bone, alarming in its whiteness, and blood everywhere, the red violent against the hard yellow of Margaret's oilskins. We managed to piece together the flaps of bloody skin across the wound by using sterile butterfly bandages. Then we bound up all the fingers. I gave the patient a codeine pill, cleaned the blood out of the cockpit, and took a slug of brandy for my shot nerves. Margaret took it all very calmly.*

We were within twenty-five miles of land, and during the afternoon a fishing trawler appeared south of us. Toward evening, fog thickened around the ship, so we hove to for the night, each of us keeping a look-

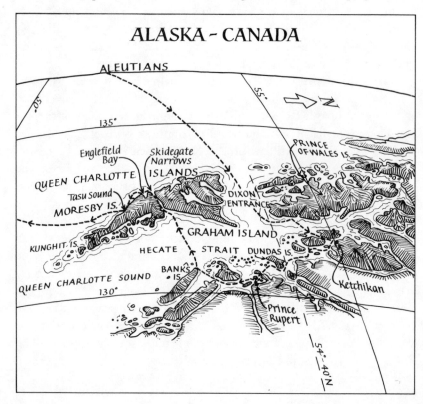

out in turn. The next morning we continued eastward, and as the sun rose the fog dispersed. At 0718 a longitude sight put us seven miles west of tiny Langara Island, at the north end of Queen Charlotte Island, and I suspected we were over Learmonth Bank, because the sea had a different feel to it and we saw fish and birds and large tangles of floating kelp.

"I see a blue swell of land off the starboard bow," Margaret announced at eight o'clock. "At first I thought it was more clouds, but what I see is stationary and solid."

Our longitude was no problem. We knew we were at the west coast of America, but we wanted to be very sure of our north-south position in case an onshore storm came up. At 0942 the position line from a second sun sight angled through Dixon Entrance, and as a wonderful landscape of bluish clouds lifted, a complex of land forms unfolded around us.

I thought back to the scenery of Japan, which, though adequate and sometimes splendid, was often shrouded in grays. Japan's landscapes had seemed as diminutive as her people, lovely but on a modest scale. The Aleutians were isolated volcanic remnants, carpeted lushly in green for the few months of summer, but essentially austere and harsh. However, the landscapes of southeast Alaska and northwest British Columbia now on all sides of us were totally big and powerful. Islands and capes and high mountains and promontories climbed above the ship on every side. We saw row upon row of hills and spurs and ridges, all on a grand scale and all forested with tens of thousands of tall and untouched conifers. We glided along calm expanses of water cut on three sides by a giant country that seemed to climb to the sky. The air was clear and we felt we could see until the limit of vision dimmed our fancy.

The earthy smell of the land was good, and the fragrance from the trees almost brought tears to our eyes. We sailed past Dall Island, headed north up Clarence Strait, and anchored in the first good bay on Prince Charles Island. Gardner Bay was completely protected from the sea, and after our crossing from Atka we slept the sleep of the dead for a day and a night to recover from the exertion of the long sail. During the nineteen-day passage we had changed headsails and reefed and unreefed the mainsail sixty-one times. We had been becalmed on three occasions for a total of twenty-three hours. We hove to five times for a total of fifty-three hours.

The principal town of southeast Alaska is Ketchikan, a haphazard collection of gimcrack houses that clings precariously to the steep southwest slope of Revillagegedo Island a few miles north of the Canadian border. The entire town of 8,000 looks as if it is ready to slide down the slope of Deer Mountain into the still waters of a tree-lined strait named Tongass Narrows. Ketchikan is about seventy miles from the Pacific and is a free-spending frontier town that lives on logging and fishing and summertime tourism. The people make vast wages, but they pay colossal prices for everything, so they are about even in spite of the flamboyant economy.

It was a busy place. Most of the transport was by air, and as we approached, our ears droned with the distant hum of jets and the nearby snort of float-equipped lightplanes, waddling amphibians, and spidery helicopters. We tied up next to the Coast Guard cutter *Cape Romain*, whose crew helped us find a doctor who took charge of Margaret's injured hand.

On the first night we thought we would eat in Ketchikan.

"Excuse me," I said to a fisherman. "Can you suggest a restaurant?"

"Well, stranger, there's no place real good, but you can try the Elks Club."

We weren't members, but the man kindly introduced us at the club, where we were led to a table and given menus engraved on thin planks.

"Why don't you have the special?" suggested the waitress, pouring water. "It's only eight-fifty each and you get—"

Seventeen dollars! We swallowed our pride and walked out. During much of our trip we had spent $50 a month for everything.

The next morning Margaret tried to buy short lengths of wool to darn our stockings.

"Oh, we don't have anything like that up here," said the woman in the store. "If people get a hole in their stockings they throw them away."

We got acquainted with the men of the Coast Guard on the *Cape Romain*, who were keen to see the yacht ("Imagine coming from the Aleutians in this!"). Chief Bosun's Mate Dick Benson helped me repair the wind vane. Quartermaster George Porter fixed us up with charts, and the skipper, Jake Jacoby, gave us a tour of Ketchikan. George Porter was a great moose hunter and every November he shot a huge animal that furnished meat throughout the year for his family. Mrs. Porter gave us a big piece of the frozen meat and we had moose roast,

moose steaks, mooseburgers, mooseballs and spaghetti, moose hash, and finally moose soup!

The area was the center of salmon fishing, and every summer hundreds of big purse seiners—worth up to $120,000 each—chugged north to Ketchikan from the state of Washington. The salmon ran thick and heavy and the fishermen made lots of money, often $3,500 for ten weeks' work. The fish boats were stout and husky, with a whopping Diesel, and generally carried a crew of eleven who worked on a share basis. Many of the purse seiners flew a broom at the starboard mast spreader to indicate that the ship had taken 100,000 salmon worth ten to twenty-five cents per pound at the cannery. We got to know some of the fishermen, ate on various purse seiners, and soon realized that most of the money the fishermen earned wound up in the pockets of the owners of the saloons and bars which lined the short, roisterous streets of Ketchikan.

A typical fisherman was Al Orton, the cook on the *Mary Elizabeth B.* Al was an amusing, chatty fellow in his fifties, very bright and friendly, and only slightly sad that he no longer worked as a lawyer.

He had run a collection agency, among other things, and over several glasses of wine he told us about the business.

"An American values his car more than his wife, children, or house," said Al. "If you threaten to repossess his automobile he will sign anything, especially if you rouse him at 0500 and confront him with a document and a sheriff."

Al's stories never stopped: "One day we were out seining and I was on my way back to the galley from the food storage box on deck. I planned to make corned-beef hash for lunch, and in addition to the meat I carried a large green bell pepper, a tall bunch of crisp celery, and several onions.

"The skipper stopped me," said Al.

" 'Say,' he said, 'I don't care for green peppers. Leave them out of the noon meal, will you?'

"O.K.," said Al, and he tossed the green pepper over the side.

"One of the crewmen spoke up. 'I'm not much on celery,' he said. 'The strings get in my teeth. Don't put celery in the corned beef.'

The cook nodded and threw the celery into the water.

" 'Oh, I can't eat onions,' said another man. 'They make my breath bad. No onions, please.'

"All right," said Al, and he heaved the onions into the sea. "The hell with you guys," he roared. "I won't eat corned-beef hash without green peppers, without celery, and without onions." He threw the meat over the side. "You can all go hungry until supper."

Our new friends urged us to look at the totem poles which were unique to southeast Alaska and western British Columbia. We went to parks at nearby Saxon and at Mud Bight, where we saw dozens of these remarkable carvings, some of which were sixty feet high. The poles were sculptured with ravens, bears, fish, owls, frogs, humans, and so forth, cleverly carved around the outside of each log. The totems had been collected from deserted villages and restored by the U.S. Forest Service with the help of Tlingit and Haida Indian carvers, who repaired and painted and in many cases entirely made anew the tall cedar logs whose strange forms sparkled with bright blues and reds and yellows. Each pole illustrated a legend, and the topmost figure symbolized the clan that owned the totem. The interpretation of the poles and legends was complex, but even with no knowledge of the individual myths we found the totems amazing to inspect. We heard that modern Indian craftsmen often carved with chain saws and used cans of spray paint, which seemed a bit disappointing but inevitable, I suppose.[44]

A few days later we sailed southward from Ketchikan and anchored at Village Island, almost on the Alaskan–Canadian border. A century ago this tiny islet was home for a tribe of Tongass Ravens who drew their canoes up on the sandy beaches, perhaps with freshly killed deer from the mainland and salmon ready for smoking. Today, however, the Indians were gone and their canoes and dwellings had vanished. Yet their totem poles remained, now largely rotten, with many taken away, and the rest grown over with scrub and trees.

The carvings we saw in their original environment on Village Island had a wonderful primitive quality about them. We looked at images that had a feeling of agelessness, of simplicity, of depth, of power, properties the modern totem poles lacked. The figures reminded us of the carvings we had seen in the Marquesas Islands and in photographs of statuary on Easter Island. Without paint, splitting apart, rotten, and vandalized, the remnant totem poles were superior in every way to the recent work we saw near Ketchikan—in spite of the chain saws and the cans of spray paint.

Sailing in the archipelago along the northern west coast was a new experience. We anchored every night and traded the sextant and *Nautical Almanac* for a hand-bearing compass and binoculars. We sailed from point to point and rejoiced in the superb charts, first-class navigational aids, and protected waters. The air was clear and the scenery grand. I would trade all the scenery in Japan for one bay in Alaska.

Logging was big business along the coast, and as we crossed into Canadian waters we often passed tugs that were pulling enormous rafts of logs toward pulp and lumber mills. A few of the logs escaped and were very dangerous, so we sailed only during the day when we were able to keep a lookout for these deadly battering rams, many of which were half again as long as the yacht.

September 19. 0830. This morning we got under way before dawn because wind commenced to blow into our anchorage near Dundas Island and we were poorly anchored in rocks. When I came on deck in the black night the stars were as crisp as new snow on a zero morning and I was glad I had pulled on long underwear and had my heavy coat tightly around me. The fragrance from the fir, spruce, and cedar forests was enchanting in the cold air. Margaret put up the main and jib while I shortened the chain. She then steered and handled the sheets while I broke out the anchor and we began to make short tacks toward the Green Island light.

There was no point in two of us being on deck, so when our position relative to the north wind improved, I sent Margaret back

to bed. The wind was 15 knots or so with a short chop, and I was
busy with the tiller, adjusting sheets, and making sure that I was
away from Whitesand Islet, a place bordered with rocks.

Red-streaked fingers of dawn filtered over the dark-blue
mountains that ringed the scene above the black water. Scattered
clouds and fog banks lay balanced above the sea in the distance,
and far away the bases of the taller mountains were hidden, making
their blue-black summits appear like islands in the sky. The water
had a surprising tumble, yet when I looked below I saw Margaret
sound asleep with only her nose and unfurrowed forehead showing
from beneath a pile of blue blankets. How peaceful she looked.

I thought of the kindness of the men of the Coast Guard in Attu
and Ketchikan. Surely if I had military service to do again I would
choose the Coast Guard. Not only is it a small organization with
superb esprit de corps but its work is worthwhile. You help
someone instead of trying to destroy him.

We headed into Prince Rupert by way of Venn Passage, a narrow
backdoor channel. I had worked out the bearings and headings beforehand, and I sat on the mast spreaders with a chart and a hand-bearing
compass directing Margaret. The day had become warm and sunny,
the wind light, and as we glided through the riverlike passage with
grasses and shrubs and trees around us, Indians from the village of
Metlakatla came from their houses to watch us.

Prince Rupert, the western terminus of the Canadian National Railway and home of a large cold-storage plant for fish, had a population of
12,000 and a splendid position on a bluff on the south side of a fine
protected bay, large enough for all the ships of Canada. But Prince
Rupert seemed a town that time had forgotten. The buildings dated
from the 1920s and I felt that nothing much had happened since—in
spite of the hopes of stockbrokers and the promises of politicians for a
new gateway to the Orient.

We discovered that the fuel barges of the big oil companies had
laundry machines, dryers, a kitchen, hot coffee on tap, and first-class
showers, toilets, and washbasins for both men and women. All were
free if you bought fuel, so we filled our tanks, although I felt foolish
buying only four gallons of Diesel oil and nine gallons of kerosene.

The Prince Rupert chart agents had poor stocks of Canadian charts
and we were obliged to ask various fishing-boat captains whether we
could buy any extra numbers they had. We got several charts from
Sergeant Lorne Musclow, the skipper of the blue-hulled *Nanaimo*, a
Royal Canadian Mounted Police patrol ship.

"Do you jig?" asked Lorne.

"Beg your pardon?"

"Do you jig?"

"Fox trot a little."

"No, no," laughed Lorne. "Do you fish for cod and snapper with a jigging lure?"

"You'd better tell me about jigging," I said.

"You use a heavy Norwegian lure about six inches long," said Lorne. "It's shiny with treble hooks and you stop over a good ten or twelve fathom patch and lower the lure to the bottom and then heave hard on it three or four times. If there are any fish around they will strike at once. If nothing happens you move on. You need spend only two or three minutes in a place to catch dinner in a hurry."

We bought a jigging lure at once, which we used with signal success thereafter, blessing Lorne each time we bit into fresh red snapper or ling cod.

The day before we left Prince Rupert we were astonished to see the Australian yacht *Calypso*, which we had tied next to in Tahiti more than a year earlier. Florence and Ron Mitchell and their son Ronald had sailed their thirty-foot Tahiti ketch to Hawaii and then to Sitka, Alaska.

"We worked up the coast to sixty degrees north and saw glorious scenery—especially in Glacier Bay," said Florence. "We caught halibut and salmon and crabs, gathered clams and abalone, and picked five kinds of wild berries. We made friends everywhere, and they almost sank the ship with kindness and gifts of meat from moose and elk and deer and caribou.

"When we sailed into Juneau, the governor personally welcomed us," said Florence. "No amount of money could have bought a happier or more exciting summer, yet we hardly spent anything at all, except a smile, a handshake, a helping hand once in a while, and the simple story of our trip."

Our friends in *Calypso* headed south while we sailed west to the Queen Charlotte Islands. It was now the end of September and time for southeast gales. We had heard many stories of fish boat disasters in Hecate Strait, the fifty-mile channel between the mainland and the Queen Charlotte Islands. Hecate Strait was shallow, the tides ran strongly, and a southeast gale against an opposing tide over the shoals could raise a maelstrom that was death for small vessels. The fishermen knew this well and never crossed the strait unless the weather was clear.

We stopped at Larsen Harbor at the north end of Banks Island, where we lay with half a dozen small gill net fishing boats that had been stormbound for five days. It had blown so hard the day before that the fish boat we rafted with had had one of its wheelhouse windows blown out. However, the weather improved and the next day we all left, the gill netters traveling together in case one had an engine failure.

The fifty-five-mile crossing was easy, although the sun had an evil-looking ring around it. We passed many patches of tangled kelp on the surface, while above us we watched dozens of geese and large, long-necked birds, white below and black above, that we later identified as western grebes. The wind was light and we didn't sight the dim outline of land until 1730. At that time the depth of the water was only thirteen fathoms and the sea sounded like a river, gurgling and chuckling in the shoal depths. We were headed for a small place named Queen Charlotte City, but the entrance was obscured by an enormous sandbar whose pass was many miles to the north.

The night was black and it began to rain hard and to blow from the southeast. We felt our way through the pass into the shelter of the bar, but the buoys and lights were different from our chart and *Pilot*. Where we sounded four fathoms we should have had twenty. An hour before midnight we anchored, hoisted a powerful light in the rigging, and turned in, to wait until morning, when we sorted out things and continued another fourteen miles to Queen Charlotte City.

A bird flying high among the clouds could tell you that the Queen Charlotte Islands look like a long, skinny triangle with its base at the north and its pointed tip curving toward the southeast. The triangle measures fifty-five miles across at the top, and the north-south dimension is 150 miles. Halfway down the triangle a threadlike east-west channel named Skidegate Narrows divides the mountainous land mass neatly in two, leaving Graham Island to the north and Moresby Island to the south. Near the southern extremity the east-west Houston Steward channel slices off the tip of Moresby Island, named Kunghit Island, making three main islands in all plus a handful of islets on the east side of Moresby.

The latitude of this ocean outpost of Canada is about the same as central Labrador or the northern tip of Holland. The Charlottes are somewhat similar to larger Vancouver Island, except that these islands are farther north and west and more offshore, a wild and unsettled place with only 3,000 people—including 800 Haida Indians—on the almost 4,000 square miles. Even today the islands have not been thoroughly explored, and each map-maker has a different story. Many sailing charts have blank spaces entirely without soundings and details.

The Charlottes have excellent natural harbors, abundant timber, good offshore fishing, and extensive deposits of hard and soft coal, copper, iron, and gold-bearing quartz. Some men reap the profits of this rich land and throw them away. Others husband what they make and become prosperous. But all the people are self-reliant pioneers, for the land is harsh and not used to the ways of twentieth century man.

We sailed into the little settlement of Queen Charlotte City near the eastern entrance to Skidegate Narrows. The day was wet and cold, with hard rain from the southeast. Purse seiners, salmon trollers, and gill netters packed the small harbor and we rafted up alongside. I thought the fishing boats were in the harbor because of the weather.

"Oh no," said Bronson Bussey, the talkative captain of a nearby fish-buying boat. "We're only allowed to fish three days a week. The season is set by the fisheries' people, who count the salmon in each river and arrange the boundaries and seasons accordingly. Their idea is to allow enough salmon to get up the rivers to spawn for fishing in the days ahead. But the officials are always thinking up new regulations and it's rules, rules, rules."

Bussey had 50,000 pounds of salmon on his fish-buying boat and could afford the time to complain.

No matter where you are the fishermen always grumble. In every port in the world you can find a collection of old salts in a coffee shop or on a dock somewhere bitching and complaining and growling. But like the farmers who always plan to get away and never go, the fishermen never stop casting their nets and hooks. In the Charlottes the herring are fished out, the sardines are gone, and nobody wants sharks' livers anymore. You can still find salmon and halibut, but the Greenland turbot have wrecked the halibut market and the fisheries' people are ruining salmon fishing with all their rules. Or so go the stories. The fish prices are low, food costs more now, the boats are poor, the fuel is bad, the weather forecasts are wrong, the sliced bread is too thin. . . .

"My brother made sixteen thousand dollars on halibut and ten thousand dollars on herring in one year," said Bill Greene, who we talked with on his gill netter *Heather*. "However, at income tax time he had to borrow money."

It was the same story we had heard in Alaska. Big money but broke. "He made thirty-five hundred dollars in two weeks, but. . . ." The biggest catch and end product was usually booze. Whether this is the nature of fishermen, a recourse when the fish don't appear, something to combat the cold, nasty, wet, hard work, or because of the loneliness and uncertainty of the job, I don't know, but show me ten bags of groceries for fish boats and I'll wager you can find eight bottles. I don't mean to be a prude, for I enjoy a hot rum on a blustery day. But the amount of uncontrolled hard drinking on the northwest coast was astounding, and a direct blow to the area's vitality.

On their days off the fishermen worked as loggers, sat around playing cards, flew to Prince Rupert in chartered float planes, or went deer hunting. We saw as many as eight deer on fish boats that had come in from remote inlets. A big deer was a heavy load for a man, especially up the steep tidal ramps that rose and fell up to twenty-seven feet. I never understood why the deer had to be unloaded at low tide.

The national bird of the Queen Charlottes was the crow. These big black fellows were all over the fish boats, cawing and hopping about, picking at fish scraps, at untended grocery bags, and at drying venison. I watched a crow drop a clam on the dock trying to knock the shells apart. The crow picked up the calm, flew into the air, and dropped the shellfish on the concrete. Again and again. What a noise a choir of crows could make!

One day Margaret went to a nearby Haida Indian village. She started to walk but was given a ride by a local resident who introduced her to Rufus Moody, a Haida argillite carver. Argillite is a rare, block-like slate that takes a high black polish. The stone was hard work to get. Rufus and his wife took a ninety-minute boat ride and then climbed eight miles up a mountain to reach the deposits, which then had to be quarried and loaded on packboards.

Rufus used a variety of tiny chisels to carve small totems that were five to eighteen inches high and cost from $50 to $180. The totems were embellished with noble-looking eagles and ravens and the usual traditional figures. Mrs. Moody gave the finished carvings an ebonylike luster by buffing the rock with black shoe polish.

A few days later we were anchored in a nearby cove when we heard an outboard engine stop and a skiff glide alongside. Someone knocked on the hull.

"Is anybody at home?" said a tall, flat-faced man who spoke with a strong German accent. "I own the laundry. You left me a note that one of the machines was out of order. I want to refund your forty cents."

"Never mind about that," I said. "Come out of the rain and have a cup of coffee."

We met Werner Funk and his ten-year-old son. Werner had emigrated from the Rhine Valley in 1952, built a home and got married six years later, and now had three sons and a daughter. Werner modestly admitted to driving a Caterpillar bulldozer and cutting logging roads, but we later found out he was the best logger in the area and had just paid $40,000 for the principal business property in Queen Charlotte City.

"It's good country here," said Werner. "Clean and beautiful. We don't see many yachts because the Charlottes are too remote from the big cities. Most boat owners don't go far anyway."

We told Werner about our trip and asked him to sign our guest register. "Our plan is to go through Skidegate Narrows to the west side of Moresby and to visit a couple of the big bays before we head south. But I wasn't able to get a chart of the channel and the *Pilot* is full of warnings," I said.

"The easiest for you is to follow someone through," replied Werner. "I could take you myself, but I think a ship is better. You need local knowledge because at low water, parts of the channel dry out. In fact, at low water we can get a bulldozer down in the channel to work on it."

We arranged to follow a fisheries' patrol vessel, the big *Sooke Post*, through Skidegate Narrows, and at first light on a day when the tidal stream was exactly right, the ship picked us up at the eastern entrance.

"Follow us closely and turn as we do," shouted Ken Harley, the skipper. "We draw nine feet, so you won't get into trouble unless you cut corners."

It was impossible to sail in the narrows. We fired up our little Diesel to the maximum and closely hugged the stern of the *Sooke Post*. I thought it was a miracle there was a navigable channel between the two great islands, for precipitous mountains shot up immediately on both sides.

The *Sooke Post* made abrupt stops at blazes on trees and at other special markers, turned sharply one way or the other, and hugged certain sides of the channel so closely that when we followed, our mast and rigging ripped off bits of tree branches.

Winding through the heart of the mountains was exciting and an adventure I never dreamed of. We passed sets of range markers and I could see Ken Harley's head snapping back and forth as he maneuvered his ship to keep the markers in line. At one place the shrubs on each bank of the channel almost touched. I thought it was the end.

"It's a mistake," I said to Margaret. "We'll both be stuck forever. Future archaeologists will wonder how two ships got entombed way up in the mountains."

The channel widened from time to time and the silent water reflected gorgeous vistas of cedar and spruce. We were at sea level, of course, but we felt as if we were up hundreds of feet. Hawks spiraled overhead and deer looked up impatiently as our little procession split the mountains.

"Look!" shouted Margaret, pointing at the *Sooke Post*. "The captain's crazy this time. He's going right for the bushes."

We watched with apprehension and incredulity until a thread of water appeared. The *Sooke Post* shouldered aside more shrubs and continued westward. In two hours it was all over. I was wringing wet from the excitement but dancing inside from such a thrilling morning.

We tied up briefly with the *Sooke Post* to thank the crew for their help. Ken Harley was a tall, beefy man who wore a white skipper's cap, a neat black tie, and a khaki uniform complete with campaign badges. He was a long-time, practical sailor and when he marked his favorite anchorages on our charts his pencil moved with the confidence of a man who had every inlet and cove and ship disaster fingerprinted on his mind.

"This chart's all wrong," said Ken, jabbing with his pencil. "The bay really goes like this. Look out for a rock here and a shoal patch there. You can tie up near this waterfall and take fresh water easily." When he finished I felt my charts were a hundredfold more valuable.

We continued down a wide inlet toward the Pacific, and as we began to feel the swells of the ocean, the *Sooke Post* left us, easily running at twice our speed while her crewmen waved goodbye. We sailed offshore a few miles and turned southeast. The English sailor Peter Pye, in *Moonraker*, stopped along the west coast of the Charlottes in 1954, and it was from his fine book *The Sea Is for Sailing* that we got the notion to visit the area.

And what a coastline! Craggy mountains climbed directly from the sea to the clouds. Wide waterfalls tumbled into the ocean. Yellow cliffs and black forests fought for space above a nervous Pacific. It was a land as rugged as Magellan's Tierra del Fuego, a splendid paradise in settled weather but an awesome hell in an onshore storm.

With a fair wind in our sails we headed southeast to Englefield Bay. We followed Ken Harley's advice and slipped around Saunder Island to Kaisun Harbor ("The way in looks impossible but keep going"), where we anchored in front of an abandoned Haida village.

Ashore we found the beaches stacked with immense logs that had been washed up in storms along with all sorts of flotsam. The village had long been gone and the only things left were a few rotting totems, a burial box in a tree, a few posts and pits, and wide patches of grass. Streamlets of water had been led to the village, and as we walked among the bear and deer tracks we wished the white man had never brought his smallpox so we could have heard the laughter of the vanished Indian children and seen the long log canoes drawn up on the shelving beach. It was lovely among the tall cedar trees with the bright sun and the blue sky, but we felt that the spirits of the Indians were looking over our shoulders.

The next day a southeast gale blew up and we took refuge in Security Inlet, a finger of the sea that reached four miles into the mountains. While the gale howled for five days we hiked around the shores, fished, wrote letters, read, and—as we had been instructed— helped ourselves to the crab pot of the *Sooke Post*. While I did a few maintenance jobs, Margaret took the big Dungeness crabs and experimented with *soufflé à la crabe, crabe à la Newburg*, and *crabe gratine*, succulent delights that she had learned when she lived in Paris. I was always awed at the miraculous meals Margaret prepared on her tiny two-burner kerosene stove.

On October 6 we left Englefield Bay and headed south, but we found that the southeast storms had set up such a strong northwest-running current that we made only ten miles in four hours, even though we sailed hard. We weren't getting anywhere, so late in the afternoon I turned back so we could make shelter before dark.

We now had a strong fair wind and soon neared the intricate entrance to Kaisun Harbor.

"Look behind us," shouted Margaret above the noise of the breakers on the rocks.

I glanced aft and saw a small white fish boat, quite near, alternately appear and disappear in the swells. I couldn't believe my eyes. First I thought the ship was running for shelter as we were, and after we turned a blind corner and she didn't appear in a few minutes we went back out to see where the fish boat was, for I thought she might be in difficulty.

Then I saw her turn out toward the main part of Englefield Bay. No doubt her skipper had seen our sail, a strange sight along the isolated coast, and had followed us to see that we got in safely. Bless his heart! How humble and thankful I felt.

The following day we tried again and found the current less and the wind more favorable. Our destination was Tasu Sound, a large inland arm of the sea twenty-five miles down the coast. The entrance to Tasu, according to the *Pilot*, was especially hard to see when approaching from the north, so we watched the cliffs and mountains carefully as we headed southeast.

When we got near Tasu we worked in to about one mile offshore. There was a good lump in the sea from the northwest-running current, the swells left over from the southeast gales, and new cross-swells raised by the twenty to twenty-five knots of wind from the south-southwest. I didn't want to get to leeward of what we thought was the entrance, so we stayed hard on the wind until we got well to windward of our target.

"O.K., helmsman," I called. "Go for that notch in the castle wall."

We rushed through the mixed-up swells and jumpy waves shoreward of the 100-fathom mark. *Whisper* pitched and rolled, and as we slammed into the short waves, spray rattled in every direction. We sailed fast in the gray and unsettled weather, for we had plenty of sail up so we would have the power to beat out in case we had picked the wrong headland. Margaret worked the tiller like an oar as the ship bounced and turned. I scrambled a little way up the ratlines and was satisfied that Tasu Sound was in front of us, for I could dimly make out a placid inland lake beyond a narrow slit in the mountains.

I glanced behind us and saw an enormous blue-black cloud rearing up astern. It looked like a biblical painting of the end of the world. Fortunately it passed rapidly to seaward of us.

"Pay attention to your compass heading," I called to Margaret. "Here comes a strong squall." We steered by the compass for a minute, and when the sharp rain passed we could see the navigational light on Davidson Point, which confirmed our position.

The wind was now dead aft and the head of the ship yawed from side to side in the turbulent water. The mainsail gybed with a crash and threatened to gybe again. A bell rang in my head and I remembered a lesson I had learned from Ed Boden in the South Pacific. When you are running hard with the wind directly aft and it's impossible to change course, pull the mainsheet in tightly and ease the headsail sheet. You retain control of the ship and have the mainsail up and ready for use in case of need.

We could see the waves hammering into the rocky headland beneath the light signal. On Tasu Head, to starboard, there was an enormous offshore rock, a low rounded dome on which the seas rose up and shattered like glass. As we neared the narrowing channel the edges of the dark sea turned into light green over the rocks along the edges.

Trees suddenly loomed above us and we hurried past the outermost part of the headland. The channel was only three cables wide and the wind hurled down on us from the mountains as squalls ran to the east. Margaret and I had to shout to talk because the waves thundered on the rocks.

As soon as we had passed through the channel into the sound we pulled down the mainsail. The water was smooth and calm inside the bay, but squalls flung their wind and rain on us and the yacht staggered under their force. However, we were safe, and half an hour later we rounded Horn and Gowing islands. We had been told about an iron mining settlement at Tasu, so we sailed in and tied up at a small dock at the little company town.

While I made fast to the float in the dying daylight a slim man in an oilskin jacket appeared out of the rain.

"Hello," he said. "My name is Peter Mylechreest. There's just time. Follow me."

Mystified, we did as we were told. Peter hurried us up the ramp and along a gravel street to a squarish building. When we went inside we realized it was a dining hall.

"Steak tonight," said Peter. "Be my guest."

Peter was the doctor for the company town whose 400 residents lived in a cheerful, new, well-planned community supplied by daily float plane flights from the east. Heavy stores were barged in from Vancouver. The town was adjacent to a deposit of thirty-three million metric tons of rich copper and iron ore which had been readied for mining by an investment of $41 million in the town, complex mining machinery, and docks. All the ore went to Mitsubishi in Japan on such ships as the *Japan Maple*, a colossal vessel that carried 55,000 tons of ore on each trip.

"This must all seem startling to you," said Peter, who took us on a tour of the big open-pit mine the next day. "I could hardly believe it when I first came."

We became good friends with Peter, who was an M.D. by profession but a wildlife biologist in his spare time. He was a studious, well-groomed bachelor from the Lake District in the county of Westmoreland in England and he passionately loved travel in the wild places of the north. One of his favorites was Foula in the Shetland Islands. He had studied trout problems in Great Bear Lake in the arctic north of Canada and had voyaged on mission ships to remote Indian villages. When Peter spoke of these places his eyes grew wide and bright and he became the

restless slave of adventure. If we had been starting out on *Whisper* I would have taken him with us at once.

Tasu was a Haida Indian word that meant "Lake of Plenty." It was a wonderful inland bay that reached into the mountains for five miles with four irregular three-mile arms that stretched sideways parallel to the coast. Except for the iron mine, which was dwarfed to insignificance, the whole area was untouched and virginal. Tall mountains wreathed with fragrant conifers sloped swiftly downward on all sides. The crystal waters of a dozen substantial streams tumbled into the smooth sound, which was home for enormous runs of salmon, along with halibut, cod, snapper, and crabs. Bear, deer, elk, and many wild creatures roamed the shores, which were tough to penetrate because of the thick rain forests of spruce, cedar, and hemlock. It seemed to me that Tasu must have resembled the San Francisco Bay of 200 years ago: largely unspoiled, the waters and shores filled with natural life, and an aura of peace and quiet over the whole place. The land before the rape by man.

One day while Peter was guiding us to a new part of the sound we slipped around a corner and saw an odd little yellow vessel at anchor. As we got closer we saw that it was a decked-over steel lifeboat with a big cabin. A smokestack puffed lustily into the chill air, and a large Canadian maple-leaf ensign strained at the flagstaff. We were waved alongside *Hiram* by a couple who appeared on deck in red shirts.

"Have you seen the eagles this morning?" called the silver-haired skipper. "More than a dozen since breakfast. Look! Here comes another."

For the first time in my life I saw a bald eagle. He was right off a silver dollar, a great black bird with a white head and white tail feathers. His flat wings stretched some seven feet, and as he passed overhead we could hear a swish as his wings dipped and raised.

We got acquainted with the owners of *Hiram*, Neil and Betty Carey, two Americans who had emigrated to the Queen Charlotte Islands. "Something I should have done years ago," said Neil, a big tough-looking ex-Navy officer with the physique of a wrestler and the soul of a violinist. The Careys owned small houses on both the east coast and on isolated southwest Moresby Island. They didn't have much money and did a great deal of beachcombing along the wild western coast, a pastime that got them both a fine collection of souvenirs of the sea and an enviable knowledge of the coastline.

Betty was a famous canoe expert who had made solo paddle trips from Seattle to Alaska in a fourteen-foot dugout canoe. She taught us much about Haida Indian village sites. "Of course you won't find an anchorage for a deep keel near a village," she said. "The Haidas looked for smooth, sloping beaches up which they could pull their canoes to safety."

When we met Neil he was working for the Canadian Fisheries Board, and for a month or two little *Hiram* putted about the west coast inlets, checking fishermen, setting fishing boundaries, and counting salmon. I went with Neil on several counting trips. With a loaded carbine to scare off the bears that were everywhere, munching on salmon, Neil led a blistering pace along the streams that were bordered by almost impenetrable rain forests. I thought I was pretty nimble in slipping through woods, but Neil put me to shame. He shinnied across moss-covered logs, ducked under leaning alders, scrambled over upturned roots, skirted boggy patches, and eased down muddy ravines at a pace I couldn't believe, all the while telling me about salmon.

"The sockeye come in June or July," said Neil. "The pinks or humpbacks arrive in August. The chums or dog salmon appear in the autumn along with the cohoes or silvers."

By means of a well-practiced sampling technique, Neil was able to estimate the number of salmon in a run.

Sometimes we looked into a deep pool and saw fifty or seventy cohoe salmon, each three feet long, each a silvery pink-bellied beauty. We saw a few about to deposit eggs and milt. The female circled over a crude scraping in the sand in a shallow place and deposited her eggs, which were fertilized by the male hovering a few inches away, culminating the life cycle of these remarkable and vigorous fish.

One night before we left Tasu we anchored far out in a remote bay, miles from anyone. There was a light rain, the clouds were low, and away from the yellow glow of our kerosene cabin lamps the night was black as death. We had been hiking in the woods and had turned in early.

Suddenly in the middle of the night I heard a strange scratching noise. I was awake at once. I pulled on a coat, slid back the hatch, and peered out. We were still well anchored, no driftwood was against the hull, and the dinghy was tied aft with two lines. The noise had stopped. I was satisfied and went back to bed.

A few minutes later I heard the scratching noise again. Now it

was louder, an eerie scraping sound. I climbed on deck with a flashlight and swept the powerful light around. Nothing forward. Nothing to the sides. Nothing aft. My heart stopped when the light hit the dinghy, for I saw a man in a rubber wet suit, a scuba outfit, climbing out of the water! My hands clenched the flashlight like a vise. My hair must have stood straight up.

Then I looked again. No! It was not a man. It was a big seal that had decided to take a fresh-water bath in the half-swamped dinghy. At midnight the big gray creature had crawled into our tender to splash around. What a fright!

We sailed from the Queen Charlotte Islands on October 10, bound for San Francisco, 900 miles to the south. It was a fine, clear day when we left, and as the great dark mountains around Tasu receded into the mist behind us I realized that the long Pacific trip was almost over. The Queen Charlotte Islands were the last of the new and unknown places. There had been so many during the nineteen-month trip: Eiao, Moorea, Aitutaki, Palmerston—seventy places in all. The memories made me a bit weak. Already there was a fair volume of correspondence from new friends.

It was good to get to sea again, and as *Whisper* heaved on the breathing ocean I felt a real kinship with the mighty Pacific. But as always the relationship was a cautious friendship, for though the old woman was capable of love she could be cantankerous and difficult.

The season of the equinoctial gales was advanced, so we headed offshore to get an offing of several hundred miles and to stay clear of the shipping lanes. We hoped for an eight- or nine-day passage, but the northwest winds that we had heard so much about seldom materialized. We found mostly calms, fog, and winds from the south.

On the fourth day the wind increased to thirty knots from the southeast, so we hove to for eight hours. At 2300 the wind suddenly died and was replaced a few hours later by an icy thirty knot blast from the northwest.

October 14. 1045. 200 miles west of Tatoosh Island on the latitude of the United States–Canadian border.
   Last night in the dim hours we fought the mainsail down, handed

*the jib, and discovered that we were humming right along under
bare poles. I knew I could never get the vane to steer with no
headsail, so Margaret dug out the 50 sq. ft. storm jib since I was
determined not to waste a fair wind. I banked on the sail, crawled
back to the mast, and began to hoist the little sail when I happened
to look aft.*

A tremendous wave was bearing down on Whisper. *Suddenly
the ship looked so tiny and the whole enterprise seemed so
insignificant. "She'll never rise to this wave," I mumbled aloud as a
puff of wind snatched the words from my lips. I watched, half-
holding my breath. The mighty wave rolled forward, the stern
lifted, and the yacht rose well, although the foaming crest boomed
on board, roared into the cockpit, and bowled along the side decks.*

*Margaret, with two safety lines around her, was in the cockpit
steering. She suddenly found herself up to her armpits in a bathtub
of water only 20° above the freezing point. I saw her spluttering
and blowing. She calmly began to take off her clothes and to wring
them out.*

*"It's your turn to steer," she said gamely. "I've had my bath for
today."*

Later we put up the trysail and continued to make good time. But
the following day we were becalmed on an utterly smooth ocean. On
the seventh day we hove to for twenty hours in a southeast gale and
on the eighth and ninth days we were becalmed for fifteen hours.

And so it went. No wind. Then too much from the wrong direction. Our daily runs were erratic and poor—57, 101, 48, 26—but like
chopping at a tree with a dull ax, you keep at it and eventually the
target tumbles. Occasionally we saw the lights of ships at night. We
constantly watched the big dusky black-footed albatrosses that
circled around and around on their thin droopy wings, day and
night, in calm and in storm. Sometimes porpoises frolicked around
the ship, exuberantly diving, rolling, twisting, jumping, and splashing.
Then in an instant they would be gone.

One night near the latitude of the Oregon–California border we
were slowly beating into a fifteen-knot southeast wind during a
rainstorm when I looked out and saw a light behind us. I immediately pulled on my oilskins and went on deck. I expected a freighter
to pass, but as the rain swept the sea the light stayed about the same.
After half an hour I realized I was traveling only a little slower than
the lights, which were gradually nearing *Whisper*. Closer now I saw
the three vertical masthead lights of a big tug pulling something. The

rain increased, but I felt safe since the lights of the tug were heading toward my starboard quarter and would safely pass to the west. Then I glanced at my port quarter and suddenly saw a *second* tug. The two tugs were on a bridle hooked to a towline that pulled something which was almost invisible but which loomed huge and awesome in the black night. *I was gradually being overtaken and surrounded by the two tugs, one pulling up on each quarter.* When the rain cleared for a moment I saw the bow waves of the tugs only a few hundred yards away.

I wasted no time but tacked to the east at once and bore off a little to get away from the leviathan that was after me. A few moments later the high sides of an enormous vessel under tow glided past. The unlighted monster would have erased *Whisper* as easily as a man could have stepped on a snail.

At the height of all this the string holding up my oilskin pants came undone. I grabbed at my trousers but only managed to undo my belt. My trousers tumbled about my ankles, which left my bare bottom out in the downpour while I worked the tiller and the headsail sheets.

When it was all over I didn't know whether to laugh or to cry.

On the thirteenth day we were near Cape Mendocino in heavy fog but slowly getting south. The cottony fog formed each morning for three days. It was thick at the surface but not high, and often we could see a sun that resembled an opalescent pearl on a cushion of dull satin.

We began to work inshore and saw more steamer traffic, but fortunately no more vessels under tow. On October 25 our position was 38° 21′ N. and 123° 30′ W., close to Point Reyes. Under vagrant westerly zephyrs, a bright sun, and a cloudless sky we crept south and east. Before noon on the sixteenth day we sighted the Farallon Islands, and a few hours later the sturdy towers and the delicately swooping cables of the Golden Gate Bridge hove into view.

How exciting it was to be within a few miles of our outbound track! At 1400 we passed underneath the bridge. The trip was in our pocket. Margaret produced a bottle of Japanese whisky and we each lifted a glass in celebration of the 18,538-mile voyage.

I toasted the Pacific. I toasted the ship. I toasted the mate.

I loved all three.

A Few Notes on Whisper

I BELIEVE A SAILING YACHT SHOULD BE ABLE TO FUNCTION without an engine. If you are becalmed at sea you simply wait, perhaps a shocking thought to jet-age travelers these days. However, a well-designed ship can do wonders in light airs. Some of my most pleasant memories are of ghosting along and dreaming and feeling very close to the sea and its creatures, something you miss entirely if you turn on a noisy engine.

I do feel that a small Diesel (with emergency hand-cranking) is a useful installation. It can drive a powerful mechanical bilge pump and is a good charging plant to supply power for a few electric lamps. Sometimes an engine is helpful in docking, although I much prefer the excitement of entering and leaving ports under sail. Where an engine is of particular help is when you are becalmed and caught in a strong tidal stream when it is too deep to anchor (I think of the Tuamotus). However, in 1,000 days of sailing this may happen only once. You may be becalmed just outside a port with dirty weather coming up. Or you may wish to go through a canal. These are legitimate uses, it seems to me, for a small engine if the weight, size, and fuel requirements don't overwhelm the vessel and use up its best space. My fifteen-horsepower, two-cylinder Volvo-Penta weighs about 425 pounds and consumes one quart of fuel an hour.

I have experimented with a long sculling oar and find that I can scull and maneuver Whisper (displacement six tons) at one knot in calm water. For a month during the Pacific trip we had no engine and managed to get along reasonably well.

The engines in cruising yachts get larger each year (along with electrical complexities) and a whole new school of cruising, a group that misses much of the spirit of the sea, it seems to me, is growing up. Instead of being sailors, these captains have to be journeymen mechanics and financiers to keep ahead of the repairs and the bills. Everything is engine, engine, engine, more and more fuel tanks, long distance radios, pressure hot water, washing machines, radar, Loran, and so on, *ad nauseam*.

I think you can make an interesting distinction between (1) a pure sailing ship, (2) a sailing vessel with a small auxiliary engine, and (3) a motor vessel with auxiliary sails that are used when the wind is favorable, a *sail-assisted vessel*. I believe that most accidents happen to category number three because many owners of so-called "full-power auxiliaries" are not sailors and don't know how to maneuver and control their ships under sail. These yacht owners often have no concept of storm management, how to sail an anchor out, how to heave to, and so on. Instead of knowledge they rely on engines that may work or may not.

I would humbly suggest that $100 be spent by each of these people to attend a dinghy sailing school. The skills learned and brought to the larger vessel will add immeasurable pleasure, safety, peace of mind, and perhaps commence to build pride in seamanship.

A principal consideration in a seagoing sailing ship is of course the integrity of the hull and deck structures. Without a sound hull and sturdy hatches, ports, cockpit, coachroof, and decks that are impervious to pounding seas, the ship will fill with water and its heavy lead keel will sink the vessel.

Whisper's hull—constructed from many layers of fiberglass mat, cloth, and roving saturated with polyester resin—is magnificent. It has never leaked a drop, and after 25,000 sea miles seems as good today (August 1971) as when it was launched five and a half years ago. However, as has been made evident in the account, I had trouble with the hull-deck joint, which was simply a bond of a number of layers of fiberglass mat placed on the inside where the hull and deck moldings met. For ordinary weekend sailing this would probably be enough, I suppose, but at sea where the stresses are sometimes awesome, the joint was inadequate.

When we returned from the Pacific trip Margaret and I removed the toerail, plugged 140 bolt holes, and radiused the outside of the joint. We then covered it on the outside with seven layers of ten ounce fiberglass cloth of gradually increasing widths set in polyester resin so that the joint would be massively strong and watertight both inside and out. In place of the low toerail we installed a $1'' \times 4''$ teak bulwark (35 feet on each side) bolted one inch above the deck on special stanchion bases spaced six feet apart. (While we're on the subject of leaks I wonder why there must be over 250 holes in the deck of a modern yacht, all of which are potential drips or worse? With a little thought you can eliminate half of them.)

In case you think I overstate my case I will say that when we crossed the Philippine Sea and bashed into head seas day after day we opened up thirty inches of the hull-deck joint at the stem, the point where the hull strength should have been prodigious. The pound-pound-pound of head seas soon uncovers any structural flaws. (The reason many cruising skippers are keen on all-steel yachts is massive strength, no leaks, and freedom from fastening worries.)

All parts of a vessel that go to sea should be painstakingly engineered, and should draw on experience at sea. You need something besides a shell of plastic for a fiberglass yacht. Naval architects who spend their careers working in warm offices have little appreciation of the power of breaking waves (oh, that the sea would get the same consideration as rating rules!). Deck structures, it seems to me, should be low and unencumbered, with generous bracing and reinforcement tied well down into the hull. Portlights should be small and strong. Better to lose a bit of headroom than to compromise with strength. (The importance of headroom is highly overrated anyway.)

Lest this sound like a diatribe against John Brandlmayr, the designer of *Whisper*, let me say that the ship sailed well and never gave me the slightest worry regarding performance. Her motion was wild many times and we had to shorten sail as soon as the wind increased, but she was a whiz in light airs and our elapsed passage times were reasonable.

Whisper's rudder is hollow and built of fiberglass shells. Some of the compartments are open to the sea and filled with water, an engineering feature I don't understand. But though I had doubts, the rudder and fittings proved adequate. When we put the ship on a coral reef at Guam the bottom of the rudder merely got crushed. If the rudder had been steel, the impact with the coral would have torn off the entire assembly. Better to have crushed a few square inches than to have lost the whole thing. I suppose the rudder of a cruising yacht should be set a few inches above the keel so the keel takes any grounding strains rather than the rudder.

This is not the place to discuss the pros and cons of various rigs, but I can say that when you cross oceans in a sloop, your shoulder development is assured, for you will make many sail changes. I would definitely fit running backstays to help support the upper part of the mast. Though *Whisper*'s mast has a reasonably large cross-section, the upper portion moves around alarmingly in a seaway. Of course if you fit backstays you might as well fit an inner headstay on which you can fly a staysail. You then have a sort of cutter rig. If you sew a set of reefing points on the staysail you have four choices of headsails without physically manhandling sails, not a small consideration. You can fly a jib and staysail, jib alone, staysail alone, or a reefed staysail alone.

I don't understand sailors who readily accept the chore of cranking enormous sheet winches yet who complain about setting running backstays—which take only a moment.

I would definitely not fit twin headstays again, for I had much trouble with (1) chafe of the headsail against the unused stay and (2) with the unused stay working open the jib hanks of the sail set on the other stay. I would make all the mast fittings of Monel, silicon bronze, or galvanized iron—in that order—rather than stainless steel, for I broke four mast tangs during the trip. The stainless steel appeared to work-harden and become brittle. Never weld stainless steel mast hardware.

It is useful to carry some sort of a swaging tool to help with repairs to running and standing rigging, both for yourself and for other small ships you will meet.

Whisper's original sails came from Rolly Tasker of Hong Kong and served us well. Our later sails were made in Seattle by Franz Schattauer whose skill and personal attention resulted in much better setting canvas. In consultation with Franz we now have stout, triple-stitched sails with hand-sewn bolt ropes and ample reinforcements. The sails are very strong, but quite light. Franz used eight-ounce Dacron for the mainsail and six-ounce for the genoa. The full cut main has three short fiberglass battens, each enclosed in envelopes of Dacron built up to three thicknesses to control chafe. For offshore cruising you need sails of the highest quality; skimp elsewhere if you must, but not when buying sails.

On future trips I will definitely take a spare mainsail (rather than the useless and expensive RDF set in which I invested) for when you get down to basics it is sailpower that drives the vessel. I prefer slab or tied reefs (three rows) to roller reefing because (1) the sail sets much better, (2) the strains on a roller reefed sail that is rolled slightly unevenly are severe, (3) you get away from dependence on a possible faulty roller reefing gear such as we had, (4) you can have a lighter boom with better sheeting arrangements, and (5) it's cheaper. Tying reefs is of course slower than using a roller reefing mechanism.

On *Whisper* we cook and heat and light with kerosene, which I think is the perfect fuel for small ships. Kerosene—or light clear Diesel fuel or stove oil which seem to be the same as kerosene and half the price—works to perfection in Primus stoves and appliances. The fuel is cheap, safe, dependable, hot, and in all ways satisfactory. (Kerosene is smelly only if you have leaky appliances.) My second choice is a Diesel stove, which is excellent in the high latitudes but a furnace in the tropics. Bottled gas is dangerous, expensive, hard to get in many ports, and the fittings on the containers are always different. Alcohol is excellent but costly and sometimes impossible to get. (I recall a yacht that bought alcohol from the pharmacy in Papeete at prescription prices.) Solid fuel is dirty, bulky to store, and often expensive and difficult to find. On a long trip you use a good deal of fuel, no matter what sort. We carry twenty gallons of kerosene on *Whisper.*

Your tastes become simple when you cruise in a small ship. It's amazing how little you really need to exist pleasantly and comfortably. The more gadgetry the more problems. Possessions as such mean little on extended trips.

Although we generally use electric lights for reading—especially in the tropics—we planned our equipment so that we can get along with no electricity at all. We had no refrigeration, not because I don't appreciate the advantages of ice but because I refuse to put up with the complex machinery and the noise of a charging plant. I recall a big all-electric yacht whose main generator was out of order and whose auxiliary generator had a broken part. The existence of the people plummeted to utter squalor since their electric toilets wouldn't work, they were unable to cook, their frozen food spoiled, they couldn't raise their anchors. . . . We finally loaned them some candles and a pressure kerosene lamp.

I carry lots of spare parts. In many cases I carry spares for the spares. My theory of spare parts is to fit the spare so you know it will replace the original. Then to tuck the original away for a rainy day.

For example I installed the spare water pumps for the galley before I left on the trip. I stored the originals, *which I then knew would fit in all ways.*

The Hasler wind vane gear was completely successful and made most of the trip a pleasure instead of a steering marathon. We lost the wind blade in heavy weather in the Gulf of Alaska, but the fault was mine, for I should have removed the blade in such weather. The vane gear steered perfectly downwind when I generally ran with the mainsail eased forward (with a guy to prevent gybing and a vang to hold the boom down to minimize sail chafe on the lee spreader). To balance the drive of the mainsail we carried a headsail boomed out on the windward side with a spinnaker pole. It is good to carry poles of different lengths to boom out a variety of sails, particularly storm sails. The use of a mainsail and a poled-out headsail does a lot to minimize rolling. We used twin headsails a few times but experienced a good deal of rolling since twins are essentially squaresails and fail to give much lateral support.

With a steering vane you must be careful not to fall over the side. In bad weather and at night we always wear safety harnesses, which we clip to a lifeline or a piece of rigging. We hang police whistles on cords around our necks for emergency signaling. We also have a long bamboo overboard pole with a flame-colored flag on top, two life rings, and a floating overboard light with a high-intensity flashing light.

Recently I have learned about small pocket-sized waterproof mini-flares, which certainly will go along on our next trip. With such a flare in your pocket you would be able to pinpoint your position to someone on a returning yacht.

I carry two radio receivers, principally to obtain time signals. We have no transmitter, for I feel that if we get into difficulty we should get ourselves out. I feel strongly about calling for help, for U.S. small-boat people have abused the privilege so abysmally that I am horrified at the whole concept. My situation would have to be very desperate before I would ask for assistance. There is the matter of *pride in doing it yourself*, a value not often thought of these days, but something I believe is important.

I can see one use for a transmitter and that would be to ask for medical advice in case of a mechanical injury or a major illness. Our battery power is modest, however, and I have none.

In general we had good weather during the Pacific trip. You plan carefully to take advantage of fair winds, summer temperatures, and seasons free from gales. The literature of sailing has entirely too much storm talk. Like the newspaper and its daily tabulation of murders, one's ideas may get distorted. The newspapers never mention how many men peacefully come home from the office, kiss their wives, and spend an evening with their stamp collections. That wouldn't be news, even though it is the truth. Likewise the sea, though sometimes stormy and downright nasty, is often smooth and easy.

Without question the most important piece of mechanical gear on the ship is the anchor windlass, in our case a Simpson-Lawrence 500 two-speed lever action device which enables Margaret or me to handle the anchors with ease and to assist in warping the ship when in harbor. We carry four anchors—two forty-five-pound CQRs, a forty-two-pound fisherman, and a thirty-pound Danforth. We generally use one of the CQR anchors, which we have arranged to be self-stowing over a stem roller. Most modern yachtsmen use CQR anchors because they hold well and don't bend, a problem with the Danforth design. The fisherman, of course, is the old standby, and though it automatically gets fouled when the ship swings on a tidal change, the anchor holds well on a short length of cable and is often good in rocky holding ground.

We generally anchor with all chain and carry thirty-five fathoms of ⅜″. We had little trouble with dragging anchors. The only difficulty in seventy places, strange to say, was over gleaming coral sand in Rangiroa atoll in the Tuamotus, where the white sand appeared to have a hard crust. We spent a perplexing hour with all three types before we got one to dig in. In the tropics I often put on a face mask and swam out to inspect the anchor after we had put the ground tackle down. I learned a good deal about anchors and anchoring. Sometimes you think you are well anchored and the chain is wrapped around and around the anchor. It is a good policy to buoy the anchor, although it is one thing more to do when you are busy sailing into a new place.

We carry seventy-eight gallons of fresh water in two tanks, plus eight or ten gallons of water in plastic jugs. This is ample, in fact more than twice what we have ever used on a passage. Two quarts of fresh water per person per day is sufficient. The best way to replenish water in the tropics is with a water-catching awning. Not only is it simple and quick but the water is clean and easier to get than rowing jugs ashore and walking long distances to catchment tanks where the water may be of doubtful purity.

Cruising yachts should have two dinghies. If you lose one you have a spare. (A small tender can fit inside a larger, or you can have an inflatable for a second.) If you are anchored out and someone is ashore with the dinghy, anyone on board is immobile unless you have a second tender. A good sailing dinghy is useful, for the distances you must row in foreign places are sometimes considerable. Also you can often take pleasant trips to far corners of a large lagoon in a sailing dinghy. Carry spare oars and rowlocks. I do not have an outboard because I refuse to have gasoline on board.

We carry no guns, which are illegal in most parts of the world anyway. Your best ally, if you are worried about protection, is a smile, a handshake, a small joke about the weather, and perhaps an offer of a cup of coffee or an inch of whisky. Guns are made for killing, not friendship.

Rather than to worry about what to *do* about people, our problem was often what to do *for* people when they had done us great kindnesses. In the future I plan to carry a number of cheap stainless-steel knives, large fishhooks, and inexpensive rope to give friends who are especially good to us. Again and again we were asked for used clothing. A Polaroid photograph of everyone is a fun gift, and a picture of the ship and crew is appreciated. People like to go for short sails. Always carry a guitar in the South Pacific.

You must take the advice of natives with caution with respect to the suitability of a place regarding depth. Most people of the South Pacific use outrigger canoes, which draw only a few inches. The natives generally have no concept of the underwater shape of ships with keels and will enthusiastically wave you in to a place with only a few inches of water. It's a good idea to put a dinghy over the side and to make a few soundings yourself if the water is unclear.

What does it cost to take such a trip? I consider that a small yacht in good condition is worth the same as a modest house. In 1966, *Whisper* cost approximately $20,000, to which I added another 25 percent—$5,000—for the steering vane, charts, navigation equipment, stores, spares, dinghies, warps, medical supplies, and so on and on. Cruising equipment is astonishingly extensive. You need *everything*, for you have to be self-sufficient in both items for living and for keeping the ship going. A vessel at sea is a miniature, self-contained world. It takes months and months to get ready.

Actual cruising costs are something else. The very nature of a long trip takes you to places where it is often impossible to spend any money at all. You find instead that you barter a pair of old trousers for two fish and half a dozen drinking nuts. Where the money goes is when you reach a large port and eat out in restaurants, something we seldom did. If you have modest resources the best scheme, we believe, is to buy first-class foodstuffs and to prepare them yourself. Even in San Francisco today Margaret and I can both eat a good meal on *Whisper* for $1 or so. If we eat out it is hard to spend less than $4 for the two of us.

I believe that in 1971 two people can cruise in a small ship for from $100 to $200 a month if the ship is well prepared beforehand, has no complex machinery or electrical gadgetry to maintain, and if you watch your expenses in every way. This means avoiding places with high port charges and in general being frugal. Often you can stock up when you find food bargains. The fun you have is of course in no way related to what you spend. We have seen the crews of yachts in the $100-a-month class have much better times than those who spent ten times more. You don't have to deny yourself sightseeing, for most places have cheap public transportation. We carried take-apart bicycles which we stored in the forepeak.

Cargo and passenger ships travel mostly between large ports where there are generally excellent aids to navigation and pilots you can hire to help you enter and dock. The smaller places, however, often have no aids to navigation and you must find your way in alone. The volumes of pilot instructions that cover practically the whole earth tend to reflect this situation. The big ports are well described, but the remote places generally have only skimpy and outdated notes. The disparity is increasing, for large ports are growing bigger while small places are falling into disuse, except for local traffic.

The only literate strangers to many small ports are the crews of cruising yachts. I feel it is important for small-ship captains to write in changes and corrections to the *Pilots*. It takes only a moment and one sentence to say that "such and such a beacon no longer exists," that "harbor X has a mean ground swell and it is better to anchor out than to lie alongside the dock," or that "you need to hire a watchman if you leave the ship." The correctness of sailing directions can be maintained only if everyone concerned helps. Who knows? Maybe your son will profit from a change you have written in.

There are many aspects of seamanship involved when you cross an ocean in a small ship. One lifetime seems hardly long enough to learn all you should. I have a theory that preparation for passage-making is worse than the actual sailing. I am always nervous and unsettled before sailing and calm and untroubled once we get under way. The contemplation of danger is sometimes far worse than the actual hazard itself. Small ships seldom get in trouble at sea. It's around land where difficulties begin. If things look nasty when you draw close to a strange coast, heave to and wait awhile. What is one more day? You have to throw away the calendar when you go cruising.

You must do all you can to stay rested and to keep reserves of energy tucked away, for a tired captain can easily make a stupid move.

I have talked enough. If you have the urge to go you will in spite of what I say. If your heart isn't in the sea you will never leave the safety of the land, a pity perhaps, but not many people have the fire of adventure in their bones. But if you want to go don't wait until everything is perfect or you'll never get away. Most adventuring is done on a shoestring. Perhaps that's part of the fun. ("If you have all the money you need, you lose the adventure," says my friend Bobby Uriburu.)

The very nature of exploration, pioneering, and adventure is quest and curiosity, not safety and security. Only a few berths from where *Whisper* is now tied up is another yacht whose owner watched us arrive fresh from the shipyard. He saw us set out on the Pacific trip, return, edit a film, write a book, give lectures, and now he sits and watches the parade of visitors from the Pacific climb onto *Whisper*. Yet he still talks of his trip and how he is going. If you have the urge by all means set a date and go!

Notes

1. J. C. Beaglehole, *The Exploration of the Pacific*, Stanford University Press, 1966, pp. 65–68. Also see *Pacific Islands*, published during World War II by the Naval Intelligence Division of the British government (B.R. 519B Geographical Handbook Series). The five volumes are a superb source for Pacific information. The Marquesas are covered in detail in Vol. II, pp. 260–99, and in Vol. I, pp. 246–47.

2. J. C. Beaglehole, *The Journals of Captain James Cook*, Cambridge, Hakluyt Society, 1961, Vol II, pp. 372–73.

3. Charles A. Borden, *South Sea Islands*, Philadelphia, Macrae Smith, 1961, p. 116.

4. Robert C. Suggs, *The Hidden Worlds of Polynesia*, New York, Mentor Books, New American Library, 1962, p. 59. A highly readable book about recent archaeological work in the Marquesas. Chapter Two has a good summary of the troubled history.

5. Willowdean C. Handy, *Forever the Land of Men*, New York, Dodd, Mead, 1965, p. 167.

6. Population figures in French Polynesia are sketchy and incomplete. See Handy, *op. cit.*, pp. 223–26. Also *Pacific Island Year Book*, Sydney, Pacific Publications, 1963, p. 151. Useful but often highly inaccurate.

7. Many small-ship sailors have called at the Marquesas and written accounts, including Stevenson (1888), London (1908), Muhlhauser (1921), Seligman (1937), Le Toumelin (1951), Crealock (1952), Van de Wiele (1952), Hiscock (1953), and Pye (1953).

8. Bengt Danielsson, *Forgotten Islands of the South Seas*, London, Allen & Unwin, 1957, p. 165. Danielsson, as Alain Gerbault did a generation earlier, demonstrates that with proper motivation—as in sports—the 'lazy islanders' have astounding energy, vitality, and endurance.

9. Bengt Danielsson, *The Happy Island*, London, Allen & Unwin, 1952, pp. 155–75.

10. For the ultimate description of Palmerston, viewed from the air, see James Ramsey Ullman, *Where the Bong Tree Grows*, Cleveland, World Publishing Co., 1963, pp. 227–28. Charts of Palmerston are difficult to get. H.O. 1980 has been discontinued. The best I have been able to find is in a little booklet, *Maps of the Cook Islands*, by the Survey Department, Rarotonga, printed by the Government of the Cook Islands (undated).

11. Data for the ocean floor around Palmerston can be found in Helen Raitt, *Exploring the Deep Pacific, the Story of the Capricorn Expedition*, Denver, Sage Books, 1964, Chapter Fourteen.

12. Commander Victor Clark, *On the Wind of a Dream*, London, Hutchinson, 1960, pp. 134–97. By far the most authoritative account of Palmerston. Clark, whose yacht was wrecked and rebuilt on the island, had an excellent chance to study the place for eleven months. His lucid account debunks the stories of inbreeding.

13. *Ibid.*, pp. 136–37.

14. W. A. Robinson, *Deep Water and Shoal*, London, Rupert Hart-Davis, 1957, pp. 115–17. Also see Ralph Stock, "The Dream Ship," *National Geographic*, January 1921, pp. 49–50.

15. *Pacific Islands Year Book, op. cit.*, p. 144.

16. *Pacific Islands, op. cit.*, Vol. II, pp. 561–62.

17. Another visitor to Palmerston was Irving Johnson, *Westward Bound in the Schooner Yankee*, New York, W. W. Norton, 1936, pp. 124–26. A view of a churchman is by Bernard Thorogood, *Not Quite Paradise*, London, London Missionary Society, 1960, pp. 66–71.

18. Jan-Olof Traung, editor, *Fishing Boats of the World: 2*, London, Fishing News (Books) Ltd., 1960, pp. 73–74.

19. The high harbor dues are typical of American shortsightedness. With a little encouragement and the most modest of facilities the magnificent harbor of Pago Pago could become the center of yachting and sailing in the South Pacific. In Papeete, long the mecca of yachts, the little ships from all over the world are made welcome and form a colorful part of the waterfront. Contrary to what some Americans think, yachtsmen are not bums and do spend reasonable amounts of money locally.

20. *Pacific Islands, op. cit.*, Vol. II, pp. 591–607. For a modern

account of the 1889 confusion, see Edwin P. Hoyt, *The Typhoon That Stopped a War*, New York, McKay, 1968.

21. John O'Grady, *No Kava for Johnny*, Sydney, Ure Smith, 1966. A delightful novel of modern Samoa that deftly reviews the conflict between old and new customs.

22. For an invaluable guide to mariners, see Captain E. V. Ward, *Sailing Directions*, Tarawa, Gilbert and Ellice Islands Colony, 1967. Price $1 (Australian). This detailed and up-to-date seventy-four-page handbook is far superior to *Admiralty* and *U.S. Pilots*.

23. Samuel Eliot Morison, *History of United States Naval Operations in World War II, Aleutians, Gilberts, and Marshalls*, Boston, Little, Brown, 1951, Vol. VII, p. 185.

24. For general information, a reading list, and statistics of this well-governed atoll colony, see *Gilbert & Ellice Islands Biennial Report, 1964–65*, London, Her Majesty's Stationery Office, 1967.

25. Sir Arthur Grimble, *Return to the Islands*, New York, William Morrow, 1957, pp. 50–51.

26. Sir Arthur Grimble, *We Chose the Islands*, New York, William Morrow, 1952, p. 174. The classic of the Gilberts, a bit exaggerated occasionally but the writing is often breathtaking and always penetrating and conscientious. Grimble should be required reading for all Americans in overseas government. For an early account of Abemama, see Robert Louis Stevenson, *In the South Seas*, New York, Charles Scribner's Sons, 1923, pp. 329–409.

27. *Ibid.*, p. 276.

28. *Ibid.*, pp. 78–79.

29. Sir Arthur Grimble, "War Finds Its Way to Gilbert Islands," *National Geographic*, January 1943, p. 85.

30. *Sailing Directions for the Pacific Islands*, Washington, U.S. Government Printing Office, H.O. Pub. No. 82, Vol. I, pp. 6–9. A handy source of miscellaneous information is *Trust Territory of the Pacific Islands*, Washington, U.S. Government Printing Office, 21st annual report, July 1, 1967 to June 30, 1968.

31. The Trust Territory is fertile ground for crusading reporters who have found plenty to write about. See Willard Price, *America's Paradise Lost*, New York, John Day, 1966; E. J. Kahn, Jr., *A Reporter in Micronesia*, New York, Norton, 1966; and Don Oberdorfer, "America's Neglected Colonial Paradise," *Saturday Evening Post*, February 29, 1964. An older and more idealistic sketch is by Robert Trumbull, *Paradise in Trust*, New York, William Sloane, 1959. For a broader background, see J. C. Furnas, *Anatomy of Paradise*, New York, William Sloane, 1947.

32. James A. Michener and A. Grove Day, *Rascals in Paradise*, London, Secker & Warburg, 1957, pp. 223–58.

33. David S. Boyer, "Micronesia: the Americanization of Eden," *National Geographic*, May 1967, p. 735.

34. Price, *op. cit.*, p. 170.

35. Ullman, *op. cit.*, p. 81. Mort Colodny, the district cooperative officer in Ponape, has made excellent suggestions for economic improvements in an eighteen-page paper *Economic Development in Micronesia* (unpublished, a copy is in the possession of the author of this book).

36. For an account of this remarkable priest, see Kahn, *op. cit.*, pp. 268–74.

37. A good synopsis of this unbelievable crop is by John Wesley Coulter, *The Pacific Dependencies of the United States*, New York, Macmillan, 1957, pp. 268–70.

38. Charles Parr, *Ferdinand Magellan, Circumnavigator*, New York, Thomas Crowell, 1964, p. 333.

39. Fosco Maraini, *Meeting with Japan*, London, Hutchinson, 1959, p. 337. This superb book is so good that one sentence can hardly sum up the depth, wisdom, information, and *feeling* of Japan. An excellent translation and first-rate photographs. A basic book is by Ruth Benedict, *The Chrysanthemum and the Sword; Patterns of Japanese Culture*, Boston, Houghton Mifflin, 1946. Helpful also is Laurens Van der Post, *A Portrait of Japan*, New York, William Morrow, 1968.

40. Maraini, *op. cit.*, p. 133.

41. For war reminiscences, see Murray Morgan, *Bridge to Russia*, New York, E. P. Dutton, 1947. A formal account of World War II military affairs is in Morison, *op. cit.*

42. *U.S. Coast Pilot 9, Pacific and Arctic Coasts*, Washington, U.S. Government Printing Office, 1964, p. 237. For a general historical sketch, see Harold McCracken, *Hunters of the Stormy Sea*, New York, Doubleday, 1957. A specialized work is by Waldemar Jochelson, *History, Ethnology, and Anthropology of the Aleut*, The Netherlands, Anthropological Publications, 1966.

43. Ted Bank II, *Birthplace of the Winds*, New York, Thomas Crowell, 1956, pp. 64–115.

44. Viola E. Garfield and Linn A. Forest, *The Wolf and the Raven*, Seattle, University of Washington Press, 1948.

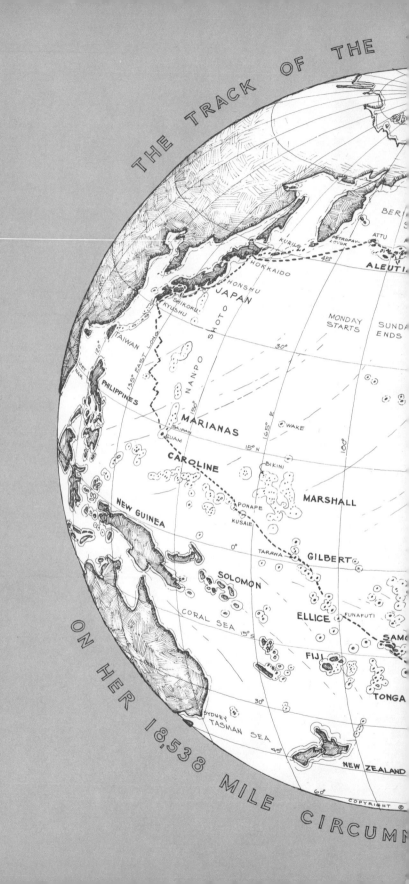

THE TRACK OF THE

ON HER 18,538 MILE CIRCUMN

BERI...
ATTU
PETROPAV-
LOVSK
KURILE
45°
ALEUTIA...
HOKKAIDO
HONSHU
JAPAN
CHIKOKU
KYUSHU
30°
MONDAY
STARTS
SUNDA
ENDS
TAIWAN
135° EAST LONG
120°
NANPO
150°
165° E
WAKE
180°
NIET NAM
PHILIPPINES
MARIANAS
SAIPAN
GUAM
15° N
CAROLINE
BIKINI
MARSHALL
PONAPE
KUSAIE
NEW GUINEA
0°
TARAWA
GILBERT
SOLOMON
CORAL SEA
15° S
ELLICE
FUNAFUTI
SAMO...
FIJI
TONGA
30°
SYDNEY
TASMAN SEA
45°
NEW ZEALAND
60°
COPYRIGHT ©